Advance Praise for *App Savvy*

"Focus on making apps that people enjoy using and want to tell their friends and colleagues about. Having customers who evangelize your products is far more important than a short-term purchase spike because you're selling your app for $0.99 rather than the price it is actually worth."

—Justin Williams, Founder of Second Gear,
http://www.secondgearsoftware.com/

"Whether you've already launched a few apps in the App Store or are someone who has a unique (and possibly great) idea for a new app, this book is a must-read. Covering all the aspects of app development, marketing, and beta testing, *App Savvy* is the ultimate guide for anyone who wants to enter the huge market of the App Store. What really impressed me is the attention to the smallest details Ken put in describing often-underrated stages like 'idea evaluation' or the importance of hiring the right team. Even if you have already released an app, you need to read this book. It will make you more competitive in the App Store. Guaranteed."

—Federico Viticci, Editor of MacStories, *http://www.macstories.net*

"Ken has outlined a comprehensive and well-grounded soup-to-nuts strategy for any company looking to create value via mobile applications. By combining solid principles for mobile strategy as well as practical guidance for execution, he makes for a great sherpa in navigating this terrain."

—Navin Ganeshan, Chief Product Strategist at Network Solutions,
http://www.networksolutions.com

"*App Savvy* is a great product management primer, focused specifically on mobile apps. It takes you from idea to getting your app in the App Store. Lots of technical tips make the book ideal for people who are just starting out creating an iPhone or iPad app, and each chapter has an interview or two with people who have actually done it."

—Steve Johnson, Product Management Evangelist at Pragmatic Marketing,
http://www.productmarketing.com

App Savvy

TURNING IDEAS INTO IPAD AND IPHONE APPS CUSTOMERS REALLY WANT

Ken Yarmosh

O'REILLY®

Beijing · Cambridge · Farnham · Köln · Sebastopol · Tokyo

App Savvy
by Ken Yarmosh

Published by O'Reilly Media, Inc., 1005 Gravenstein Highway North, Sebastopol, CA 95472.

O'Reilly books may be purchased for educational, business, or sales promotional use. Online editions are also available for most titles (*http://my.safaribooksonline.com*). For more information, contact our corporate/institutional sales department: (800) 998-9938 or *corporate@ oreilly.com*.

Editor: Brian Jepson	**Indexer:** Angela Howard
Production Editors: Rachel Monaghan and Holly Bauer	**Cover Design:** Karen Montgomery
Copyeditor: Audrey Doyle	**Interior Design:** Josh Clark, Edie Freedman, and Nellie McKesson
Proofreader: Sada Preisch	**Compositor:** Nellie McKesson

Printing History:
First Edition: October 2010.

ISBN: 978-1-449-38976-5

[M]

To Daddo.

This all started with Q*bert.

Psalm 136:2

CONTENTS

LAUNCH

TIPS AND TOOLS

Foreword

Is an App a Tool or a Behavior?

Back around the turn of the Internet—oh, I don't know, 2005—I started religiously recording interviews with experts for the Duct Tape Marketing Podcast. I did it in part because it looked to me like the next new thing and I wanted to make sure I was part of it. As time wore on, I found that I just sort of liked doing it and eventually built an audience that liked getting their content that way.

More recently, I gave in to the siren's call of the app for my podcast. I mean, I was an iPhone-toting devotee of all things appish, after all, and thought I really should have my own app. I created it and decided to price it at $2.99 just for grins. Now, understand, it pretty much has the exact same content that I publish weekly on iTunes for free.

I was immediately struck by the number of people, including current podcast subscribers, that snapped it up at $2.99. I would call this a light bulb kind of moment for me and my relationship with apps.

The lesson for me was that people want apps for things because they allow them greater control.

I don't think developers should look at apps with a "new, new thing" or "hottest water-cooler download" mentality. Apps are on their way to supplanting the Web in general as the provider of information, games, experiences, and productivity—and control.

While my podcast content is out there to be had for free, it's out there in the wild. An app user of my content has much greater power over how they consume, interact, destruct, and transport that content, and that's perhaps the larger point of this book.

The first step to becoming *app savvy* is to recognize why the app category is red-hot and here to stay, and why you need to think in terms of tapping app behavior to package, repackage, purpose, and repurpose everything that a mobile social consumer wants to do—and even a few things they don't know they want to do.

When you come to view your app ideas and execution with a "feeding a behavior" mindset, ideas and the carrying out of those ideas will flow more freely.

Creating apps may become your gold mine, and this book will certainly show you how to make it so, but step away from the "get rich" desire and focus on creating apps that allow people to do the things that need doing in ways that give them far greater control, and you'll be well on your way to unlocking a flood of potential.

I met Ken way back in those wild days of 2005 or so, and it was clear to me then that he was on a mission to embrace, connect, and commune with all things digital, so I wasn't the least bit surprised when he showed up on my doorstep with a book you need to read right now for the reasons I've outlined above.

Whether you plan to build an app yourself or hire someone to build one for you, this book will make you smarter about the things that matter.

—John Jantsch
Author of *Duct Tape Marketing* and *The Referral Engine*

Preface

HISTORICALLY, THERE HAVE NOT BEEN MANY product books—that is, books that deal with topics beyond the creative or programming aspects of the software development process. The ones that do exist have been fairly conceptual. They often don't get into the details and instead focus exclusively on frameworks for building software. Details are necessary, however, for those who want to go from idea to software product, or in this case, from idea to iPhone app. This book includes those often-missing details. While providing a broader perspective of iOS application development, this book also covers the specifics of taking an idea and subsequently launching an app into Apple's App Store.

Yet that statement is oversimplified. People don't want to just take *an idea* and launch *an iPhone app*. Instead, the typical goal is to take what is believed to be a *unique* or *great idea* and launch a *successful application*. The latter element, success, can vary but is usually easy to define. It may include financial gain, notoriety, career advancement, personal satisfaction, or similar outcomes.

How to achieve these desired outcomes by launching an application, however, is not as straightforward, and hence, failing to achieve them is common. Failures often result because of the false assumptions that an idea is indeed unique, great, interesting, financially lucrative, or more generally, appealing to someone beyond the person with the idea. This problem is not specific to launching an app into the App Store and it is a major reason why most new business ventures of various shapes and sizes flounder early in their existence.

Thus, critical to turning an idea into an app that people beyond you—customers—really want is an understanding of how to assess whether an application actually does that. Some preliminary items need to be handled before that can begin to occur. The good news is that regardless of role, job, background, or skill set, anyone can complete these steps.

Who Should Read This Book

It's possible that you are a "product person" like me, who can't create designs or write code, but has an idea. Or you could be a designer or developer who has either launched an app to no fanfare or realized that those skills alone won't guarantee success on the hyper-competitive App Store. You might even be tasked to build an app at work. Regardless of your background, this book distills my experience, as well as that of the larger iOS development community, to provide you with a practical guide to launching awesome customer-inspired iPhone and iPad apps.

I don't claim to have the market cornered on *the* right way to build an app, but what's in this book is not merely a guess of *a* way to do it. In fact, throughout this book, I am going to refer to two of my apps that have done well—AudioBookShelf and Tweeb—highlighting the principles of this book in practice.[1] Beyond AudioBookShelf and Tweeb, I will also point to the apps of those interviewed in this book, as well as several others, so that you can see the apps' evolution throughout the development process.

Although I've had my own successes, my knowledge, experience, and apps alone wouldn't be enough to prove that what you read in this book is a smart way to build your app. So, you'll be happy to know that I have interviewed the very best developers in the App Store. And when I write "the very best," I mean the very best. These developers include the likes of Smule, the creator of Glee, Magic Piano, and I Am T-Pain, as well as tap tap tap, maker of Camera+, the Digg iPhone app, Convert, and Where To? Both of these

---

1 My interests in Tweeb were acquired by the development firm Mobomo in June 2010.

developers have had a handful of *the* top paid apps in the App Store throughout their history. These interviews are well worth the price of admission. You'll find them exceptionally insightful and complementary to the content of each chapter, starting with the "Interviews" section in Chapter 1.

What You Need to Use This Book

This book assumes that you are a registered iOS developer and enrolled in Apple's iOS Developer Program, which allows you to develop and distribute iPhone and iPad apps on the App Store. If you are not, refer to this book's Appendix on how to register and enroll. Although you can begin developing your app without being part of the iOS Developer Program, you'll want to enroll in it now and start the process early, especially if you want to distribute a paid app. There can be some back and forth between you and Apple to complete the contractual, tax, and banking information.

Unless you are the person who is doing the actual programming of your app, you don't necessarily need to be working on a Mac. If you use a Windows-based PC, however, you'll be missing out on some nifty tools developed by Apple and third parties that can help you through this process. This includes Apple's freely available *iOS SDK* (software development kit) that has tools such as the iPhone Simulator and requires an Intel-based Mac for installation.

If you don't have a Mac but you have some funds for one, consider looking for a used machine on eBay or Craigslist. You might also look at Apple's lowest-priced Mac, the Mac mini, which is perfect if you already have a monitor, keyboard, and mouse. Of course, if you are planning to invest in app development over the long haul, take a look at higher-end models too (*http://www.apple.com/mac/*).

Refer to the Appendix to learn more about the iOS Developer Program, installing the iOS SDK, and which tools are available to you. Unless you are the one doing the programming and testing, the SDK and tools are not absolutely required. They are extremely helpful, however, as you become more familiar with building apps. At the expense of being a little more involved in the technical details, you'll free yourself from relying on others, especially your developer, and generally will be more informed about what's happening with your app.

I don't want to overlook a more basic requirement, which is to have an actual Apple iOS device. You should have an iPod touch, iPhone, or iPad. For the first two devices, I recommend at least a third-generation iPod touch or a third-generation iPhone (3GS). Although it is not required, if you have one of these devices for personal use, you may want to consider purchasing a separate one just for development purposes. That device will be useful if you plan to install the latest pre-release iOS software that Apple makes available to developers only. Chapter 2 covers the hardware differences among these devices.

How This Book Is Organized

I wrote this book so that you can use it from idea to App Store sale, while at the same time being able to refer to it for a particular topic. This second goal is particularly important for those who may already have an app or are just stuck. For example, discussing how to differentiate your app from others is addressed in Chapter 2, while improving your app before it is submitted to the App Store is covered in Chapter 6.

What is not initially apparent from the sequential nature of this book is that Chapter 8—the marketing chapter—actually begins being referenced in Chapter 3. As you move forward, you'll learn that marketing, or what I call your *marketing crescendo*, actually occurs in parallel with the development of your app. This approach highlights something that many developers miss. Namely, that many either do not market their apps or believe that marketing begins only after they have built the app or gotten it approved by Apple. If you start marketing your app at that point, you'll miss out on a key opportunity for your app, because the launch into the App Store presents one of the biggest moments for exposure and you need to fully maximize it.

Thus, the initial culmination of your marketing crescendo will be reached when your app is approved into the App Store. To reach that point, I will continue to direct you to Chapter 8 throughout the book to perform your *marketing checkups*—marketing activities that occur in parallel with your app's development—which consist of five phases. By the time you finish submitting your app to Apple in Chapter 7, you will have already referenced most of Chapter 8 and will immediately jump to Phase 5 of your marketing crescendo.

I also want to highlight that the process you are going to follow is essentially one complete pass through the life cycle of an app. This process starts with an idea and ends with updating your app once it has been launched. Some parts of the development process may require you to *iterate*; that is, you'll need to repeat what you are doing and get it right before moving forward (see Figure P-1). This can include validating your idea until it resonates with customers, revising a screen until it is easy enough to use, or improving the performance of your app before you submit it to Apple. While your decision to continue to invest in your app won't necessarily take you back to the beginning of this process, the conclusion of this book may seem somewhat anticlimactic because you'll already have been through all the steps at least once. This means that at the end of the book, the next step may actually be a previous step from an earlier chapter.

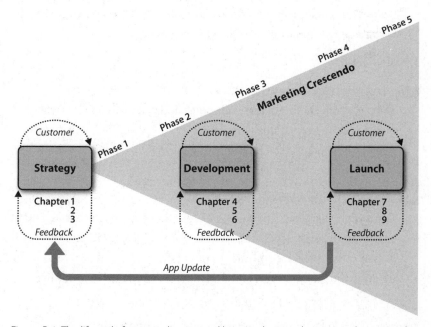

Figure P-1. The life cycle for an application and how it relates to the various chapters in this book; notice how you will be referring to Chapter 8 throughout the book, performing your marketing activities and developing your app in parallel

With this background, it's time for you to begin exploring your idea. Here's how the rest of the book breaks down.

Strategy:

Chapter 1, "You Have an App Idea...Now What?"
You don't start building an app...by building an app. You first need to wrap your mind around the vastness of the App Store ecosystem and discover whether your app idea should be more than just an idea.

Chapter 2, "Finding Your Inner App"
To build an app, you need to fully understand Apple's touch devices—the iPod touch, iPhone, and iPad—and how you plan to differentiate your offering from other options.

Chapter 3, "From Idea to Concept"
With the initial assumptions about the device you are targeting and the features you want your app to have, you'll immediately turn to customers to start validating these ideas. Of course, you'll first need to know who those customers are and how to find them.

Development:

Chapter 4, "For Hire: Identifying Help"
Having a concept for an app and some validated ideas about it will expedite your conversations with people or companies that will actually build it. Beyond understanding your app, you'll need to know how best to find and then vet designers and developers.

Chapter 5, "Getting a Working App"
Once you have a team in place, you'll use the assets you've created up to this point to begin developing your app. You'll dive more into the details of specific features the first version of your app will have, and begin defining the look-and-feel and functionality as you drive toward getting a working version of your app.

Chapter 6, "Making Your App Better Before It Reaches the App Store"
To improve the features and functions of your app, you and your customers will test it extensively before it is submitted to the App Store. To install an app outside the App Store, you'll create a special version of it that you can distribute for testing.

Launch:

Chapter 7, "Preparing for the App Store Submission"
> After you are satisfied with the first version of your app, you'll need to submit it to Apple for approval. Before running straight to Apple, though, you'll gather everything you need to make the App Store submission process as smooth as possible.

Chapter 8, "Building Your Marketing Crescendo"
> By the time your app is approved, you'll have your pre- and post-launch marketing checklist in place and start checking those items off to maximize the visibility and reception of your app when it first hits the App Store.

Chapter 9, "Measuring Success and Future Development"
> Comparing the criteria you defined at the start of the process with the feedback and data you now have allows you to assess how your app is doing. You'll be watchful of early warning signals and avoid problems by keeping customers engaged and excited about your app.

Tips and tools:

Appendix, "Tips and Tools"
> Those daring enough to get slightly more technical will be rewarded with some tips and tools that will make their involvement in app development more efficient and enjoyable.

Conventions Used in This Book

The following typographical conventions are used in this book:

Italic
> Indicates new terms, URLs, email addresses, filenames, and file extensions

---

This signifies a tip, suggestion, or general note.

Out with the Old, in with the Apple

As you can see from my tweet in Figure P-2, it's hard to keep up with the pace of innovation at Apple. In fact, I had to consistently rewrite, edit, and update various parts of this book while it was in progress because of the frequent changes to Apple's devices, software, and tools. While I've done my best to stay a step ahead of Apple, parts of this book are bound to become outdated.

Figure P-2. One of my tweets during the writing of *App Savvy*, revealing my attempt to keep up with Apple

Apple needs to stop being so innovative. Trying to write a book here! #iPhoneAppsBook

4:44 PM Apr 5th via txt

Delete

kenyarmosh
Ken Yarmosh

I've addressed this problem in a couple of ways. The first is that I wrote this book in a format that allows updates to some digital versions of it (e.g., O'Reilly eBook) and I plan to update the most significant changes and keep those versions as current as possible. On an ongoing basis, however, you should bookmark a special part of my website that is dedicated to keeping you app savvy: *http://kenyarmosh.com/appsavvy*. This site includes some complementary book materials that I've developed and I'll refer to that URL throughout the book.

Terms

The following words and phrases are used in this book:

iPhone
> "iPhone" is generalized to refer to the iPhone, iPod touch, and iPad unless noted otherwise.

App
> "App" or "apps" is short for application or applications, respectively. Apps are available for download and installation from Apple's App Store.

iPhone app

"iPhone app" is generalized to refer to iPod touch, iPhone, and iPad apps unless noted otherwise.

Third-party app

The term "third-party app" refers to all apps in the App Store. It is used only when comparing these apps to the Apple-provided apps such as Calendar and Mail.

iPhone developer

"iPhone developer" or "developer" refers both to the person(s) responsible for bringing an app to the App Store and to the person who possesses the programming abilities to write actual iPhone software code. The context will dictate which usage is being implied.

iPhone development

"iPhone development" or "development" refers both to the process of bringing an app to the App Store and to a specific task called "development" that is performed by the person who possesses the programming abilities to write actual iPhone software code. The context will dictate which usage is being implied.

Development team

Often, multiple people will be involved in the development process. Instead of the term "development team" or "team," though, the word "you" will generally be used to represent all of these persons unless another team member is specifically referenced.

Customer

"Customer" and not "user" is the preferred way to describe a person who will download and use an app. The word "customer" will generally be used to refer to prospective and actual customers, of both free and paid apps.

Safari® Books Online

Safari Books Online is an on-demand digital library that lets you easily search more than 7,500 technology and creative reference books and videos to find the answers you need quickly.

With a subscription, you can read any page and watch any video from our library online. Read books on your cell phone and mobile devices. Access new titles before they are available for print, and get exclusive access to manuscripts in development and post feedback for the authors. Copy and paste code samples, organize your favorites, download chapters, bookmark key sections, create notes, print out pages, and benefit from tons of other time-saving features.

O'Reilly Media has uploaded this book to the Safari Books Online service. To have full digital access to this book and others on similar topics from O'Reilly and other publishers, sign up for free at *http://my.safaribooksonline.com*.

How to Contact Us

Please address comments and questions concerning this book to the publisher:

> O'Reilly Media, Inc.
> 1005 Gravenstein Highway North
> Sebastopol, CA 95472
> 800-998-9938 (in the United States or Canada)
> 707-829-0515 (international or local)
> 707-829-0104 (fax)

We have a web page for this book, where we list errata, examples, and any additional information. You can access this page at:

> *http://www.oreilly.com/catalog/0636920010012*

To comment or ask technical questions about this book, send email to:

> *bookquestions@oreilly.com*

For more information about our books, conferences, Resource Centers, and the O'Reilly Network, see our website at:

> *http://www.oreilly.com*

Acknowledgments

This book would not be possible without a number of people. First, my beautiful wife, Stephanie, put up with me spending considerably more time in my man cave than normal. Without her support and understanding, this book would probably have been completed sometime in 2012. Similarly, I must thank my parents, family, and friends because even though I didn't talk with many of them through the first half of 2010, they decided not to disown me.

Of course, I wouldn't even have had the opportunity to alienate my loved ones without my editor, Brian Jepson, taking a chance on a first-time author. From my first interaction with him, Brian showed incredible interest in my ideas, super-fast responsiveness, and a desire to collaborate; that hasn't stopped. To that extent, Brian reflects the demeanor of the entire O'Reilly team, who impressed me through every step of this process.

Along with Brian, my technical reviewers, Jeremy Olson of Skookum and Chris Brown of Millennial Media, wrestled with the earliest version of the text and provided extremely detailed and insightful criticisms. Jeremy and Chris were initially interviewed in the book, but continued to provide some of the more helpful feedback after their interviews were finished. They were asked to do a formal technical review of the book once the first draft was completed.

I'm extremely grateful to everyone who agreed to be interviewed, and their names are listed in each of their respective chapters. There are others, though, that were not interviewed but were always willing to chat about anything and everything related to apps and this book. These people included David Smith, Doug Kushin, and Trace Johnson. A special thanks also goes to Thanny Young for her amazing design work on a couple of my apps, Bert Bates for his editorial comments while working on his own book, Graham Dawson for his perspectives on App Store rankings, Kevin Dewalt and Brant Cooper for their reviews of the customer development principles described in Chapter 3, Cody Fink of MacStories for his thoughts on estimating development costs, and Eric Ries for his generous introductions.

O'Reilly's Open Feedback Publishing System (OFPS) provided a great way for interested people to provide comments on the in-progress draft. I'm thrilled that many took the time to comment, but am especially indebted to Sean Mountcastle and Yixin Qiu for the amount of time they spent reviewing the book, both in OFPS and, later, with me directly.

Finally, this book represents a culmination of many, many years of personal and professional encouragement and love. These acknowledgments would be unbearably long if I expressed my appreciation to everyone who has been a part of this journey. To those I have not mentioned, and you know who you are, thank you.

Strategy

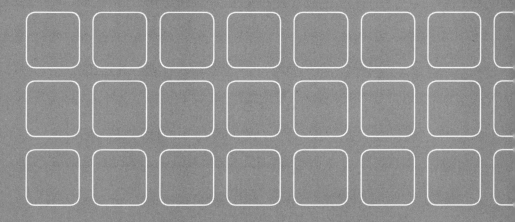

1

You Have an App Idea…
Now What?

IF YOU SOMEHOW ESCAPED the runaway success of the iPhone, iPad, apps, and Apple's App Store, you probably wouldn't be reading this book. It's likely that a family member, friend, colleague, some random person on the street, or Apple itself got to you. As a result, you've learned about people leaving their day jobs to pursue their dreams in Steve Jobs' App Store. You've seen—or rather heard—sophisticated apps such as the infamous iFart. You may even be talking about mobile and apps at work just as people did 10 years or so ago with the Web.

On that point, it's been suggested that mobile is the new Web. What is meant by such a statement in the context of the current mobile market is that mobile *apps* are the new Web. That is, apps—these small pieces of software that run on mobile devices—represent the next opportunity to fundamentally shift the way business and society use technology. This is perhaps a brash perspective for an upstart like the App Store, which is less than three years old. And yet, research shows that the iPhone has grown faster than other market-disrupting launches. For example, the iPhone and iPod touch subscriber base is already eight times larger than AOL's was two years after its launch.[1]

---

1 *http://www.morganstanley.com/institutional/techresearch/mobile_internet_report122009.html*

If that seems absurd, that's because it is. Since July 2008, when Apple opened its App Store—the marketplace where consumers can browse and install free or paid iPhone and iPad apps—the number of apps has grown so drastically that it's not even worth trying to keep track anymore. In about a year, the App Store went from fewer than 1,000 apps to about 50,000. In July 2010, the App Store's two-year anniversary, there were more than 200,000 apps that were downloaded more than 5 billion times in total.

Apple's "There's an app for that" marketing campaign has arguably been as successful as the company's idea for an App Store. Unlike with most marketing campaigns, however, Apple's campaign statement is somewhat true. There really does seem to be an app for almost everything, and that's where the trouble begins.

The "New" App Store

Not only is there a metric ton of apps in the App Store today, but everyone seems to have an idea for a new one. As in the dot-com era, the success stories and accessibility of the medium have enticed would-be entrepreneurs to think, "Why not me?"

In fact, it didn't take much effort to put some nice cash in your pocket when the App Store first opened. Earning a royalty check from Apple wasn't as simple as sneezing, but most of the apps that people bought then aren't even being downloaded for free now. At the launch, it was a simple case of supply and demand, with a relatively small number of diverse enough apps available compared to the large number of people who were intrigued by the newness of iPhone apps.

Circumstances are different today. The App Store is a highly competitive marketplace consisting of a delicately balanced interplay among Apple, developers (those who build the apps), and consumers (those who download the apps). Whereas Apple absolutely relied on a small, select group of developers to help populate the App Store when it launched, that's no longer the case. Estimates put the developer count at over 50,000, with Apple reviewing more than 15,000 new apps per week.

Looking at the Numbers

Within the context of the new App Store ecosystem, anecdotal evidence as well as actual analysis confirms that a get-rich-quick mentality to developing apps can be emotionally devastating and financially costly. It's true that the top developers do extremely well, with the most popular apps with the broadest appeal—typically games—such as Angry Birds and Doodle Jump yielding 4 million and 5 million downloads, respectively. Given the $0.99-per-download cost and the focus on these colossal hits, it is easy to look at the App Store and see nothing but dollar signs.

These tremendously popular hits, however, skew the realities of the more typical App Store application. The analysis that is available is fairly striking, and reveals that half of all paid applications receive fewer than 1,000 downloads and, after Apple's cut, earn just less than $700 per application per year. Those numbers may even be optimistic, because the downloads for the very top applications—such as Angry Birds and Doodle Jump—are so much larger when compared to most apps.[2]

Does that mean that if you are new to apps or building software in general, you should give up now? Not necessarily, but I do want to give you a reality check: recognize that with the current environment of the App Store, there are few who venture into it and launch an extremely popular app the first time around. That does not mean it's impossible for that to happen, but many successful iPhone developers create at least one app before building one that achieves their goals. Part of the value in pursuing your first app, in particular, will be the experience and process of building the app itself. Even with the head start you are getting from this book, the knowledge and experience of others cannot substitute for your own.

This reality check may be troubling to you, but my advice is to think broader than an app. Build something that has value to you beyond just the app. Successful developers usually decide from the outset of entering the App Store that they will be committed to it over a period of time, viewing app development as an investment opportunity and not a lottery ticket.

---

2 *http://communities-dominate.blogs.com/brands/2010/06/full-analysis-of-iphone-economics-its-bad-news-and-then-it-gets-worse.html*

The more experience you gain and the more time you spend in the App Store, the smarter you will be at identifying the right opportunities. By approaching the App Store as an investment, you'll cultivate important relationships with peers, customers, and the media, as well as create development and design assets that can be reused for other applications. In conjunction with the reality of the App Store's economics and the collective wisdom in this book, these relationships and assets are going to provide you a considerable advantage over those wandering into the App Store. Unlike others, you will not approach the App Store emotionally charged and with visions of grandeur about the viability of your idea. Instead, you will, as objectively as possible, assess the opportunity for your app and figure out if you should invest your time, money, and effort into it.

Evaluating Your Idea

To fully evaluate the viability of your idea, you should understand the landscape of apps on the App Store, assess what the value of launching your app is to you, and be realistic about your ability to get it into the App Store. I'm using the words "you" and "your" here, but this might include multiple people such as a team at work or friends and contacts who are working with you on this idea. Whether you are evaluating this idea by yourself or with others, the following framework will provide you with a more structured approach toward thinking about your app.

The App Store

The App Store really is the starting point for gauging your app idea. The App Store—whether on iTunes or the App Store app on the iPod touch, iPhone, and iPad—is not just a place to browse and download apps. It's a battleground, a place to gather intelligence behind enemy lines and learn from those who are doing things right (and wrong).

Apple has made it easy for you to start mixing it up in the App Store. If you have an iTunes Store account, you'll be able to use those credentials to install free or paid apps from the App Store. You can also create that account directly from your device (*http://support.apple.com/kb/ht3575*).

Make it your business to know what's happening in the App Store. Apple typically does a more substantial refresh of its Featured apps toward the end of the week. Featured apps are an extremely small subset of apps that are carefully selected by Apple and highlighted across all the stores each week (see Figure 1-1). This is a great way to see the types of apps Apple considers unique or interesting. Continue to visit the Featured apps section of the App Store after you've done your initial research so that you'll always be aware of what's grabbing Apple's and, subsequently, consumers' attention.

Look at the apps they pick and you'll begin to notice patterns across them—they're simple, they're creative, they have a great design, and they're well built. The Featured apps aren't always the most unique, but they are better—for one reason or another—than other similar apps. When an app is "Featured," it's a game changer for that app. The amount of visibility, and thus the increased number of downloads, for an app featured by Apple is sizeable, and is one of the more rewarding accomplishments an app creator can ever hope to achieve.

Figure 1-1. The Featured area of the App Store

Categories and search

Beyond the Featured section, you can browse the App Store through Categories. There are 20 categories total, with the Games category also having 20 subcategories. When you browse on a device (iPod touch, iPhone, or iPad), each category highlights the top 100 paid and free apps in it (Top Paid and Top Free). When you're on iTunes, you'll see the top 200 paid and free apps. There's also an overall Top Paid and Top Free listing called Top 25 on the iPhone and Top Charts on the iPad.

The Categories view is possible because developers must assign their apps to a specific category. More technically, apps are assigned to a primary and secondary category (see the section "Version Information" in Chapter 7). Choosing the category for an app is a strategic decision. Books, games, and entertainment have the highest number of applications, and thus more competition. For example, if an app could exist in both the Lifestyle and Entertainment categories, placing it in the former would offer a better chance for it to move onto one of the top lists. Getting too creative, however, could result in the app being ignored by consumers. Check out 148Apps (*http://148apps.biz/app-store-metrics/*) and uquery (*http://www.uquery. com/stats*) for breakdowns of all apps by category to get a better sense of the most crowded categories.

Figure 1-2 shows a graph from 148Apps. Notice that the Books, Games, and Entertainment categories have the largest number of apps. That does not imply that you should give up on your idea or place it in a completely unrelated category. Just be aware that you'll face higher competition in those three categories.

Figure 1-2. A breakdown of categories from 148Apps

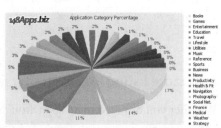

Remember that one of your main purposes in exploring the App Store is to identify and learn from applications that are similar to your idea. So, although the Categories view will be helpful to discover apps that are somewhat related, from a competitive research perspective the Search area of the App Store will be the most useful to you. Unlike Categories, Search will reveal any apps that are more directly comparable to your idea.

Search operates in three ways: querying by application name, by company name, or by *keywords*. Of course, if you don't know the names of the apps you consider competitive to your idea, searching for them by name will not be particularly useful. And even if you *think* you know all the competitive apps, there might be a few surprises waiting for you.

So, try typing in some keywords: words that describe the features, functionality, or uses for an app. Like a category, Apple requires developers to assign keywords to their applications (see Chapter 7). So, if your idea is to create an audiobook app and you type "audiobooks" into the search bar, Apple will return a list of apps with "audiobooks" in their name along with apps in which developers specified "audiobooks" as a keyword. Due to the number of applications in the App Store, though, the search results are also weighted by the popularity of the apps. This means that searching by keyword will help you find your top competitors.

Figure 1-3 shows a keyword search. The results will appear as you type letters and words into the search bar. Try various combinations and even non-obvious alternatives to find all the apps comparable to your idea.

You can also use resources such as Appsaurus (*http://www.appsaurus.com/*), Appolicious (*http://www.appolicious.com/*), Appsfire (*http://appsfire.com/*), and App Advice (*http://appadvice.com/*) to discover apps in the App Store.

App Store listing and customer feedback

Whether you browsed to an app through Categories or through Search, you will eventually arrive at the app's *App Store listing*. Understanding the anatomy of the App Store listing is important both in this research phase and later, when you will submit your own app to Apple (see Chapter 7).

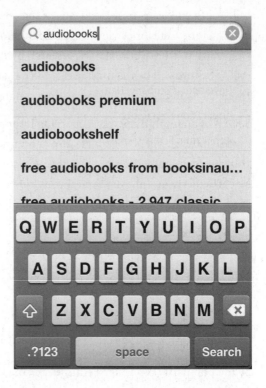

Figure 1-3. Searching for audiobooks

The App Store listing consists of a number of items that the creator of the app controls, including the application icon, application name, developer (company) name, application description, and application screenshots. The App Store listing reveals the sum total of how a developer markets his app to be downloaded. Give special attention to the language and features in the description area and the screenshots that are highlighted, as this information emphasizes what the developer considers most compelling about the app.

Figure 1-4 shows an App Store listing and its various components. Components labeled in white are controlled by the application developer while those in orange (labels 6 and 7) come from customer feedback about the app.

Key for Figure 1-4:

1 Application Icon

2 Application Name

3 Developer (Company) Name

4 Application Description

5 Application Screenshots

6 Customer Ratings

7 Customer Reviews

Figure 1-4. App Store listing on the iPhone for AudioBookShelf

The customer feedback areas of the App Store listing—Customer Ratings and Customer Reviews—are populated by the input of customers who download the app (see Figure 1-5). Apple verifies that a person owns the app by requesting that a customer verify account credentials before a rating or review will be shown. This also allows the customer to update the rating or review going forward.

An app's rating ranges from one to five stars, with five being the best. The review includes a title and a description, along with the name of the reviewer. Explore the Customer Reviews section for any app that is competitive or complementary to your idea. In this area, you can read the pros and cons of an app and what customers like or dislike. In particular, identify what customers are frustrated with or what they feel is lacking, as these represent opportunities for your app.

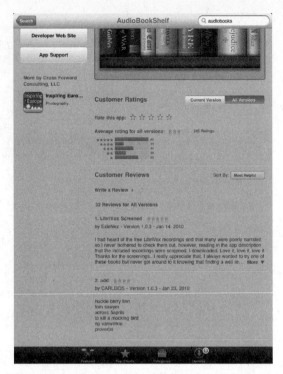

Figure 1-5. The Customer Ratings and Customer Reviews areas for an App Store listing on the iPad

Ongoing awareness

At some point, you may consider your exploration of the App Store and the app landscape done. Remember that hundreds and hundreds of applications are submitted to Apple every day, with the same amount being approved into the store. So, you'll want to be sure to keep track of these new entrants by viewing apps through the Release Date area of the Categories view for your primary category at least once a week (see Figure 1-6). On a weekly basis, you should also continue to review the top apps for your category and the new Featured apps.

Figure 1-6. Sorting a category on the iPad by release date, which shows newcomer apps comparable to yours

I can't stress enough how fanatical a consumer of apps and a student of the App Store you should be. For example, don't be stingy about installing paid apps. Give yourself a budget dedicated to checking out apps that you find interesting, are featured by Apple, are mentioned by press outlets, or you consider competitive to your idea. There's no better way to understand the app ecosystem than to continually be immersed in apps.

Overall, the goal of investigating the App Store is not to help you identify how to make an awesome app. Instead, it should be to help you get a sense of how many apps are similar to your idea and whether there is a highly competitive or a nonexistent market for it. Both of those extremes have implications. If you found many apps related to your idea, you'll have to build an app that is supremely better or more compelling than alternatives. If you found no or few apps, there's a chance that your app idea has little demand. I'm making generalizations in both cases. The good news is that even when dealing with these extremes, you will see examples of app developers who succeeded in crowded categories or by being pioneers.

Quantifying Your App

There's a reason, or some number of reasons, you want to build your app. Maybe you are interested in experimenting with new technology. Perhaps your job has required you to oversee the building of your company's app. Whatever those reasons may be, you still need some sort of justification for it—or what I'll refer to as "quantification"—because as mentioned earlier, building an app will require time, money, and effort.

Before going further, I want to articulate two nongoals of this quantification:

Determining exact download numbers
> In fact, that's not really possible, and even if it were, the numbers would fluctuate extremely rapidly.

Validating the features that would warrant someone downloading your app
> You are still in the idea stage. You will begin to build assumptions about features and validate them in Chapter 3.

Be sure you are clear on why you are pursuing your app. Are your motivations personal or professional? Is your objective to maximize downloads or revenue? Do you want to drive awareness of a charity or complement an existing product? Whatever you determine as your goals, they will influence how you proceed in quantifying your app and will be particularly important in the type of revenue models you select for your app.

Revenue models

A big issue with the Web is that even some of the most popular websites have struggled with turning a profit because of the absence of a simple payment mechanism. That's not a problem in the App Store because payment is facilitated through an iTunes account and Apple has reported it has 150 million credit cards on file.

There are a number of pricing methods for distributing an app in the App Store. Some are explicitly defined by Apple and others are clever ways of avoiding Apple's policies and limitations. Choosing the style of your pricing or, for that matter, deciding to make an app available for free should flow directly from your goals and the market data you've researched.

The Apple-defined pricing methods include an app being free and paid. There's also a feature called *In App Purchase*, which allows a customer to purchase something from within the application itself. Initially, In App Purchases were only allowed for paid apps, but Apple changed that restriction so that they also are allowed in free apps.

With so few options, you might think that choosing a revenue model is straightforward, but that's not the case. Even allowing In App Purchases for free apps and the launch of the iPad have drastically changed the way developers think about pricing and distributing their apps. Entrepreneurs also saw opportunities to bring other revenue streams such as advertising to the iPhone platform. Apple joined in the advertising game by purchasing mobile advertising platform Quattro Wireless in January 2010. Apple integrated Quattro's technology to create the *iAd* platform, which was announced as part of iOS 4. The following are the various revenue model options:

Free

Releasing an app for free may be a mystifying prospect to you. Why give anything away for free that involves any amount of effort? The answer relates directly to your goals.

The App Store may just be another channel for you or your organization to have a presence. If it is, it is less important to make money from your app. The Gap has apps for its various brands that it gives away because it wants to sell clothes, not apps. Facebook—one of the more popular free apps in the Social Networking category—is free because its website is free. The Salvation Army's app—its famous bell—is free because it wants to raise awareness of its cause and mission.

Free + Advertising

I'm going to immediately bias you about advertising as a way to monetize an app you release for free. Unless you have a large number of apps or an extremely successful app to advertise in, you are likely going to make more money charging even a nominal price for your app.

Many advertising options, including Apple's iAd, take 40% of the revenue generated. If you do decide to integrate an advertising platform into your app (see Chapter 7), make sure you do it in a way that is not intrusive or you will frustrate customers. Ensuring that the advertisements are relevant will also reduce the number of annoyed customers.

The Pandora music app is a good example of how to properly leverage advertising. Apple's iAd is addressed in more detail in "iAd" in Chapter 2.

Paid

A paid app is the second of the Apple-defined pricing methods. For paid apps, Apple takes 30% of any app sale. As I'll cover in Chapter 7, Apple uses a tiered pricing model, with each tier associated with a particular price (ranging from $0.99 to $999). Pricing your app appropriately is both an art and a science. It's one of the few elements that can quickly impact the number of downloads, and thus the revenue you make from your app. I'll provide more detail about initially pricing your app later in this chapter, and will cover promotional pricing strategies in Chapter 8.

Lite and Pro

Allowing customers to demo or try software before buying it is a fairly common practice. A major criticism of the App Store is that it lacks this function. Consumers can't try out paid apps and have to purchase them to use them.

Although it is less popular today due to the availability of In App Purchases for free apps, during the earlier days of the App Store developers began to circumvent the absence of a trial function by offering separate "lite" and "pro" versions of their apps. Typically, but not always, the lite version is free and the pro version is paid. Lite versions, as with trial software, usually either will not have all features available or will have some other limitations (e.g., a game may have only one level).

In App Purchases

In App Purchases is the final official Apple method for monetizing an app. As with paid apps, Apple takes 30% of any In App Purchase. Since Apple changed its policies to allow In App Purchases for free apps, the lite and pro model has increasingly become abandoned in favor of this option. Many developers use In App Purchases to turn on additional "premium" features or sell new levels in games. Using this approach versus a lite and pro model gives developers significantly more options to control how customers interact with and experience the app. Check out ngmoco's We Rule (*http://werule.ngmoco.com/*) and notification service Boxcar (*http://boxcar.io/*) for good examples of how to integrate In App Purchases.

New Versions

Once a person buys your app, she owns it indefinitely. If you continue to invest in that app and produce *updates* that help improve it, any customer who owns the app will receive the updates for free through the Updates area of the App Store (learn about updates in Chapter 9).

That process has been another sticking point for developers because it's a common software practice to charge customers for significantly different or enhanced versions of an application. Under the Apple App Store system, unless In App Purchases are used, the lifetime value of a customer is the initial price paid for the application. That means an app that cost a customer $0.99 will yield a total of $0.70 for a developer and never a penny more.

Although not extremely common on the App Store—except in the case of iPad apps—some developers decided that system doesn't work for them. So, after improving a version of an application for some period of time, they released a brand-new version of it under a different app name. Consider it a sequel of sorts.

Two examples of this approach include the popular Twitter client Tweetie (now owned by Twitter and renamed Twitter for iPhone) and a puzzle game called Enigmo. In the case of Tweetie, developer Loren Brichter felt so strongly about how much time he had invested in the next major version of his app that he shut down the first version and removed it from the App Store after launching Tweetie 2.[3] Enigmo pursued a slightly less controversial path, which was to think about the next version as a true sequel; both Enigmo and Enigmo 2 are still available on the App Store.

It is worth reiterating that the Tweetie case is bold. Removing the original version of the app from the store meant the app name could not be reused (as defined by Apple) and the ratings and reviews for the app would not transfer. Be very careful about this approach. Although it can offer the possibility of higher revenue, it could alienate existing customers if pursued solely for that reason.

---

3 *http://news.atebits.com/post/199400544/bigbird-redux*

For some more background on how to select a revenue model, including specifics around advertising, see the interview at the end of this chapter with Krishna Subramanian, cofounder of the mobile advertising exchange Mobclix.

Table 1-1 summarizes the various revenue model options.

Table 1-1. Summary of revenue models

Revenue Model	Uses	Examples
Free	Used for brand awareness apps or where the app itself is not the end goal	The Gap; Facebook; The Salvation Army Bellringer
Free + Advertising	Used for apps with a large number of customers and high interactivity	Pandora; Flixster
Paid	Used for the majority of apps; 70% of the revenue goes to the developer	—
Lite + Pro	Unofficial method to let customers test app without paying for it; now less common due to In App Purchases	Labyrinth Lite; Labyrinth
In App Purchases	Used to let customers buy new features	We Rule; Boxcar
New Versions	Unofficial method to persuade customers to pay for new versions of an app	Enigmo; Enigmo 2

App type

Currently, three types of apps can be submitted to Apple: iPhone, iPad, or Universal apps.

iPhone

iPhone applications work on the iPod touch, iPhone, and iPad. When on the iPad, iPhone apps run either at their original iPhone resolution (1× mode) or at twice the horizontal and vertical resolution (2× mode), to account for the larger iPad resolution. In 2× mode, your app will not appear very crisp, as each pixel is scaled up to occupy 2 × 2 pixels.

iPad

> iPad applications are the simplest of cases. They are apps that are built for the iPad and run on it only. When browsing the App Store you will see that complete iPad application listings will appear in iTunes and the iPad App Store but not on the iPhone App Store.

Universal

> Universal applications run on the iPhone and iPad as optimized applications using a single *binary* (see Chapter 7 to learn more about binaries). That is, a Universal app submitted to Apple knows how to function properly on whichever device it's installed on. Universal apps are supposed to help developers avoid maintaining two separate codebases—but can reduce the opportunity for additional revenue. On that point, Universal apps are consumer-friendly because customers pay one price for an app that works properly on the iPhone or iPad.

With the launch of the iPad, the "new" versions of apps, mentioned in the "New Versions" entry in the earlier list, have become more common. Many developers found that developing for the iPad is unique and that the amount of effort to make an iPhone app work on the iPad was not always trivial, making Universal apps less desirable. As a result, many iPad-specific versions of apps were developed. For apps that already existed on the iPhone, developers began adopting labels such as "HD" and "for iPad" for the iPad versions of their apps. "HD" generally is used for game titles while "for iPad" is a typical choice for apps in other categories. For example, the popular iPhone app game Flight Control was launched as an iPad version called Flight Control HD.

More details about differences between developing for the iPhone and iPad will be explored throughout the book, but especially in Chapters 3 and 5. For now, recognize that the option(s) you choose will impact your revenue potential.

Mike Rundle, creator of Digital Post, provides some context on choosing the right app type and working with Universal apps in an interview at the end of this chapter.

Pricing

At this stage, you only need to understand a general price point for your app. Your new familiarity with the App Store and the apps comparable to your idea should provide you a good sense about pricing. For instance, if others are charging $3.99 for similar apps, you probably won't be charging $14.99, but could charge $5.99 provided you did something that made your app worth the extra money.

Due to the general price sensitivity of App Store consumers, your app's price will have a significant impact on the number of downloads for your app. Even small changes such as shifting an app's price from $1.99 to $0.99 can impact download numbers. And yes, these are the sorts of pricing numbers most of you will be using for iPhone apps. The average paid iPhone app price is around $1.99. iPad apps are priced higher because the apps are often more complex, and in some cases they can even feel more like traditional desktop software. The average iPad app price is closer to $4.99.

Beware of pricing your app at $0.99. The lowest price in the App Store can lead to quick, impulse purchases. People buying your app before understanding what it is about can result in an onslaught of negative ratings and reviews when they find it doesn't do what they expected.

It's useful to think about some scenarios behind price points, especially if you are preparing to invest in the App Store over the long term. Consider an iPhone app that is priced at $2.99. If, on average, that app received 15 downloads per day over the course of a year, its gross sales would be around $16,000 ($15 \times \$2.99 \times 365$) with the developer's portion being around $11,000 ($16,000 \times .70$). Bumping the price will almost always reduce downloads because rankings typically worsen with higher prices. For the sake of this example, consider that a $4.99 price cut sales by one-third, to 10 downloads per day. The result may not be intuitive, but the gross sales would actually increase to approximately $18,000, with the developer's take being around $12,500.

Figure 1-7 shows an analysis from Distimo that provides anecdotal evidence that a higher price negatively impacts rank. Once this developer raised the app's price to $1.99 (shown as $2 in the figure), the rank plummeted outside the top 25, reducing the app's visibility, and potentially, its overall revenue. You should experiment with price to determine what yields the most revenue for your app. That won't necessarily be the lowest price with the highest rank and most number of downloads, but it could be.

Figure 1-7. Distimo analysis of price versus rank

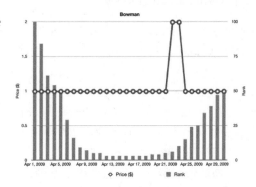

For many of you, if you're launching only a single app, these numbers would reflect a losing financial proposition based on what it will cost to build an app. But if you have a portfolio of apps, these economics can scale nicely. A second app that had similar success could begin producing supplementary income for many individuals.

Your app's best-case scenario

You can use your app's revenue model, app type, and price to size the market opportunity for your app. One way to do that is by calculating an *addressable market*. Your addressable market is a best case scenario for your app, where every possible customer downloads or purchases your app. The addressable market is a theoretical ceiling of the maximum downloads or sales of your app, which is equal to the number of customers for your app multiplied by the price associated with it.

What may not be clear to you initially is how to discover the "number of customers" for your app idea. Jonathan Wegener's excellent article "The Definitive Guide to iPhone App Market Sizing" (*http://blog.jwegener. com/2009/08/03/million-dollar-iphone-app-market-sizing/*), discusses an example of how to discover this type of information. Jonathan writes a blog called Back of the Envelope and is the creator of the iPhone app Exit Strategy NYC (*http://www.exitstrategynyc.com*). While I was preparing this book, I spoke with Jonathan, and he shared an update to the scenario in his original guide, providing a detailed example of how to calculate an addressable market:

> *Exit Strategy NYC is the ultimate tool for New York Subway riders. The application shows you exactly where you should be on the train to exit efficiently (for example, stand at the second door of the third car and you'll arrive directly in front of the station's exit). Using the app shaves minutes off each subway trip.*

> *Before starting the project, I ran some market sizing to make sure the sales would potentially be worth the effort. If I were launching the application today, here's how I would estimate the potential sales.*

> *First, see how many Apple devices there are in the world that could potentially buy the app—start by getting the latest sales numbers. As part of its iOS 4 announcement in early April 2010, Apple said 50 million iPhones had been sold to date and an additional 35 million iPod touches. Exit Strategy NYC works equally well on both of these devices, so we can use the combined 85 million figure. If every single person bought our app at $0.99, we could potentially have gross sales of $85 million. But our app has a limited appeal: it targets New York City subway riders.*

> *Next, let's see how many of these devices are in the United States. AdMob's Mobile Metrics report shows that roughly 50% of the devices are in the U.S., which means 43 million devices. There are 300 million Americans, so 21.5% of the population has either an iPhone or an iPod touch. Now, let's figure out how many of these devices are in our target market of NYC Subway riders. There are 8 million NYC residents and the MTA's website tells us there are 5 million subway riders on any given weekday. So, let's say 6 million ride the subway. Given the 21.5% device penetration we calculated earlier, this means there are 1.3 million devices among subway riders.*

But how many people will buy the app? To determine an upper bound on app sales, look for sales figures from top app sellers. Doodle Jump, a popular game, sold 3.5 million copies through early 2010. Across the 80 million devices, this represents an app penetration of around 4%. So, we can reason that if Exit Strategy NYC does well, it might get on 4% of the devices in our addressable market, which would be 1.3 million × 4% = 52,000 users. If it were a $0.99 app, it could potentially earn $52,000— before Apple's cut. And if it were priced higher, it could potentially earn even more!

Similarly, market sizing can also help you figure out if you're targeting too small of a niche. Perhaps you want to make an app to help wheelchair-bound Boston residents better navigate the city. Consider that Boston has 750,000 residents and about 0.5% are in wheelchairs, which means a target market of 3,750 people. If 21.5% have Apple devices and 4% at maximum will buy the app, that's about 32 customers. You obviously won't get a return on your investment serving those 32 customers.

If you plan to release an app with In App Purchase, be sure you use the sum of all possible purchases in your calculation (initial purchase plus all available In App Purchases). Similarly, account for a Universal app—one price for two apps—or if you are going to offer a separate iPhone and iPad version of your app. Although I am focusing on sales, an addressable market explicitly reveals the number of potential customers for an app, so it is useful for free apps as well, where the metric is not sales but downloads.

I want to reiterate that the addressable market number is not a promise of how much you will make from an app. Instead, it reflects the app's maximum potential by showing the possibilities if every single person interested in your app downloaded or purchased it.

Several good industry sources provide the number of devices running Apple's iOS. These include AdMob (*http://metrics.admob.com/*), Flurry (*http://blog.flurry.com/*), and Distimo (*http://www.distimo.com/report*). Flurry's VP of marketing, Peter Farago, is interviewed in Chapter 9.

Gleaning insights through rankings

Rankings are another way to assess how your app might fare on the App Store. Check the overall and category rankings through the Top 25 (iPhone), Top Charts (iPad), and Categories views—Top Paid, Top Free, and Top Grossing—to see if competing or complementary apps you've identified are showing. Rankings are important because they generally correlate to the number of downloads an application receives. Downloads, in turn, dictate the amount of revenue earned by the application.

Although viewing the rankings of these apps is not very scientific and won't reveal the actual download numbers for them, the rankings do provide another source to evaluate your idea. If you see that apps like the one you want to build are not ranking for their category, this may indicate that:

- There's not enough demand and interest for the type of app you have in mind because these apps are not being downloaded very often.

- There's an opportunity for you to do better.

In the iTunes App Store, you can view the top 200 apps for a category, while on the device App Stores you'll see only the top 100. The App Store is only a snapshot of what's happening now, though, and provides no sense of historical rank trending. To overcome this limitation, you can turn to tools such as PositionApp (*http://positionapp.com/*), MajicRank (*http://majicjungle. com/majicrank.html*), Mobclix's App Ranking (*http://www.mobclix.com/ appstore/*), or APPlyzer (*http://www.applyzer.com/*), which can show you extended rankings across all stores.

The data available to you in apps such as PositionApp and MajicRank is invaluable. Later, you can use these tools to track the rankings of your own apps. Now, however, you will want to track all the apps you consider competitive or complementary to your idea.

MajicRank, shown in Figure 1-8, provides you the opportunity to track comparable apps' rankings over time. If you track a fairly well-done app that has positive reviews, yet you find that it's not ranking, it could indicate that there's no market for the app. Conversely, apps ranking on any of the top charts show a promising market with the downside being the existence of viable competitors.

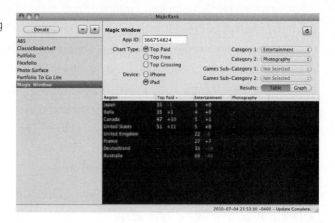

Figure 1-8. Tracking app ranks with MajicRank

Know Thyself and Thy Resources

You may have the next must-have iPhone or iPad app with a persuasive ad-dressable market, but if you can't take your idea and execute against it, it's just an idea. The good news is that even if you do not possess the experience to transform your idea into an app, you can find others who do. Still, when evaluating whether to proceed with your idea, you can't overlook inexpe-rience, or conversely, your prowess, in designing and launching software products *similar to* apps for the market you are entering.

Looking in the mirror

The ideal situation is for you to have experience both in the market or in-dustry where your app will be relevant and in producing digital products. If you have experience in neither of these areas, you'll have a harder time launching an app.

Birthing ideas from problems you experience daily, and thus knowing the mindset of the person who will use your app, is indispensable. You will definitely have the opportunity to learn from customers throughout the process of building your app. But being a customer yourself will start you with a solid set of assumptions and features for your app. Familiarity with your market or industry should also provide you with a nice list of potential customers, partners, and press contacts for your app.

If you have an idea that is outside your particular area of knowledge, try to surround yourself or consult with subject matter experts. That could be as easy as working with those who are using similar apps. The same holds true if you are clueless about building websites, software, and other digital products such as iPhone apps. Find accomplished designers and developers who don't just talk about app development, but show you their apps on the store. Team building and identifying help will be explored in Chapter 4.

Looking in the wallet and at the watch

You don't know exactly what your app is going to cost you yet…and that doesn't matter. It could, for example, cost you a grand total of zero dollars if you are building the app at work or with friends. There are still costs in both of those cases, though. In the first situation, your employer is footing the bill. In the second, you and your friends have an opportunity cost for something else you could have done with your time instead of building the app.

It's unlikely that a quality app would cost less than $10,000. This varies significantly based on features, complexity, and your experience with building software. Estimating app costs will be discussed in Chapter 4.

An app costing you no money out of your pocket highlights a key point. Independent of the amount of money you'll need to turn your idea into an app is a commitment to actually submitting it to the App Store. That commitment could cost you your nights and weekends if you're developing the app as a hobby. The commitment might also represent your company heavily investing in mobile and apps as a strategic initiative.

Thus, money is not the only thing to be lost in unsuccessfully launching your app, and yet it is *something* to be lost. When considering that half of all apps on the App Store make less than $700, you can start to understand why it's important not to invest too much in a single app. Regardless of what you'll learn about the costs to develop your app in Chapter 4, be firm in terms of what you are willing to invest into building an app, especially your first app. Start with a conservative budget and let the app prove itself on the App Store before using any of Junior's college fund.

Interviews

Digital Post: Mike Rundle

APP: Digital Post

POSITION: Creator (design and development)

BACKGROUND: Digital Post is a virtual newspaper application for the iPhone and iPad. The iPad application debuted as part of the iPad App Store launch in April 2010.

LINKS: *http://flyosity.com/digitalpost/; http://twitter.com/flyosity*

Ken: *Describe where you got the idea for your app, Digital Post. What were your goals in launching it? Do you feel you achieved those goals when it launched?*

Mike: Digital Post started out as a very different type of application with a different name and totally different concept. In early March 2010, I had the idea to build a dedicated "Internet search" app for the iPad, called SearchPad, with the goal for it to be available in the iPad App Store on the first day. I planned on pulling down information from Google (regular search results) as well as pictures (Google Image search) and displaying them in a nice way, better than you'd find if you used Safari. I had some interesting interface ideas for the image search; images would drop onto the screen and then could be manipulated using Multi-Touch gestures like in the movie *Minority Report*. The regular Google search results would be displayed in a list view, similar to how they're shown on the Web, but with better typography, spacing, and colors to make it more polished and feel like an app and not a website.

The more I thought about this concept the more I realized I was approaching the device in the wrong way, an easy thing to do when you're developing for a device you've never actually used before. I thought about how people would use the iPad and then tried to match it with the overall idea for SearchPad, and it just didn't mesh well. Before its launch, the iPad was mainly seen as a device for casual consumption of information: movies, emails, tweets, music, games, etc. It was being billed as an entertainment appliance where interesting information would be displayed for you to interact with. SearchPad wasn't going to display anything interesting to you when it opened; its first screen would essentially be an empty void until you typed in a term. SearchPad wouldn't be an app you launched when you wanted to be entertained for a few minutes, and after a few days of careful thought I realized that "instant interestingness" is the niche I wanted to be in, so I scrapped SearchPad and started thinking about similar concepts.

Many months ago I began an iPhone application called, simply enough, Interesting for iPhone. It would cull various RSS feeds that I predetermined and show what was interesting on the Web at the moment. I never finished it, but I took the kernel of that idea and applied it to the iPad. For information sources, I thought I'd use newspaper articles since they're of a high quality and precurated, and then it struck me to build the interface as a pseudonewspaper design.

My goals for Digital Post were simply to build something I was proud of and perhaps to make some money. I'm definitely happy with how it all came out, especially since I went from idea to 1.0 in about three weeks' time, only working nights and weekends. The sales have been good and fairly consistent as well, which was a shock to me. I thought there would be a huge jump at the beginning and then a tapering, but with Digital Post that was not the case.

Ken: *What sort of background research did you do to assess that Digital Post was a good idea? What convinced you it was the "right" app to pursue?*

Mike: The iPad lends itself to media consumption and the newspaper idea seemed to make a lot of sense for the form factor. I knew that the *New York Times* had an app in the works, but from seeing the interface when the iPad was introduced I saw a lot I could do to improve on the concept of simply browsing news articles. Their single-article view is excellent, but on the main view they try to emulate the newspaper version too much and only show four to five articles due to long excerpts. From my background in usability testing (and especially eye tracking), I know that people mainly read headlines to determine how interesting something is, so showing paragraphs of text for an article they don't want to read is a waste of space. In Digital Post, I use a list layout and display many more articles per screen, so it's easier to scan for something interesting to read. As soon as I knew it'd be an app that I'd use myself I knew I was on to something.

Ken: *With the launch of the iPad, Apple began offering the option for developers to create Universal apps. Digital Post started on the iPad, but you decided to build an iPhone version too. Will it be Universal? What went into that decision-making process?*

Mike: When Apple first announced Universal apps I thought they were a terrible idea, and so did many of my developer friends. Why would someone completely rework the interface for the iPad's resolution with brand-new features and not make it a separate app with a different price, especially if they have to rehire a designer to do it all? It didn't make sense to me at the time, but I'm slowly coming around, mainly because it makes your current users really happy, and that keeps the buzz and word of mouth going. From reactions on blogs and on Twitter, users are ecstatic when a developer releases a Universal version, because it's like a reward for being an early customer.

For Digital Post, I'm planning to have separate iPad and iPhone versions. That decision is based purely on price and the economics of each store. At $2.99, I think Digital Post for iPad is priced pretty well in the News category, and also relative to other apps in the App Store. For an iPhone app, however, a $2.99 price is definitely on the expensive side, considering the functionality it has. It's not a big enough app to warrant people thinking $2.99 is a good price for it. My plan is to do an iPhone version and price that at $0.99. In the future, I may drop the iPad version's price to $1.99, but that's not really for sure.

Ken: *Share some perspectives on how best to price an app. More specifically, how did you determine the price for Digital Post?*

Mike: The economics and business of the App Store interest me more than anything. Because the iPad was brand-new, no one really knew what the prices for apps would be like, so it was an exercise in game theory—your app's price is partially based on everyone else's price—and you don't want to look too expensive or too cheap. OmniGroup gambled the most and put out a $50 app, which seemed to raise a few eyebrows, whereas the big media companies had some great apps available for free. I priced Digital Post at $2.99 because some existing news apps in the iPhone App Store were around that price and it felt right to me for the amount of effort I put in and how much value someone would get out of it.

Ken: *Since you have a background developing software on other platforms, what makes the iPhone platform different? Where will those who may have experience in other media get tripped up when first dealing with Apple's iOS? Conversely, what will they enjoy more or find easier, if anything?*

Mike: When I first started learning Cocoa it was for Mac application development. It wasn't until later that I got into the development APIs for the iOS. I also have a deep background developing apps for the Web. I never learned C, so learning Objective-C meant I had to learn header files, pointers, and memory management as well. It's a challenge, especially since Objective-C's syntax is quite different from other languages someone may be coming from (Java, PHP, Ruby, etc.), but once you get the hang of it, you can fly. The Cocoa Touch frameworks are excellent and extremely high-level; you can do very complex things in one line of code. Apple's known for quality interface design, and they provide developers a wealth of built-in components that you can use without any customization to build solid apps. Of course, if you want to go the extra mile and do custom interface development, that's very straightforward as well.

The iPhone is one big constraint—no keyboard, small screen, few buttons—so designing applications for the iPhone is an exercise in building smart, simple software. It's all about removing everything until you still have the main features available and then executing those perfectly so that the interface is pixel-perfect and the overall user experience is smooth and flawless. Bloated apps full of half-baked features don't do well in the App Store, so it's better to omit a feature than to not get it exactly right. Compared to Android apps that I've used, an app's interface matters far more on the iPhone, so make sure it's a top priority.

Building applications for the iPad is very interesting; it uses the same frameworks as the iPhone, but applications feel so different. They feel more like full-screen desktop applications than simple mobile apps. However, the same elegant design principles from iPhone development apply, and the screen is very large, so there's more room for error. It's fairly simple to use the default built-in interface components for an iPad app, but when they're blown up to full-size they look awkward. Developers can create decent iPhone apps without hiring a designer, but you just can't get away with that when building an iPad app since there are more pixels to fill and errors are magnified. Hiring a designer to work on your iPad app is a must.

Ken: *Besides being tech savvy and a designer/developer, you're very involved in several different technology-oriented communities. All are huge assets that make putting an app into the App Store a somewhat less risky proposition compared to someone who is just starting out with app development. What advice would you give to those who find themselves in that position?*

Mike: As with all products, the better they are the more they do the marketing for you. If you don't have an exciting, engaging product, it takes more to convince people to write about you and spread the word. I'll be the first to admit that a curated, filtered news reader isn't the most exciting application in the App Store, but I did my best to execute the concept as well as I could. That's the only variable you really control: quality of execution. A decent idea with world-class execution will do well; however, the very best app idea in the world can be spoiled with poor execution.

How do you get world-class execution in an app for the App Store? Pay attention to the details: every pixel, every color, every font, every button. If you're not the type of person who can do this, make sure you hire the best interface design person out there, and no, they're probably not that expensive. I personally know people under the age of 20 who I'd consider world-class designers, guys with half my experience but twice my skills who are just insanely talented. Every few months or so one of them gets snatched up by Apple. These are the types of people you want on your project, not some gigantic iPhone consulting firm with a dozen people on staff treating your project like a paycheck. Unless you're building the next killer 3D platform, your app can probably be built with just a few people working on it if you get the right people. Finding these people is tricky, so you have to go where they are, such as forums like Dribbble and deviantART. Quality interface design is what turns a so-so idea into a fantastic app, and a great idea into a million-dollar app.

Ken: *What are three "to-do" items to put developers on a path to success?*

Mike: My three "to-do" items for success would be these:

- Build an app that you will love to use every day.

- Sweat every single detail or hire someone who will.

- Always remember the constraints of the platform since you don't want your app looking out of place (or people saying it belongs on Android!).

Mobclix: Krishna Subramanian

COMPANY: Mobclix

POSITION: Co-founder

BACKGROUND: Mobclix is one of the largest mobile ad exchanges, enabling 20+ ad networks to reach a targeted ad inventory across apps on the iPhone platform, Android, BlackBerry, and mobile web.

LINK: *http://mobclix.com*

Ken: *Mobclix has been a leader in the mobile advertising space. Having seen many apps across multiple platforms, what are some of the characteristics of successful apps? Conversely, what traits are evident in apps that struggle or fail?*

Krishna: Apps that serve a simple purpose and do it well are always successful. Casual games that are fast-paced, like ngmoco's Maze Finger, keep users engaged. Apps that make use of the rich features of smartphones are always exciting—Need for Speed, for example, incorporates the iPhone's accelerometer. Meanwhile, apps that tap into users' online social circles can become extremely viral. For instance, Newtoy's Words with Friends and FlipSide5's Touch Hockey both allow users to play against each other over network connections.

Consumers only want to spend three to five minutes to perform a task or interact with data and objects. Understanding this behavior has been essential to the developers who've made successful apps. This is because the longevity and sustainability of an app can be determined by its ability to invoke high levels of consumer engagement (e.g., magazine apps and multiplayer games), help users perform a task well (e.g., productivity and navigation), check and consume data (e.g., Twitter clients and instant-message clients), or interact in an entertaining fashion (e.g., casual games). Likewise, apps with simple designs and good functionality can also expect to do extremely well on the App Store.

Apps that fail or fall out of favor with users have three main traits in common:

- "Me-too" apps

- Too complex

- Not enough functionality

Me-too apps are apps that try to replicate the behavior of successful apps. Often, these copycat developers will miss key features or will fail to understand the key mechanics needed to engage their users. Two good examples of this are Doodle Jump and PapiJump. Both apps have the same functionality; however, Doodle Jump succeeded by providing consistent updates and engaging their customer base. PapiJump, on the other hand, released updates at random intervals that didn't make any significant changes to the app. Moreover, apps that serve as app wrappers of web content, soundboards, or joke cards don't provide enough user value to have a sustainable life cycle in the App Store.

Ken: *Choosing a revenue model (e.g., free, paid, In App Purchase, advertising, etc.) is often confusing for new developers. Based on Mobclix's experience, how should developers approach determining what works best? Can a business model change over time?*

Krishna: When the App Store first launched, developers were only able to release paid apps and free apps. In other words, they had two distinct audiences that they could market to. Free apps typically drive the widest audience for developers and guarantee them revenue through advertising. In the early days of the App Store, we heard of one-off companies making millions on $0.99 apps (e.g., iShoot, Pocket God, etc.). Most of the time, developers would first focus on maximizing the number of downloads of their free apps, and then try to drive those users to download the paid version of the app.

As of late, we are seeing more traction in the In App Purchase model across free apps, largely because this model offers quicker and increased revenues via in-app incentives.

Ken: *When does it make sense for a developer to choose advertising as the right business model to monetize an app? For those that fall into that category, what are some good practices for incorporating advertising properly? What should developers definitely not do when choosing to use advertising?*

Krishna: Best practices include leveraging all of the available types of advertising. This means having a good mix of banner, interstitial, and rich media advertising. That being said, developers need to think about advertising and how it will fit into the app from day one by building the user experience around ad creatives. Often, developers wait until the very end to add in advertising, making for a poor user experience. Right now, we are starting to see developers create better engagement around the banner ads as a way to drive higher click-through rates (CTRs). ngmoco's GodFinger app is a good example.

Developers also need to understand that impressions are not the only or even most important drivers of revenue. The mobile advertising ecosystem is still evolving, and CTRs are an important measure of performance right now.

Ken: *Related to the previous question, what are some ways for developers to estimate what they might be able to make from advertising in their apps? Is there any market data or tools available to help them have even a broad understanding of whether their app can offer a better return on investment through paid downloads versus advertising?*

Krishna: Some good tools include the estimators and calculators that are available via Mobclix. A good rule of thumb is to take 70% of the expected purchase price and compare that to the total estimates that advertising can provide.

Ken: *How will the launch of the iPad affect the app economy? How will this impact mobile advertising? What will be the new opportunities for advertising on the iPad?*

Krishna: The iPad will provide a new user base for developers to attract and make great apps for. Mobile advertising will continue to grow and innovate, and with the proliferation of the iPad device, it will continue to drive marketers and advertisers to devote more of their budgets on mobile. Advertisers will be able to leverage the iPad's functionality to drive higher engagement with creative ads.

You will also start to see a shift from mobile ad networks to online ad networks in terms of ad dollars being driven to the iPad since the ad unit sizes correlate more to IAB (*http://www.iab.net/*) standard sizes.

Mobclix provided the first monetization solution on the iPad and has the largest display inventory across the board on the iPad today. We were able to do this by leveraging our online ad network relationships to help developers start generating revenue when the iPad App Store launched.

Ken: *How will the introduction of the iAd impact Mobclix and other mobile advertising options? Does the iAd appeal to all developers and advertisers or to only certain segments?*

Krishna: There are certain types of advertisers looking to reach a certain type of app and iAd will bridge that gap. For sure, the iPhone platform advertising market will continue to flourish and have multiple winners. iAd will increase the overall advertising earnings available to iPhone and iPad app developers. At the same time, scaling rich media campaigns across 30 billion impressions will be a monumental challenge. Plus, HTML5 creative adoption will be an ongoing process. At the end of the day, advertisers will continue to focus on cost to acquire new customers and brand equity.

Whether they use a rich media brand buy or a targeted text ad, they will want to answer the same question: how much is it costing me for a new user? As for developers, the best plan of action for them will be to have multiple sources of revenue to maximize the value of their user base.

Recap

When deciding whether you should move forward with your idea, consider everything you learned or uncovered in this chapter. To help you keep track of this information, I created a way for you to logically organize your research. It's available at *http://kenyarmosh.com/appsavvy*, and I think you'll find it helpful to see all of your information in one place.

Don't be discouraged if you've gone through the steps in this framework and subsequently decided that your app idea is not worth pursuing. The same is true if your app was already in progress but you shut it down. Should you find yourself in either of those scenarios, you are to be applauded because you've successfully digested and applied the content of this chapter. Ultimately, you've saved precious resources being applied to a failing proposition. The likelihood is that you'll get another idea soon. If that one leads you to a brighter conclusion, you'll be in a better position to explore it.

2

Finding Your Inner App

NOW THAT YOU HAVE MORE THAN AN INSTINCT that your idea
has some merit to it, it's time to start defining some details about your app
and how it might stand out in the App Store. To do so, you'll need to be
more familiar with the unique aspects of the iPod touch, iPhone, and iPad
devices.

In this chapter, you'll explore:

- The uniqueness of Apple's touch devices
- Specifics about the iPod touch, iPhone, and iPad
- What's new in iOS 4
- How to approach developing an innovative app

Getting Familiar with Apple Devices

Before That…Think First, Design Later

After browsing the App Store and thinking about the potential of your app,
you may be excited to get started. Many people assume "getting started"
means jumping straight into what the app is going to look like and how it's
going to function. Doing that is one of the biggest mistakes you can make.

First, a person who is not a designer or developer will need to collaborate on the creative and functional aspects of the app with people who do possess design and development skills. Trying to work on either of those now will only lead to frustration. Second, just as there was a structure to vetting your initial idea, there's a structure to developing it.

I promise that you'll get to how your app will look soon enough. In the meantime, you need to continue to refine your idea and create a set of assumptions about it. That starts with understanding more specifics about the iPod touch, iPhone, and iPad devices.

Breaking Down Devices and Device-Related Features

Part of what makes creating an app and developing on the iOS platform more unique than working with other software is a higher dependence on the device. Your app's functionality will rely on the device it runs on and will need to be built to accommodate it.

Although in the following sections I will review the common features across all devices, and subsequently the features specific to each device, it is ultimately the designer's and developer's responsibility to properly implement them. I provide this information for context so that you have a more comprehensive understanding of what you can incorporate into your app. The intricate technical details regarding how these features are integrated into your app shouldn't cause you angst.

The "touch" generation

Next to apps themselves, what has made Apple's iOS devices so successful is *touch*. Sure, the ability to interact with a device through some sort of physical touch metaphor existed previously. It just hadn't been created "the Apple way."

The two biggest differentiators for Apple's approach included a large keyboard-less display—now fairly common for mobile devices—and *Multi-Touch*. Multi-Touch allows the device to recognize more than one touch or gesture on the screen at once. It is what powered the revolutionary *pinch to zoom* feature on a map or photo.

Apple didn't stop there, though, as even the more basic touch capabilities were improved, allowing "endless scrolling" by swiping up or down and left or right on the screen. The point is that Apple raised the bar dramatically, redefining how someone could interact with standard functions (e.g., email and voice mail), and eventually apps. All new smartphones and touch devices launched today have to at least try to compete on this front with the iPod touch, iPhone, and iPad.

You definitely don't want to underestimate the significance of how the Multi-Touch paradigm will impact the experience of your application. Although the mouse and point-and-click have been the predominant experience for consumers for the past two decades or so, controlling an app via touch is exceptionally more personal and intimate.

The same is true with the device itself. People hold and experience their devices and apps while on the bus, in bed, and yes, even in the bathroom. They slip them into their pockets and slide them into their bags. They customize every aspect of them, from the background to the order of the icons on their Home screen. The Home screens of an iPod touch, iPhone, and iPad are little customizable worlds crafted and shaped in every way and everywhere, tap by tap, touch by touch, and swipe by swipe. These devices present a means to be perfectly unique reflections of their owners (e.g., see *http://firstand20.com/*), and it all starts with the experience of touch.

The iPod touch and iPhone allow for five simultaneous touch events. Developer Matt Gemmell discovered that the iPad more than doubles the number of touch events (see Figure 2-1), with 11 simultaneous touches (*http://mattgemmell. com/2010/05/09/ipad-Multi-Touch*), indicating that Apple clearly developed it for Count Tyrone Rugen (see the section "Fundamentals of all devices" on page 54).

Figure 2-1. Matt Gemmell's analysis of the number of simultaneous touch events for the iPad

Fundamentals of all devices

A number of elements are standard across the iPod touch, iPhone, and iPad. I'll cover these first and then address each device individually.

Apple no longer officially supports first-generation devices such as the original iPhone. Older devices and operating systems (pre-iOS 3.x) are increasingly becoming statistically insignificant, especially with Apple making iOS 4 a free upgrade. Thus, the following sections assume a baseline of second-generation devices running iOS 3.x. Because of the relative newness of iOS 4, it is addressed separately.

Hardware

The three hardware features that are available on all Apple devices are WiFi, Bluetooth, and the accelerometer. The first two are probably familiar terms to you and relate to network connectivity. The significance of WiFi as a baseline is that certain devices will have access to the Internet only when a WiFi network is present. Thus, network connectivity cannot always be assumed.

It might seem odd that Bluetooth is a common element to all devices, especially when most people use it for hands-free headsets and the iPod touch and iPad do not have phone capabilities. Bluetooth is included on all devices because Apple relies on Bluetooth for peer-to-peer connectivity, most often taken advantage of in games. Bluetooth also allows the later-generation devices using iOS 3.2 and later operating systems to connect to a Bluetooth keyboard.

You are likely more familiar with what an accelerometer does than with the word itself. The accelerometer is what detects the movement and orientation of a device. In the former case, the device can detect side-to-side, up-and-down, and more sporadic shaking movements. The more basic function, however, is that the accelerometer powers apps to flip from portrait to landscape mode depending on how the devices are being held. If you are a physics geek, the accelerometer can offer a playground. Take a look at Illusion Labs' games Labyrinth 2 and Labyrinth 2 HD, which showcase the accelerometer in all its glory.

Apps

Most of the functionality of the Apple-provided apps (see Figure 2-2) is accessible to *third-party* apps (like yours) through various *technical frameworks, kits*, and *application programming interfaces* (*APIs*). Since detailing those is both beyond the scope of this book and irrelevant to you, I'll review the functions of Apple's apps and how they are made available to you. I'll continue to use the term "third-party" throughout this section to help distinguish the apps in the App Store from Apple's apps.

The *Contacts* apps house all the contacts of a device. When in a third-party app that accesses the device's Contacts, depending on what is selected (e.g., phone number), an app may close and activate some other action such as a phone call. In that case, the app will not necessarily re-open once that action is completed. In other cases, such as emailing, if *in-app email* is used, the device's *Mail* app will open a new message and return to the app once it is sent or canceled.

Another popular function incorporated into third-party apps comes from the Safari web browser. Using Safari's functions, a user can open links from within an app without having to leave it.

Closely related to Safari is web video content. With YouTube being the Web's most popular video destination site, Apple worked with Google to create a *YouTube* app optimized for Apple devices. Clicking on a YouTube video from within a third-party app will open the YouTube app; the app will return you to the third-party app when you are done with the video.

Continuing with media, the *Photos* and *iPod* app libraries are available to third-party apps. Developers often use these libraries when their app would benefit from including a photo from a device's *camera roll* or from customizing sounds (e.g., an alarm clock app). Other media functions available include playing audio and video clips, as well as recording audio.

Another popular application func-tion that's available across Apple's devices comes from the *Maps* app. Apple again partnered with Google to bring a customized version of Google Maps to Apple devices. Leveraging Maps' features, devel-opers can embed maps into their apps. Obviously, that's typical for apps in the Navigation category, but this functionality is not used exclusively by navigation-based apps.

Figure 2-2. Features of Apple's apps, which are made available to develop-ers to use in the creation of their own apps

Utilities

Recall that I mentioned the "keyboard-less" display before. Obviously, most apps would be completely useless without some way to input text or numeric content. Apple provides apps with several different on-screen keyboards that can be shown based on usage needs, including ones customized for entering a web address and phone number.

Beginning in iOS 3.0, *Cut, Copy, & Paste* was introduced and became an instant success. Although Apple has it enabled in most of its apps (wherever it makes sense), developers don't always incorporate it. When they fail to, they hear about it from customers. To a lesser extent, the same holds true for keyboard *auto-correction* and *auto-capitalization*.

Services

Mentioned in Chapter 1, In App Purchase is one of the more significant technical frameworks provided by Apple. It facilitates payment authorization through Apple without having to leave the application. Developers have found many uses for it, including selling new levels in games and turning on premium features such as push notifications.

On that last point, push notification is another technical framework that has a substantial customer-facing impact. Its official name is the *Apple Push Notification Service* (*APN*), and it sends or "pushes" an alert or notification to a customer's device. The push notification can include a message, a sound, a *badge number*, or a combination of all three depending on the developer's preference (see Figure 2-3). Push notifications are useful for encouraging a customer to re-engage with an application depending on whether a particular event has occurred. With the launch of iOS 4, Apple has released local notifications.

Figure 2-3. Notification settings in the NotifyMe iPhone app

All devices also have general location-based services available through WiFi. Through WiFi signals and access points, devices use technology from Skyhook and Google to calculate location in Apple's apps (e.g., Maps), as well as third-party apps.

iPod touch

In many ways, you can think of the iPod touch as the baseline Apple device. As such, there really aren't device-related features to detail, so I'll focus only on the hardware specifications.

The second-generation iPod touch models have a 533 MHz processor. That's actually faster than the iPhone 3G. The third-generation 32 GB and 64 GB iPod touch devices have the same specifications as the iPhone 3GS, namely a 600 MHz processor and 256 MB of RAM.

These specs, as well as the ones that follow, aren't pointless. The performance and speed of an app can vary significantly across devices because of these hardware differences. Keep that in mind when you begin testing your app, which I'll address in Chapter 6.

---

iPhone

The iPhone includes all of the features of the iPod touch plus some additional capabilities. I'm not going to highlight obvious differences, such as support for phone calls and text messages. Instead, in the following list I'll focus on the essential device-related features for the iPhone 3G, iPhone 3GS, and iPhone 4:

iPhone 3G

The "3G" in the name "iPhone 3G" stands for "3G network." Essentially, it allows faster data delivery speeds through the cellular network compared to previous generations (that's the "G") of networks. This means the iPhone, unlike the iPod touch, can access the Internet outside of WiFi. Connectivity and speeds will vary based on network demands and availability.

Although all devices have basic location-based services through WiFi, what others do not have is the more precise positioning of GPS. GPS became a killer feature for Maps, allowing turn-by-turn navigation based on current location.

Beyond obvious uses, apps will often associate *geolocation* data from the available location-based services (WiFi or GPS) when creating content such as notes or photos so that a person can see the date and place where he jotted down a thought or snapped a picture. Of course, to snap a picture, you need a camera. The camera is the final major differentiator between the iPhone and iPod touch/iPad.

iPhone 3GS

The "S" in the name "iPhone 3GS" unofficially stands for "speed." Compared to the iPhone 3G's 412 MHz processor with 128 MB of RAM, the iPhone 3GS has a 600 MHz processor and 256 MB of RAM, giving it a fairly sizeable upgrade on both fronts. With these specifications and support for up to 7.2 Mbps cellular data link speeds (compared to 3.6 Mbps for the 3G), the download speeds for the 3GS have been clocked to be as much as three times faster than for the 3G.[1]

Apple also added a *Compass* app to the iPhone 3GS via a new electronic compass chip. But what made people considerably more excited was the 3-megapixel camera upgrade (from 2 megapixels) with support for video recording. These latter two additions are more commonly incorporated into third-party apps than the compass functionality.

iPhone 4

As with the launch of the iPhone 3G compared to the original iPhone, the iPhone 4 was a major product update to the iPhone line and its iPhone 3GS predecessor. The design changes alone are significant, with the iPhone 4 being 24% thinner than the iPhone 3GS and constructed of stainless steel and glass rather than plastic. The engineering changes did not stop with the design. While making the iPhone 4 smaller, sleeker, and sturdier, Apple also considerably upgraded the specifications and features of the 3GS.

---

1 *http://www.tuaw.com/2009/06/25/speed-test-comparing-iphone-3g-3g-s-and-palm-pre-has-surprisin/*

The upgrades start with Apple's A4 processor—also used in the iPad—suggesting a 1 GHz processor speed and 512 MB of RAM. They continue with the introduction of a new high-resolution display called *Retina display*, a 5-megapixel camera, HD video recording, a front-facing camera that helps power *FaceTime* (Apple's WiFi-based video chat), and a gyroscope, which in combination with the accelerometer allows for six-axis motion sensing.

Although the number of those additions is stunning, the one with the most immediate impact to you as an app developer is Retina display. It essentially places four times the number of picture elements—*pixels*—into the same screen size of the previous iPhone models. The result of this higher pixel density is a super-sharp display that makes text and graphics look extremely crisp. To take advantage of Retina display, though, you'll need to prepare an additional set of design assets, as is required if submitting a Universal application (see Chapter 5).

iPad

The differences in the iPad start with how you engage the device. Its display is more than 2.5 times larger than the iPhone, so unlike an iPhone, the iPad is not extremely functional when you use it with only one hand; you need to either use both hands or rest it on a surface. And where the iPhone and iPod touch are predisposed to being portrait-oriented, the iPad appears more natural and useful when in landscape mode.

In terms of hardware specifications, the iPad was the first device to adopt Apple's A4 processor, confirmed at 1 GHz. Ironically, the bigger iPad actually has only 256 MB of RAM, meaning that it has the same amount of RAM as the iPhone 3GS and half the amount of RAM as the iPhone 4. Similarly, although the display is more than 2.5 times larger than the iPhone, its pixel resolution is 1024 × 768, which is not as striking a difference against the iPhone 4's 960 × 640.

Whereas iOS 4 has a software toggle for portrait mode lock, a device control unique to the iPad is *screen rotation lock*. As mentioned earlier, the iPhone, as a phone, has a somewhat natural association with being portrait-based. That's not the case with the iPad, and so Apple created a button that allows the screen to be locked in portrait or landscape orientation. When you shift the button to the lock position, the screen no longer will shift orientations when the device is rotated. Although this is helpful to consumers, it adds another variable for developers. This control is the primary reason Apple recommends iPad apps be able to operate equally well in portrait and landscape modes.

Aside from differences in its size, processing power, and memory, the iPad has similar device components to the iPod touch, including the accelerometer, Bluetooth, push notifications, and so on, all properly adjusted for the iPad. Most of the Apple-provided apps are also on the iPad, but each app has been customized for the device. Apple's iPad versions of its iPhone apps are the best examples that designing apps for the iPad requires its own approach.

Carl Loodberg, CEO of Illusion Labs, on Developing for the iPad

"Developing for the iPad is, in most ways, very similar to the iPhone, but there are some differences. The largest differences are more in the UI and interaction design areas. The larger screen size means that more information is presented at once and that a lot more graphics are present in the UI and the game. That in turn means that a lot more runtime memory for these graphics is needed. To fit all of it in memory, care has to go into optimizing memory footprint.

"The HD version of Labyrinth 2 differs a great deal from the iPhone version, but, of course, some code is still shared between the two. We felt that the Universal version approach would be hard to achieve while still staying under the 20 MB 3G download limit, which we feel is important."

For more information on Illusion Labs, see *http://www.illusionlabs.com/*.

The essential device-related features for the iPad follow:

WiFi

> By now, you likely deduced that the iPad WiFi model does not include a cellular connection and relies exclusively on WiFi for access to the Internet. As a result of not having that, it also is missing GPS and precise location positioning, using the more basic WiFi location services.

WiFi + 3G

> As I alluded to earlier, the WiFi + 3G model also includes GPS for use in Maps and third-party apps. This model is identifiable by the black strip across the top of the device and the micro-SIM card tray on its side. The micro-SIM card, which identifies you to the cellular network, enables the 3G cellular data connection.

This section on the iPad is short, for two reasons:

• As mentioned previously, beyond physical dimensions, the iPad does not have many unique device-related features. The biggest changes from the iPhone are not the more obvious hardware differences, but rather how the iPad substantially affects the design and development of apps.

• Since both iPad models share the same processor and memory specifications, there's nothing to highlight as there is with the different models of the iPhone.

Summary

To help with all the differences between the iOS devices, Table 2-1 summarizes the key technical specifications of the iPhone, iPod touch, and iPad.

Table 2-1. Summary of the iPhone, iPod touch, and iPad features

Device	Model(s)	Processor	Memory	Display (diagonal)	Pixels	Pixels per inch	Network
iPod touch	Second generation	533 MHz	128 MB	3.5 inches	480 x 320	163	WiFi
iPod touch	Third generation	600 MHz	256 MB	3.5 inches	480 x 320	163	WiFi
iPod touch	Fourth generation	1 GHz	256 MB	3.5 inches	960 x 640	326	WiFi
iPhone	3G	412 MHz	128 MB	3.5 inches	480 x 320	163	WiFi; cellular
iPhone	3GS	600 MHz	256 MB	3.5 inches	480 x 320	163	WiFi; cellular
iPhone	4	1 GHz	512 MB	3.5 inches	960 x 640	326	WiFi; cellular
iPad	WiFi	1 GHz	256 MB	9.7 inches	1024 x 768	132	WiFi
iPad	WiFi + 3G	1 GHz	256 MB	9.7 inches	1024 x 768	132	WiFi; cellular

iOS 4

The latest operating system for Apple's touch devices, iOS 4 is significant and deserves to be addressed separately. As in the previous section, I will highlight how iOS 4 impacts end-user functionality. You'll be especially happy to not have to focus on the inner technical workings of the 1,500 API changes.

Since there are upward of 100 new features in iPhone OS 4, I'm only going to outline the most important ones. These were also identified by Apple in its initial introduction of the new operation system, as part of the so-called seven "tentpole" features. Having worked with iOS 4, I can safely inform you that these really are the ones to focus on when familiarizing yourself with the new operating system.

iOS 4 is not compatible with first-generation iPhone and iPod touch devices. Certain features, such as multitasking, will only work with the latest devices, including the third-generation iPod touch and iPhone 3GS, which, as you may recall, share the same processor and memory specifications.

Multitasking

The inability to multitask on Apple's touch devices has probably been the biggest criticism of the operating system from both developers and consumers. Apple introduced its version of multitasking as part of iOS 4.

I'm going to editorialize for a moment on the topic of multitasking and relate that back to Apple's approach. Although it's less true for the iPad because of its larger display, for the iPhone, iPod touch, and more generally mobile devices, multitasking carries a different importance compared to traditional computers. Unlike with their predecessors, mobile devices have considerably smaller screens and are exceptionally more portable. People use them to perform discrete tasks, whether they are functional or fun, and quickly move on to some other activity.

There are few cases in which this does not hold true. This includes when several related tasks must occur together or when a task is ongoing. Prior to iOS 4, Apple actually addressed these issues for its own apps. You probably don't realize this, but apps such as Mail and the iPod always ran in the background pre-iOS 4. This was most evident with the iPod app because you could listen to music, for example, while also using other apps. So, what Apple did for multitasking in iOS 4 is essentially allow third-party apps to also take advantage of these functions.

Multitasking allows third-party apps to run in the background, meaning the apps continue to work even though they are not shown on the screen. Running in the background is especially useful for audio (e.g., playing an audiobook), VoIP (e.g., talking with someone on Skype), and navigation apps (e.g., getting directions to a location). Consumers can access these apps, and more generally, work across several apps simultaneously through Apple's *fast app switching*, which reveals a taskbar of all running apps when you double-click the Home button (see Figure 2-4). Although it's debatable whether this implementation captures common expectations of true multitasking, I would argue that Apple has addressed the core of multitasking and appropriately redefined it for mobile devices.

Included under the multitasking umbrella are task completion (e.g., download a file and inform the user when the download is complete) and local notifications. Local notifications are similar to push notifications but are triggered at specific times and remove the requirement to communicate with a server. Consider, for example, scheduling a reminder for taking medication or for watching a TV show.

Of course, there are some technical requirements to implementing the new multitasking features. During Apple's iOS 4 announcement, Pandora founder Tim Westergren came on stage and stated that his team fully integrated the multitasking capabilities within a day and his app heavily leverages the background function.

Figure 2-4. Multitasking via fast app switching in iOS 4, which occurs by double-clicking the Home button

Game Center

Games are much more fun when played with other people. Apple helped facilitate that through peer-to-peer Bluetooth connectivity, but the capability was limited in many ways, including the fact that all players needed to physically be in the same room. Thus, game networks sprouted, which allow consumers to not only find and play against other players, but also have their profiles, stats, and other related information saved. This information is then accessible across any game that is part of the network. OpenFeint (*http://openfeint.com*), ngmoco's Plus+ (*http://plusplus.com*), and Scoreloop (*http://www.scoreloop.com/*) are some of the most popular game networks.

A big announcement, as part of iOS 4, was Apple's unveiling of *Game Center*, the company's new game network. Game Center effectively offers the same functionality of the aforementioned game networks. This comes at some cost to the existing game networks since they invested so heavily into this infrastructure. At the same time, some of them have embraced Apple's entrance into this arena, stating that they will begin shifting focus to new areas.

For you, the major benefit of Game Center over other options is that it will streamline your access to these social gaming features. In other words, you won't necessarily have to explore the third-party options. At least in the short term, however, the existing game networks have a much larger adoption than Game Center, so you shouldn't automatically dismiss them.

iAd

In the long run, for developers, the iAd Network has the *potential* to be the biggest part of the iOS 4 release. This relates back to the bias I described in the preceding chapter, which is that for the majority of developers, advertising as a way to monetize a free app is largely not viable. Apple has suggested the purpose of iAd is to change that, by creating mobile advertising that is both more emotionally engaging and more interactive than other options.

Part of Apple's advantages over other mobile advertising platforms is that it is able to more fully leverage device capabilities and knows more consumers than third-party advertisers. At a more basic level, iAds ensure that consumers always remain in an app, which Apple believes encourages more people to explore the app. That, in combination with Apple's revenue model, which includes charging one price to the advertiser for the ad being served and another for the iAd being tapped, already increases the number of opportunities for a developer to make money. And the likelihood of consumers actually choosing to tap on an iAd increases since Apple leverages its iTunes download history to serve the most relevant ad. This tactic is commonly referred to as *behavioral targeting* and other advertising platforms use it too, but they don't necessarily have the same depth of information that Apple does.

As mentioned earlier, a lot is going on behind the scenes in iOS 4. Therefore, ensure that your developer takes advantage of the new tools that help automate testing (UIAutomation Instrument) and that provide better performance and power analysis of your application (Time Profiler and Energy Diagnostics Instruments).

Advertising, In App Purchase, and Push Notifications

The following list highlights some of the most important information and resources you should know about integrating advertising, In App Purchases, and push notifications into your app (which are tasks for a developer). Although you are still in the early stages of learning how to build your app, these items are addressed in this chapter and you should consider them when you start developing your app.

Advertising

If you decide to pursue advertising, make sure you include relevant, unobtrusive ads. You may also consider cross-promoting your own apps instead of using third-party advertisers. As mentioned before, unless you have a number of apps to advertise in, you are making money on volume, or you have an extremely successful app, advertising may not be the most profitable option for you.

Beyond Apple's iAd platform, popular advertising platforms to integrate include AdMob (*http://www.admob.com/*), Mobclix (*http://www.mobclix.com/*), Millennial Media (*http://developer.millennialmedia.com/*), Fusion Ads' Touch Network (*http://fusionads.net/touch-network/*), and Jumptap (*http://www.jumptap.com/*).

In App Purchases

For you, the technical aspects of how to integrate In App Purchases are less important than the way you execute them in your application. How the customer experiences your In App Purchase will directly relate to how many complete the purchase.

As mentioned earlier, one of the most popular game developers—ngmoco—offers an elegant integration of In App Purchases. Start up a kingdom in We Rule (*http://werule.ngmoco.com/*) and observe how ngmoco makes In App Purchases seamless and intuitive. You may want to consider integrating a third-party solution such as Urban Airship (*http://www.urbanairship.com*) to simplify supporting In App Purchases.

Push notifications

Since the App Store already has many great push notification apps, including App Notifications (*http://www.appnotifications.com/*) and NotifyMe (*http://www.powerybase.com/notifyme*), it's likely that you won't be building an app focused exclusively on push notifications. Most apps that include push notifications do so as an added feature, where it makes sense.

As development costs (e.g., time) are inherent for supporting push notifications (and In App Purchases), developers who see it as a feature versus a core function of an app have the option of integrating drop-in third-party solutions such as Urban Airship (yes, the company does In App Purchases and push notifications), Notifo (*http://notifo.com/*), or Boxcar (*http://boxcar.io/*). Remember that with the release of iOS 4, you also have the option of using local notifications. A good background on when to implement local versus traditional push notifications is available on Urban Airship's blog (*http://blog.urbanairship.com/2010/04/09/looking-forward-to-iphone-os-4-0/*).

Approaching App Innovation

You've been focused on gathering information about your app landscape and app idea, as well as learning about Apple's devices and new operating system. Consider these to be some of the raw inputs required to build a fully functional app. Now you need to synthesize these inputs so that you can form an initial set of assumptions about your app.

Creating these assumptions will help communicate how you are trying to make your app a different and compelling offering in the App Store. That is, you'll have a set of benefits your app proposes to customers compared to other options they have available. Being able to articulate these differences will allow you to incorporate outside perspectives, which will help you validate the assumptions you have about your app.

Your Heart and Brain

Being passionate about your app is an important part of launching it into the App Store. I can guarantee you that there are going to be moments where you question what you are doing, you wonder why you are spending nights and weekends in front of a computer while others are relaxing, or you are frustrated that the development of your app is not going according to plan. Above all else, your passion and commitment to your idea will keep you going through these moments. And because you actually quantified your app, you will have some sense of the actual rewards possible, which will motivate you to stick with what you are doing.

More relevant to the current discussion is that being passionate about your idea likely equates to you also being knowledgeable about the market or industry where your app is relevant. You have been further expanding that knowledge and should continue to do so for the life of any app you build, but you probably have some sort of starting point. That's a huge advantage, because solving a problem or filling a void in a market that you are intimately familiar with is one of the best ways to lead you down a path where you create something useful and compelling. In short, build an app to solve the problems you experience firsthand.

Of course, passion can trip you up by making you think that your way to meet needs and solve problems in the form of your app is *the* way to do it. Few companies and businesses have the right to think that way—Apple is one of them. For you, proceeding with that perspective alone can cause you to squander a potentially great opportunity in the App Store market.

If you abide by the strategic framework that follows and the customer-driven mindset that I'll begin outlining more heavily in Chapter 3, you'll have the proper balance of validated innovation. On the one hand, you'll be Apple-like in that you will seek to be market-disrupting. On the other hand, you'll also include customer perspectives to validate the strong set of assumptions you've developed about your app before actually building it. This means your customers will have seen your app before it appears on the App Store. This approach marries these two somewhat contrasting schools of thought: promoting bold innovation while reducing the possibility of your assumptions being dramatically wrong.

When Being Blue Doesn't Mean You're Sad

It would be easy yet wrong for me to simply write that you should make your app "unique." I don't think anyone launches an app into the App Store because she thinks it will be boring or uninteresting. So, requesting that you make your app "unique" is simply not helpful.

At the core of uniqueness lies the concept of innovation. To become unique, one must alter or change the essence of what exists—innovate—to bring something new and exciting to the market. As you can imagine, this subject is comprehensive, and entire books have been written about it, some of which, ironically, aren't particularly innovative. *Blue Ocean Strategy: How to Create Uncontested Market Space and Make the Competition Irrelevant* by W. Chan Kim and Renée Mauborgne (Harvard Business Press), however, has fundamentally shifted my approach to building products (and not just "apps") for the past five years. I'm going to highlight some of what has been most relevant to me and offer it as a more strategic approach to discovering the opportunity for your app.

Blue Ocean Strategy

Competitive markets, being innovative, and related subjects have been re-searched, analyzed, discussed, and written about for decades. Admittedly, people much smarter than I am have thought more extensively about these topics. With that in mind, consider what I'm about to lay out for you to be a sampling of the core aspects of what you need to keep moving forward with your app idea. So, although *Blue Ocean Strategy* is a great addition to your bookshelf, you don't need to read all of it before you can proceed with the process of creating your app.

"Blue oceans"

The core lesson of *Blue Ocean Strategy* is to move out of the "red ocean" of competition and into the "blue ocean" of uncontested market space. That might seem intuitive, but the reality is that most businesses—and in the context of our subject, app developers—wind up taking on com-petition directly by only marginally improving the existing features of an app. The result is twofold:

- Developers wind up fighting over the same customers.

- Price becomes a primary means for customers to distinguish among apps.

The second point is part of what caused the so-called "race to the bot-tom" in App Store prices. That is, in a competitive App Store, when there is little to differentiate an app, developers turn to lowering price as a means to win customers. A price war can ensue until prices can go no lower than the $0.99 minimum. The outcome is good for customers but bad for developers.

Moving to uncontested markets

Of course, the solution to not getting caught in that cycle is to not enter it. The *Blue Ocean Strategy* authors emphasize that "the only way to beat the competition is to stop *trying* to beat the competition." To do that, your mindset needs to change from focusing on existing demand to demand generation, from customers to noncustomers, and from competitors to alternatives. Ultimately, you are not looking to win existing markets, but to make competitors irrelevant by moving into uncontested market space in the App Store.

Value innovation

Moving your app into a blue ocean starts with the concept of *value innovation*. Unlike a value proposition, which focuses on benefits for customers only, value innovation considers actions that positively affect both you and your customers.

You can generate value innovation by raising features customers like, creating ones they've never seen, and reducing or eliminating ones that don't really matter to them. Reducing or eliminating features is what will benefit you, because this will lower the cost of bringing your app to the App Store. That may mean, for example, that pricing your app lower than competitors' actually won't impact your bottom line. Unlike them, you will operate at a lower cost structure, saving time by not developing expensive but inconsequential features.

Strategy canvas

Part of the reason I asked you to begin familiarizing yourself with the apps in your market in Chapter 1 is so that you can construct your *strategy canvas*. A strategy canvas is a visualization that does two things:

- It maps out the features currently offered by competitors' apps.

- It will soon help you identify the areas to innovate.

Think about a strategy canvas as being a simple graph, with features (*competing factors*) for existing apps listed horizontally and the amount of investment in each feature by a competitor rated on the vertical axis from low to high (*offering level*). By rating the investment into each feature for each comparable app in your app landscape, you'll be mapping out the *value curve*. The value curve is a representation of how an app performs across the key features of the app landscape. See Figure 2-5.

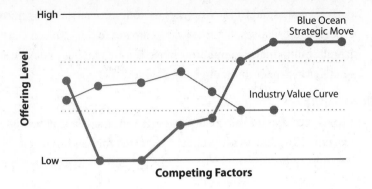

Figure 2-5. Blue Ocean Strategy canvas: value curves for industry versus blue ocean (source: *http://blueoceanstrategy.com/abo/strategy_canvas.html*)

Alternatives and noncustomers

Remember that your goal is to move from a competitive to an uncontested market. In its current form, the value curve you constructed on your strategy canvas focuses only on the features relevant to the current app landscape. It may not be instinctual, but to create a blue ocean, you'll need to shift focus, "from competitors to alternatives, and from customers to noncustomers…in order to gain insight into how to redefine the problem [your app] focuses on and thereby reconstruct [customer] value elements."

The *Blue Ocean Strategy* authors spend considerable time building the case for this idea and defining "alternatives" and "noncustomers." To more quickly communicate this idea, it's easiest to understand this unconventional concept through an illustration. I'll point to the extremely successful application developer Smule. Smule has produced such apps as Magic Piano and I Am T-Pain (see an interview with Smule co-founder and CEO, Jeff Smith, at the end of this chapter).

One example of why Smule exhibited blue ocean strategies is that its first app was the 19th virtual lighter on the App Store, yet it quickly rose to the #1 position on most App Stores around the world. Unlike developers of existing lighters, Smule recognized that lighters in and of themselves catered to only a small population of customers. Smule's innovations included creating a social and musical component, which it calls "expressive audio." Its Sonic Lighter iPhone app had the ability to "ignite" other flames on iPhones around the world, which could be seen within the app on its now-famous globe view. The flames could also be controlled via the built-in microphone of the device (know those device features!).

Smule's leveraging of the social aspects found in other alternative apps, typically games, and creating this "expressive audio" helped the company move away from focusing solely on the existing competing features of similar apps. Instead of just developing a more visually appealing lighter, it redefined the value elements of why people wanted an app like a lighter. By doing so, it significantly broadened the appeal of the app to noncustomers, which is a large part of what pushed the app quickly up the App Store charts.

One last note on "alternatives": while you are developing an app, it can be helpful to think about your app landscape, including alternatives available, outside the App Store. This could include websites, desktop software, or even nondigital solutions.

The Four Actions Framework

Analyzing alternatives and noncustomers will allow you to add new competing factors on the bottom of your strategy canvas. For example, Smule's strategy canvas (see Figure 2-6) could have started with items such as price, ignition, brightness, flame type, and sound. As part of its expanded understanding of the market, it could have included social sharing and expressive audio.

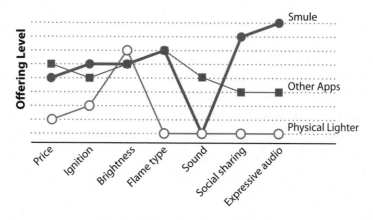

Figure 2-6. Smule's strategy canvas

The goal in adding these factors of competition is that you will be defining a new value curve—but this one will be for your app. For that to occur, you will leverage the Four Actions Framework, which includes four key questions (edited to be app-focused):

- Which features taken for granted in the app landscape should be *eliminated*?

- Which features should be *reduced well below* other features in the app landscape standard?

- Which features should be *raised well above* other features in the app landscape standard?

- Which features should be *created* that the app landscape has never offered?

If you recall, your value innovation benefits both you and your customers. The main value for you is to lower your cost structure in two ways:

- By not building features that are assumed to be useful or important but actually aren't

- By not building features where existing apps appear to be highly competitive

In the second case, the *Blue Ocean Strategy* authors note that trying to win on those factors will "overserve customers, increasing…cost structure for no gain."

The first two questions of the Four Actions Framework deal with the situations in the paragraph immediately preceding this one. The second two already surfaced in what Smule uncovered: that is, how to raise customer value and create new demand. Combining the answers to these questions, you will be able to plot a new value curve for your app by considering how to eliminate and reduce certain features, raising others, and creating new features from your assessment of alternatives. The result should be identification of an uncontested market space through a distinct value curve.

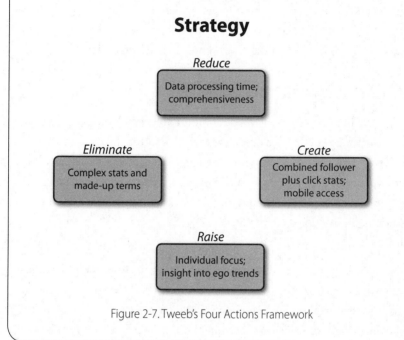

Four Actions Framework Example

As you'll see throughout the book, what you are reading is not theoretical. I use these exact principles in the development of my clients' apps, as well as my own.

Figure 2-7 shows the Four Actions Framework I created for Tweeb when I was at a similar stage in the exploration of that idea. This image comes from a slide I created in Keynote, which is part of Apple's iWork suite.

Strategy

Reduce
Data processing time; comprehensiveness

Eliminate
Complex stats and made-up terms

Create
Combined follower plus click stats; mobile access

Raise
Individual focus; insight into ego trends

Figure 2-7. Tweeb's Four Actions Framework

Making it more practical

If you are having trouble grasping the ideas in *Blue Ocean Strategy*, let me describe it more succinctly.

You are forming a set of assumptions about what's important to your customers by analyzing the app landscape. The initial competing factors for your strategy canvas represent the features in the existing apps and other solutions that help solve your customers' problems today. Assessing complementary or alternative solutions and thinking about noncustomers will broaden your perspective. You'll then be able to develop a set of ideas (i.e., the assumptions about your app) that will not only better serve customers, but also transition you to the "blue ocean" of uncontested markets.

Some of these concepts may have formalized the way you thought about your app landscape and how to make your app unique. Being dogmatic about using these tools is less important than applying this lens to your app. For example, even if you don't create a strategy canvas, be sure you understand the competing factors for your app landscape and recognize that focusing on existing customers and competitors alone will keep you swimming in the "red oceans" of the highly competitive App Store.

Other Differentiators

Understanding the factors of competition for your app landscape and the value curve for your app is a crucial aspect of defining the assumptions about your app. However, you should not get lost in the formality of the framework. Just because you are thinking about your app in a structured manner doesn't mean you should forget the very human aspects of the app development process.

You previously saw how touch transformed Apple devices and how this and the social element of Smule's Sonic Lighter were game-changing additions. You need to recognize that your customers are people. Beyond offering the right set of features to them, you need to realize that they like to have fun and to laugh, they are engaged by content, they are enticed by attractive visualizations, and they like it when things are easy to use and work properly. I will address some of these points as I guide you through the process of building your app. For now, I want you to remember two things:

- Your customers are emotional beings called humans.

- Even the right set of features or assumptions alone won't make your app successful; you'll also need to properly execute (i.e., design and develop) them.

The second element is discussed more extensively in Chapters 4 and 5.

Interviews

Smule: Jeff Smith

COMPANY: Smule

POSITION: CEO and co-founder

BACKGROUND: Smule is a leading application developer focused on interactive audio media, producing such mega hits as the apps Sonic Lighter, Ocarina, I Am T-Pain, Glee, and Magic Piano.

LINK: *http://smule.com/*

Ken: *When did you first come up with the vision for Smule? Did you know right from the start that you wanted to focus on a particular genre of apps and consumers or did that evolve over time?*

Jeff: The company's cofounder, Ge Wang, and I believed it was time to redefine what music meant, and that a commercial platform could substantially amplify some of the research in computer music at Stanford and Princeton. Music is inherently a social experience. There are opportunities now afforded by amazing new platforms such as the iPhone to explore the creative and expressive side of people, in the process forging new social experiences. Having said as much, our initial focus was to not focus and instead to experiment. We lacked conviction on whether our vision would be appealing to the masses. We also had several theories we wanted to test in the process. Yet the heart and soul of the company from inception is the exploration of a new social medium through expressive audio.

Ken: *Discuss the first app Smule ever created. What were the biggest challenges and lessons learned from that experience? What are you doing differently now after having launched seven apps?*

Jeff: Our first application was Sonic Lighter, the 19th virtual cigarette lighter in the App Store and one of the few paid lighters. Miraculously, Sonic Lighter catapulted to the #1 position in nearly every major App Store geographic market. I think people were fascinated with the ability of one iPhone to ignite another iPhone, in our case sending network instructions over sound via the built-in speaker and microphone. I also think people loved the globe view, now famous in our apps, where you could track actual ignitions of others across the world. It seemed there was some solace offered to people to see others igniting their flames. For a while, Paris dominated in kilojoules burned per day, but alas, Tokyo unseated Paris a few weeks later.

Ken: *Looking across Smule's suite of apps, including I Am T-Pain, Leaf Trombone, and Ocarina, you seem to have a recipe for success. Without revealing any Smule secrets, how have you built so many successful apps? Is there something in your process that helps you ensure there's demand or interest for an idea you have?*

Jeff: We found that our belief in the creativity of our users has been a winning formula. If we set the conditions right and give them a little nudge, it's amazing what our users can do with our products. I think people are exploring music and exploring how they might express themselves, be it singing "I'm In Luv (Wit a Stripper)" along with T-Pain, or simply igniting their flame in the *Quartier Latin*. If people actually want to use our products and share that experience with others, then we have a winner.

Ken: *When it comes to incorporating external perspectives (e.g., users or advisers) into developing an iPhone app, what is your advice to new iPhone app developers that don't have something like the Smule brand behind them? That is, where did Smule start with finding these groups before there was a "Smule," and how can new developers do the same?*

Jeff: Well, we think a lot about how users are going to find us, and how they are going to find each other. If you are considering these issues after you've built your product, you are too late. If, instead, you are thinking about this before you write a line of code, then I think you have a good shot at truly empathizing with your users and exploring what experiences they might develop with the products. We also test this with actual users. In fact, this past winter, we were three months into a project we terminated after the feedback of the first user test. We probably ate $500,000 of development and art costs. [That was] not an easy decision, and thank goodness we had an understanding from our board of directors. But unless we believe we have a compelling experience, we don't want to put our name on it.

Ken: *Describe how Smule determines when an app has enough features to be ready to launch into (or be updated in) the App Store. How do you ensure that you don't spend time building features that won't help you sell more apps?*

Jeff: We try to identify the most compelling use cases out of the gate, and… as soon as we can test these, we do. We then study our analytics data for all applications in a postmortem of sorts, constructing what we call a *usage waterfall*. This table of graphs helps us compare our hypothesis at launch to actual usage data. From this, we can take some of the learning and apply it to future products. For example, we were astonished to learn that our users of the Leaf Trombone cared little for the achievements, [and] instead simply wanted to go judge others on the world stage. We could have saved about a month of development time if we knew this in advance!

Sophiestication Software: Sophia Teutschler

COMPANY: Sophiestication Software

POSITION: Founder

BACKGROUND: Sophiestication Software is a small software design and development company, which is run by Sophia Teutschler, who describes herself as one of those "rare female developers."

LINK: *http://www.sophiestication.com/*

Ken: *Your app, Articles, entered a category that already had other solidified Wikipedia companion apps. Despite that, not only did you proceed with launching Articles, but you were able to do so with incredible success. How did you identify the opportunity that there was space for another Wikipedia app?*

Sophia: When I'm brainstorming new app ideas I always start with the question "What do I miss on my iPhone?"

The idea for a dedicated Wikipedia reader dates way back to early 2008, when I collected the first ideas for iPhone apps I wanted to make. A shopping list, a package tracker, a tip calculator, a Twitter client, a wiki app… nothing really groundbreaking was on my "want list." Yet these were all apps that everyone would want to use.

I successfully implemented the ideas for the shopping list and the tip calculator. Over time, I lost the desire to implement some of the other app ideas, like the Twitter client and package tracker. I use great apps by other fellow developers now.

However, I never found a good solution for Wikipedia on the iPhone. Everything that was available was mediocre at best. I make apps, so the decision to fix the situation was crystal-clear to me.

Ken: *What were some of the shortcomings you saw with other Wikipedia app options? What aspects did you want to improve or focus on less with Articles?*

Sophia: Without any exception, it's always the UI that bugs me with other apps. I'm not talking about the looks, but about the app's behavior and interaction with the user.

There are many examples of how to improve a UI for use on the iPhone. One particular case for Articles is how it presents images. On Wikipedia, you usually tap on an image to open its dedicated page. There you are presented with an enormous amount of metadata you don't really care about. The image itself, however, is still displayed in a rather small resolution. So, you have to tap on a thumbnail again to finally see it in full size. Yet it's still presented with a bright white background and the blue Safari toolbars... sigh.

On Articles, tapping on an image simply zooms into the photo in full-screen mode. That's the kind of simplified user experience I'm targeting.

Ken: *Articles has a great app icon, a very polished design, and an intuitive user experience. Was this part of what you thought would make your app better? In general, what is your perspective and philosophy about designing iPhone apps?*

Sophia: Making apps is my job, and my only job. This is what I'm doing all day long. I don't want to waste my life doing something mediocre. I want to be proud of what I make and feel the joy when hard work finally pays out.

Some people paint pictures, others form sculptures. I make apps.

Ken: *Articles exists on the iPhone and iPad. Discuss your considerations and concerns in developing the iPad versus the iPhone version. In your case, was creating the iPad app more of a design or development task?*

Sophia: The iPad was not even announced when I started developing Articles. I hoped for a device like this, but it was far too early to tell how it could turn out.

Creating the iPad app was definitely a design and a development task. Finding a great design and coding up the necessary changes was a considerable job, but mainly due to the time constraints I had in order to hit the submission deadline to be in the iPad App Store on day one. Being there on day one is a chance you only get once in your life!

Articles is sold as two separate versions for the iPhone and iPad. Releasing the app as a Universal binary was, sadly, not possible in this case since I had to make use of iOS 3.2-specific features. So, I had to test it on an iPhone running OS 3.2, which was only available for the iPad at that time. Apple basically made the decision [of whether] I should go Universal or not with Articles for me.

Ken: *How early do you include your customers in getting validation of and feedback for your apps? Do you show them nonfunctional concepts or only present them with a working app when it's ready? How long before Articles went into the App Store had people been using the app?*

Sophia: I usually start off by showing several early mockups to family and friends. I try to explain what I want to do, how this and that should work, and why it would be better compared to a solution that might already be available.

During development, I widen the audience with other fellow developers and app experts. I usually end up with about 50 people testing the app toward the end of the final development cycles. Developing Articles took rather long. A handful of people already had pre-release versions of the app back in July 2009. This feedback helped a lot for me to understand how people, besides me, use Wikipedia on their iPhones, and therefore helped to shape the UI to its final shape.

The first beta versions went out to testers about a month before the app finally hit the App Store. The app was pretty much usable at that stage.

Ken: *Putting bugs aside, what is the key feedback you receive from those who look at or test your app? How does that impact what goes into the initial version you submit into the App Store?*

Sophia: The key feedback is definitely about how each person uses the app and the iPhone in general. Some people love typing with the keypad in landscape mode; others solely keep it in their hand and navigate with their thumb. It might not sound important at first, but things like these help me to find the ideal UI for the majority of customers. Though it might be worthwhile to mention that I never intend to please every single one. That's simply impossible.

Recap

Here's what you learned in this chapter:

- Apple's unique approach to its devices—including offering a larger keyboard-less display with Multi-Touch capabilities—fundamentally altered the marketplace.

- Although there are device-related features, the iOS provides a number of common frameworks and features that are available across devices. Knowing both the common elements and the device-related features is key to building your app.

- iOS 4 brings a tremendous number of changes "under the hood," but many of those changes have the largest impacts on consumers. Multitasking and the iAd are the most significant consumer-facing changes.

- It's not enough to want to create a unique app. Using the strategic framework in *Blue Ocean Strategy* will guide you through understanding the competing factors for your app landscape and help you identify a distinct value curve for how to innovate in the App Store.

- Defining the assumptions of your app by using the tools and frameworks available in *Blue Ocean Strategy* represents one aspect of building a successful app. You'll also need to properly execute those ideas once customers have validated that they are indeed correct.

3

From Idea to Concept

ONCE YOU'VE ARTICULATED the initial assumptions of your app, you'll need to test them with customers. The feedback you receive from customers will help transform your assumptions into a validated concept. The concept will not be a functioning app, and in fact, it might even look more like a "blueprint" of an app. The goal of the concept will be to test your revised assumptions in further discussions with customers. Of course, before that can happen you'll need to know who those potential customers are.

In this chapter, you'll explore how to:

- Keep customers front and center

- Identify potential customers

- Have customers validate initial app assumptions

- Create a concept app

Customers Are the Key

I've been tossing the word "customers" around fairly liberally. For some of you, that's fine, because you already have customers through an existing app, product, business, organization, and so on. For others, pursuing your app may be the start of your first venture, and not only do you have no app, but you also have no customers.

That's OK. I'll show you some ways to start identifying who your potential customers are. And even if you have existing customers, many of these strategies will be helpful in engaging them further. On this point, you also should not assume that your existing customers for some other service or product will necessarily be interested in your app. To keep it simple, I'll continue to use the word "customers" in this chapter to signify both existing and prospective customers.

Why Customers? Why Now?

From the subtitle of this book—"Turning Ideas into iPad and iPhone Apps Customers Really Want"—you might have an inkling that staying customer-focused is *the* key part of successfully bringing your app to the App Store. Yes, I've asked you to do some research, quantify your idea, and think strategically up to this point, but that was all done for the purpose of interacting better with your customers. The voice of the customer is what will mitigate the risk of you launching an app that no one wants to download.

Interacting with customers this early in the development of your app will provide several benefits. First, customers will be instrumental in validating the initial assumptions you have about your idea. Although you've done a pretty intensive analysis of the market and now have a set of assumptions about the features you'll need to focus or not focus on, it's still possible that you have missed the mark. Customers are people, and people are highly opinionated. If you've over- or underestimated the importance of a problem your app is trying to solve, you will hear about it.

In addition to validating assumptions, you will learn what customers consider the primary reasons your app will be worth downloading or buying. If you do your job right, they will become your chief advocates in the App Store and on the Web. They will continue to promote and support you, and provide ideas and feedback well after your app becomes available on the App Store. Thus, the second motivation for you to begin engaging them now is that these interactions will be the first investment in a long, mutually beneficial relationship. Besides the fact that you will be trying to build an app these customers find useful or fun, you will be surprised by how excited they get about testing apps (and later, features) before they are available on the App Store. So, don't think that their involvement in the process is a chore or task for them. In fact, if you get a sense that it is, you probably aren't dealing with the right kind of customer.

The last major benefit of interacting with customers even before you have an app built is that this will officially begin the marketing of your app. You didn't misread that. Your marketing will begin the moment you start talking with your first customer.

Don't be concerned if you aren't a "marketer." By focusing on building a compelling app, you will find that marketing the app will come more easily and naturally to you. This approach is proven inside and outside the App Store. If you embrace this philosophy, your marketing efforts will progress as the development of your app progresses. In this sense, you should think about the marketing of your app as a crescendo. Anticipation and demand for your app should continue to build, until a sort of climax occurs when your app launches on the App Store.

Although I discuss marketing in Chapter 8, I wrote that chapter so that it parallels the development of your app, so you should begin referring to it now. Turn to Chapter 8 and read up to the section "Your Marketing Crescendo," and then come back here. I know this approach can result in a somewhat disjointed reading experience, but the benefits are worth it. Please don't ignore this advice and arrive at Chapter 8 sequentially, or you will miss out on key opportunities for generating interest and buzz for your app.

Who Are Your Customers?

Before you can search for customers, you need to have a basic sense of who they are. Your app may appeal to a particular demographic (e.g., 30-something females) or interest group (e.g., gamers). If you consider these factors to be particularly important, you'll want to avoid those who fall considerably outside these spheres.

If you think your app has a more expansive appeal, you can use your knowledge about the existing app landscape and the solutions or alternatives that are available to help develop your understanding of who your customers are. To give a better structure to your observations, you might create a description of who your customers are, or more simply, write down the distinguishing factors you've identified.

Although it is more extensive than you really need at this point in the process, the approach taken by Bryan Eisenberg and Jeffrey Eisenberg more fully describes how to generalize information and behaviors about customers by creating "personas." In their book *Waiting for Your Cat to Bark? Persuading Customers When They Ignore Marketing* (Thomas Nelson), the authors describe the use of personas in marketing—but the philosophy behind creating them is most relevant: to *segment* or group customers based on shared qualities and attributes.

To reiterate, at this point you only need a basic sense of who your customers are. You should consider this exercise anecdotal and not scientific.

Traits of the right customer

The iPod touch, iPhone, and iPad are popular devices, but they are not ubiquitous; a large percentage of those who own them are tech savvy. The most active consumers of apps comprise a subpopulation within the universe of device owners, representing another level of sophistication. They don't exhibit typical consumer behaviors—and that's a good thing, because at this early stage in the life of your app, you are not going to want to talk to your "average" customer.

Steve Blank calls this overall process *customer development*. He labels the customer you want to talk with at this stage the *earlyvangelist* (see the sidebar "Customer Development Model and The Lean Startup" on page 89). In his book, *The Four Steps to the Epiphany* (Cafepress.com), he outlines the five characteristics that earlyvangelists exhibit:

- The customer has a problem.
- The customer is aware of the problem.

- The customer has been actively looking for a solution.

- The customer has "cobbled" together a solution due to the painfulness of the problem.

- The customer has the funds or can acquire them to solve the problem.

He argues that the truest of earlyvangelists are those exhibiting the last two characteristics. Their frustration with the lack of a proper solution has propelled them to action, to the point where they may have even created their own solution. In the App Store, since the cost of most apps is so low, it's likely that their solution probably is either an app or some number of apps; that still counts. For example, someone who has one or more alarm clock apps but is frustrated with the available options would be an excellent earlyvangelist for a developer who wants to build a new alarm clock app.

People with these traits are going to be willing to take a risk and spend time playing with your new app because of its perceived usefulness relative to the painfulness of their problem(s).

Customer Development Model and The Lean Startup

Steve Blank's customer development model is discussed extensively in his book *The Four Steps to the Epiphany*. The customer development model focuses on helping organizations of various sizes launch new products in a way that incorporates customers throughout the development process. Eric Ries further advanced these ideas on his blog (*http://startuplessonslearned.com*) for web startups in particular, describing his contribution to and evolution of customer development as "The Lean Startup."

While I never articulated these ideas with the clarity or depth of Blank and Ries, their approach resembles how I've approached products over the past decade (and more recently, "apps" specifically). Like me, however, many proponents, thought leaders, and practitioners now embrace the "customer development" and "lean startup" monikers because they better capture and communicate this product philosophy. One such person is Cindy Alvarez (*http://www.cindyalvarez.com*), whose interview about customer development appears at the end of this chapter.

How to Find Your Customers

Now that you have a basic understanding of who your customers are and you have a sense of the traits they should exhibit, it will be easier for you to find them. You don't need to talk with hundreds of customers. In fact, for independent developers who are creating consumer-oriented apps, engaging with as few as 7 to 10 customers may be sufficient. Depending on the scope of and budget for your app, you may want to talk with up to 30 or 40. The general guideline for when to stop talking to customers is when you start hearing the same feedback over and over again.

Along with knowing traits about your customers, you may have some instincts regarding where best to find them. In general, using your contacts to make referrals and leveraging the Web will be the best methods for doing this, considering the more tech-savvy audience you'll want to engage.

I'll get to how you introduce yourself to customers and what you will be discussing with them momentarily, but for now, I'll outline some ways to find them.

Your network

You might not be one of those "important" people with a large and influential network to tap into—but you don't need to be "important." Start with your family, friends, and colleagues and think about people they know who fit the characteristics of your customer. Explain that you are looking to interact with people to get feedback on a new idea for an app (you might mention it's for the iPhone and/or iPad). Ask if they can provide you with the names and preferred contact information of relevant people, or have them make an email introduction for you. Referrals are powerful. If someone can't introduce you, be sure to mention the person who referred you when making your initial contact with a prospective customer.

Your network may also include those whom you meet at events or interact with online. Don't forget to reach out to these contacts. If you don't have an online identity or are not familiar with sites such as Twitter and Facebook, you'll still be able to leverage these tools, but will do so in a different way.

Surveys and the "social" web

Referrals are probably the best way to find prospective customers, but you may not want to bother your network. You might also want perspectives from people outside your network, just to verify that they are completely unbiased. Thankfully, discovering these types of customers is infinitely easier today because of how "social" the Web is.

I am compelled to put quotes around "social," because to me, the Web has always been about being social. It just evolved over the years, and is now epitomized by *social media* sites such as Facebook, Twitter, YouTube, WordPress, Delicious, Digg, and other similar services. At the core of all these social services is search; search is what will help you find your customers.

Unlike with referrals, you'll now be focused on generating a list of customer names yourself. You'll do so by using social media and traditional web destinations to get visibility for a brief survey that you will create. The goal of the survey will be not only to get names, emails, and possibly phone numbers from prospective customers, but also to quickly vet them by asking some relevant questions.

Survey tools

A number of free survey tools are available on the Web. I prefer to use Google Docs to create a form, but Wufoo and SurveyMonkey are also good options and are tailored more specifically to surveys.

Survey requirements

The survey should include some basic introductory text explaining the purpose of the survey. For example, "Give feedback about how you deal with _____ problem," or "Share your thoughts on a new [iPhone or iPad] app that can help you deal with _____ better." It should also include text entry fields for the respondents' name and email address.

You should state that the email address will be used only to follow up with the respondent. You might also consider requiring respondents to provide their phone number, and if you do, requesting the best time of day to call. You can take a more casual approach by asking if the customer would prefer to interact over the phone or through IM. In this case, you can get that information from customers once you follow up with them in an email.

Additional survey questions

Depending on how successful you are in making your survey visible, it's possible that you will get a number of responses. You need some way to further sort through your responses. The best way to do that is to include two or three required questions that deal more specifically with customer behavior.

These questions can be more general, such as "What are you currently using to solve your _____ problem?" or they can be a little more app-specific, such as "What Apple devices do you currently own?" or "Select which of the following apps you have purchased." You don't want to lower the completion rate of your survey, so keep these questions short and simple.

Survey incentives

Because some customers may be hesitant to provide information such as a phone number, or they don't want to spend time talking with you on the phone, you may need to motivate them to complete your survey. One way to do that is to offer a gift certificate to a popular consumer destination site such as Amazon.com. Since you are probably dealing with Apple fans, you may also consider offering an iTunes email gift certificate. For best results, title the survey with this incentive, including the dollar amount of the gift certificate (e.g., "Receive a $15 iTunes gift certificate for giving 15 minutes of feedback on the phone"). Whether it's in the title or not, the incentive needs to be prominently displayed.

Other motivating factors could include providing a free version of your app when it is completed. That's a little risky, though, because unforeseen events can cause your app to be delayed. In either case, you are spending cash to talk with customers. Even if it costs you upward of $20 per customer (a very compelling offer), realize that this could save you significant money in the long term. Learning what customers' problems are and how they react to your app idea now is priceless feedback that may prevent you from launching an app that no one will download.

Survey visibility

Publish the survey you created and copy the link to it. You are now ready to use various online channels to drive people to your survey. You may want to use a mixture of these options, or try them individually to see what works best for you.

Although some of the sources mentioned here will provide natural means to hone in on the right customer, not all of them will. For that reason, you may want to consider leveraging the paid features offered by tools such as SurveyMonkey and Wufoo that will allow you to filter survey results and limit responses based on certain criteria (e.g., by IP address).

Twitter

If you are someone who "doesn't get Twitter," I suggest that you "get it" pretty quickly, because it's a great place to find customers and interact with them on an ongoing basis. I won't be covering the basics of Twitter here, so if you need a more extensive tutorial on how to use it, I suggest you check out *The Twitter Book* (*http://oreilly.com/catalog/9780596802820/*) by Tim O'Reilly and Sarah Milstein (O'Reilly).

Twitter is the ideal place to find customers, for several reasons. First, the Twitter demographic is still more of a cutting-edge, early-adopter crowd. Although I'm generalizing here, you can think about the average Twitter user as the person who camps out to see a movie, is first in line to buy a product, and is always looking for the next big thing.

Second, Twitter is real-time and transparent. When a person publishes a tweet, a 140-character message on Twitter's website, he is expressing a thought or interest *now*. You can view a person's stream of consciousness via his *timeline* (e.g., *http://twitter.com/kenyarmosh*), as well as view what other Twitter accounts he *follows*. This gives you a tremendous amount of insight into the person's interests.

The final importance of Twitter is how searchable it is. Visit *http://search.twitter.com*, enter some keywords related to your app, and click the Search button. Twitter will return relevant tweets containing those keywords and will show you who posted the tweet. That's where things get interesting, because you can now visit the profile of that person and see if he tweets about these keywords regularly. If he does, you may want to follow and *reply* to him, using the format *@username* (e.g., I'm "@kenyarmosh") with a pointer to your link. You only get 140 characters for your tweet, so make it succinct. For example, "@username I saw you often tweet about _____. I'd love your advice about it. Can we chat? http://bit.ly/shorturl." That strange-looking link uses a *URL shortener*, to give you more space in your tweet.

There are a couple of other good places to identify relevant people on Twitter, including WeFollow (*http://wefollow.com*) and Twiangulate (*http://twiangulate.com/*). WeFollow is a directory where people associate themselves with a particular keyword interest. Twiangulate provides a variety of search-related tools. It's particularly interesting once you've found several relevant Twitter accounts because you can see if there are mutual "friends" among them, possibly representing additional people to engage.

It's time for your first "marketing checkup." You need to get much more comfortable with Twitter. Check out the "Phase 1" section of Chapter 8, because Twitter will serve as a vital channel for interacting with your earlyvangelist customers.

Craigslist

Using the popular classified site Craigslist requires much less upfront work than an option such as Twitter. Your base will be less targeted, though, and you will simply be broadcasting your survey to everyone. So, you'll want to ensure that your survey includes some of the filtering questions I described earlier.

Another difference with Craigslist is that since it is geography-oriented, it does offer you the opportunity to meet with customers in person. You can post the link to your survey in the "community" area under "volunteers." For example, here is the volunteers URL for the New York metro area: *http://newyork.craigslist.org/vol/*.

Mechanical Turk

If you use an option such as Amazon's Mechanical Turk (*https://www.mturk.com/*), you will not need to offer a gift card incentive to people for completing your survey because compensation is built into the system. Mechanical Turk (MT) is based on the idea of paying people extremely reasonable rates to complete tasks.

In this case, the task will be to complete your survey. Note that MT has its own survey tool, but it's easier to use one of the options mentioned earlier, link to it from MT, and then ask a specific question related to the survey to verify the task was completed. To get familiar with MT, you may want to peruse Amazon's "Best Practice Guide," which also includes a pricing formula that might be useful for pricing your task.[1] Having used this option extensively in the past to vet new-product ideas, entrepreneur Kevin Dewalt (*http://kevindewalt.com*) recommends using $0.10 to price a survey-related task. His experience also dictates that you'll want to use the "Location" criterion to get better results (see Figure 3-1).

Figure 3-1. Location criterion in Mechanical Turk task creation

Paid advertising

Both search engines and Facebook offer some of the better ways to target the type of customer you are looking for and also bring your survey the most visibility. Search engine marketing can feel overwhelming for those who haven't done it before. To keep it simple, you'll be bidding on keywords that will display advertisements on search engine results pages. Start slow and consider only spending $20 to $50 per day with keywords that cost you less than $2 per click. Since your budget is small, focus on Google AdWords, which will give you the highest distribution.[2] Google's Inside AdWords blog has some great tips and resources

---

1 *https://requester.mturk.com/mturk/resources/howto*
2 *http://adwords.google.com/*

to help you get started: *http://adwords.blogspot.com/*. If you want to invest more heavily in learning about paid search marketing through Google AdWords, check out *Ultimate Guide to Google AdWords*, Second Edition, by Perry Marshall and Bryon Todd (Entrepreneur Press).

If you have only limited experience in online paid advertising, Facebook Ads will probably be more intuitive for you to create.[3] Your results can vary, however, since Facebook Ads is a much newer platform and it tends to better engage a younger demographic (which might be great depending on who your target customer is). Again, the best approach with all of these options is to test what works best for you; that also sometimes depends on what you have the most experience and comfort using.

Depending on how defined you feel your idea is at this point, you may want to rely more exclusively on surveys to get much more feedback more quickly. For example, you could ask a larger number of questions covering how many apps people purchase per month, specifics about proposed features, and price points. Conversely, if you are still struggling or are unconvinced about your app idea, you could opt for longer phone conversations and allow discussions with your prospective customers to uncover the problems they are having and where you need to focus. Ideally, however, you will always use some combination of surveys plus phone calls or in-person meetings.

Longer surveys versus more follow-up phone conversations should show you that surveys can be helpful beyond the stage of identifying customers. Eventually, your idea will be more defined; when that time comes, you can use the same principles to launch a new survey focusing on those revisions. Similarly, once your app is in use, you'll consider adding new features, revising or adding new screens, and be back in this "testing" phase where you'll want to actually talk with your customers at length to solidify ideas. The difference then will be that you should already have a pool of customers to start interacting with, although it won't hurt to continue to infuse new ones into these interactions.

---

3 *http://www.facebook.com/ads/*

If you are an organization that has a physical presence (e.g., a local coffee shop) or your app idea is less consumer-focused (e.g., business-to-business), you'll likely be relying more exclusively on referrals from colleagues, peers, partners, or even existing customers. If you skimmed through this section because of that fact, make sure you at least review the section on Twitter.

What to Discuss with Your Customers

Getting the names of customers to contact is half the battle. I'd argue that it's also the more boring half because it's logistical in nature. Once you actually have a list of those you want to talk with, you'll get back to focusing on how to improve or validate your app idea.

Making initial contact

At this point, you'll have a list of contacts comprising referrals from your network and from the survey results. In either case, when initially contacting these customers, you'll want to remind them of how you got connected to them to increase the likelihood of their responding.

I find that in today's crazy, schedule-driven world, the best way to make initial contact is to send a brief introductory email. Here is a template you can use to reach out to a contact you learned about through a referral. Note that referrals typically do not need financial or monetary incentives to help you.

Referral Email Template

Subject:

Your Insight: Referral from Matt

Message:

Richard:

I'm working on a new idea about _____, and Matt from Blue Shirts, Inc., said you'd be a great person to contact. I'd really appreciate ____ minutes of your time to gain some insight into how you are dealing with this problem.

To show you my thanks, I'd be happy to give you early access to what I'm building when it's finished. If you're interested, let me know the best time to give you a call and your preferred contact number.

Best,

Ken

Here is a template you can use to follow up with customers who participated in a survey:

Survey Email Template

Subject:

Survey Follow-up: $15 Gift Certificate for 15 Minutes of Your Time [edit your gift certificate amount and time as needed]

Message:

Vincent:

You recently completed a survey found at _____ [your survey URL] regarding a new idea I'm exploring. I'd really appreciate 15 minutes of your time to gain some insight into how you are dealing with this problem [edit time as needed].

As stated in the survey, to show you my thanks, I'd be happy to give you a $15 gift certificate to Amazon.com [edit your gift certificate information as needed]. If you're interested, let me know the best time to give you a call and your preferred contact number.

Best,

Ken

As mentioned earlier, in the case of referrals, it's best to have your contact make the email introduction for you. You can tailor your template so that it is better suited to that case and then ask your contact to forward it for you.

Customer interviews

The words "customer interview" are important because they emphasize that you shouldn't do most of the talking. You're finally at the place where your prospective customers will give you feedback; don't prevent that from happening by talking too much.

Your conversations don't need to be too structured. In fact, unstructured conversations are great at the early stages of an idea. You will, however, need to keep in mind what you are trying to learn from this potential customer and how to properly frame the entire discussion.

Remember that you are trying to validate the assumptions you created by analyzing the app landscape. If you created the strategy canvas for your app and used the Four Actions Framework (both discussed in Chapter 2) to identify your unique value curve, you'll already have all the information you need:

- The customer problems as evident in the competing factors

- Available solutions (apps or otherwise)

- Your app's proposed innovations

When these elements are taken together, Blank calls them the *customer problem presentation* and suggests that you create a single slide that focuses on the top three for each category.

The first and perhaps most important part of starting the customer interview concerns creating an environment that promotes open and honest dialog (e.g., "Please be very blunt with me. You won't be hurting my feelings. My feelings will be hurt more if I launch an app that's not useful."). Unless you are meeting face to face, you may want to request a video call through Skype, FaceTime (if you and the person you are talking with have an iPhone 4), or something comparable so that you can better facilitate that sort of connectedness. Seeing someone's face will also allow you to gauge the person's reactions and interpret facial expressions. As you continue to outline the operational aspects of your conversation, ask for permission to record the conversation so that you can come back to it later.

You'll essentially be stepping through the customer interview by first presenting some information and then listening to the customer. Come to the discussion trying to take away three "must learns" about your app. Start with outlining what you've identified as the customer problems and ask the customers if your list matches their views, if there are other problems they are looking to solve, and how they would rank them. Be a good listener and don't bias your customer with your perspectives.

For available solutions, you'll want to understand whether customers are using the available solutions (apps or otherwise) and how they use them. Your goal is to figure out how they are currently addressing their problems, what solutions they are aware of, and why certain solutions are preferable. From here, you'll transition into very broadly sharing how you are going to approach the solution through your app—the third and final part of the customer problem presentation—and again solicit a response from the customer.

Blank recommends asking two critical summary questions at the end of the interview: "What is the biggest pain in how you work?" and "If you could wave a magic wand and change anything [about] what you [currently use to solve your problems], what would it be?" Depending on the focus of your app (e.g., entertainment or game-focused), you'll need to tailor these questions while maintaining their essence.

When the interview is over, set some expectations with the customer about moving forward. If you promised an incentive such as a gift certificate, tell the customer when she'll be receiving it. You should also ask the customer if she'd be willing to help again in the future, and if she'd like to be notified about the app's progress through your mailing list.

Even if you received permission to record the conversation through audio or video, do some immediate housekeeping post-interview. Make sure you captured the customer's responses to each part of the problem presentation and the answers to the final two critical questions. Synthesize your notes for that particular customer. Once you've talked with all the customers you planned to engage, revise and reprioritize your initial assumptions as needed.

If you want a "cheat sheet" on customer development and Steve Blank's book, take a look at Brant Cooper's and Patrick Vlaskovits' *The Entrepreneur's Guide to Customer Development*, available at *http://www.custdev.com/*.

Creating a Concept App

With the revisions you made from the feedback your customers provided on your initial assumptions, you are ready to take the first step of visualizing your app. I want to be very clear that this task is *not* about design. If "visualization" to you means colors, fonts, and the aesthetics of your app, let me use a different word. For this stage of your app, let visualization mean "blueprint." Think functional rather than finished. Drafting your concept will prepare you for the design (covered in Chapter 5), but for now, I want you to think of yourself as an architect who is creating a vision and not as a designer who is bringing life to that vision.

Artistically Challenged

I'm ashamed to admit that way back in middle school I stayed after school for extra help…in art class. I was a bit of an overachiever, but generally speaking, where the rest of my family seemed gifted in painting and drawing, those skills just never came naturally to me. In spite of that right-brain deficiency, I went on to oversee multimillion-dollar websites, build highly visible startups, launch successful apps, and more generally make a livelihood being creative.

The reason I share that embarrassing anecdote is that if you don't have artistic abilities, this doesn't mean you won't be able to help architect your concept app. Although I've come a long way since making my poor art teacher stay after school, I owe part of my success to realizing how best to focus my energies. Where I add the biggest benefit, and where you can too, is not in making things look pretty; there are extremely talented people who will help you do that. You will make better use of your time and progress your app further overall by being disciplined in attending to the larger vision and *not* the design details.

Understanding Wireframes

Depending on your exposure to design, and in particular, to web design, the term "wireframe" may or may not be familiar to you. In the web world, wireframes (see Figure 3-2) are visual guides that highlight key elements, structures, and relationships among the web pages of a website. Wireframes are typically created in black and white, with little or no use of font styling (beyond font sizes) or images, instead keeping the focus on the architecture and layout of the site.

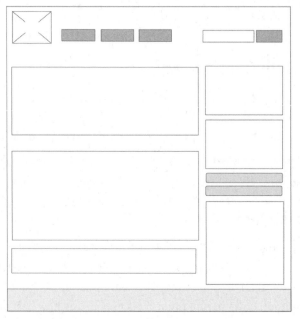

Figure 3-2. Example of a web wireframe

Of course, the larger idea behind wireframes was not birthed with the Web, nor does it stop with it. Ultimately, the advantage of including wireframes in any development process is to focus on getting the structure and functionality right, before spending significant time making it visually appealing. When mixing structure and design, it's possible to bias customers with something that looks good but is not necessarily easy to use. Similarly, it is significantly harder to revise a concept that includes design elements.

Consider, for example, how much easier it is to move a room in a house when you're working with a blueprint than it is after you've started building the structure. Since you'll be using wireframes to develop the first draft of your concept app, keeping the wireframes focused on the structure and flow will allow you to quickly *iterate* and revise the design when you get additional feedback from customers.

The secondary benefit to wireframing your app goes back to my point in the preceding section. You won't get wrapped up in ensuring that the app looks right and instead will focus on the two or three key screens and functions of your app.

Creating wireframes

Creating wireframes is considerably easier today than in the past, thanks to the graciousness of the larger development community and some significant advances in software tools developed specifically for wireframing and rapid prototyping. For this reason, I do not advocate wireframing on paper, although some people may be more comfortable with that. Just remember that you'll want to continually edit and share your wireframes, so having a digital copy will make this process smoother.

It's much harder to wireframe if you are designing a game versus most other apps, because significantly more artwork is required when dealing with games. You still should spend some time thinking about the game mechanics, rules, and flow, which can be captured in a wireframe. It also might be useful to either sketch character ideas (if needed) on paper, or hire someone who has a relevant background, such as a graphic artist, to do that for you.

In creating your wireframes, start with one or two screens that focus on what you discussed with your customers. These should be the defining screens of your app, representing the core of your offering. As questions arise about how the user should interact with elements on the screen, add those thoughts to the wireframe as an *annotation* or note. Don't get caught up in trying to answer all those questions now; at this point, it's more important to identify questions and problems than it is to answer them. It is also sometimes helpful to include screenshots from competing apps or apps you admire as a page within your wireframes. These can be used to remind you of what other apps are doing and also serve to inspire your own *user experience* (UX).

In the following list, I'll highlight a sampling of some of the wireframing tools I've used or recommend. Each tool relies on stencil libraries—a collection of shapes you can use in the wireframe—which include the core UI components for the iPhone and iPad. I list them in order of simplicity and usefulness, although your experience may dictate differently. Having been a PC user for many years, I am sympathetic to those using that platform. Thankfully, a more popular choice—Balsamiq's Mockups for Desktop—is also available for those using a PC. The others require a Mac, iPhone, or iPad.

Wireframe Example

To give you a frame of reference for what an app wireframe looks like, here is a screen (see Figure 3-3) from a final round of wireframes for my app Tweeb. I've been wireframing for some time now and this definitely represents a more polished and sophisticated wireframe using a more advanced tool (OmniGraffle for Mac).

Based on feedback I received from customers, this wireframe went through about five to seven rounds of revisions. At this stage or even at the end of wireframing your concept app, you won't need to get to this level of detail. I'm including it to show you how much can be communicated in a wireframe without really focusing on the design. In Chapter 5, I'll show you how this wireframe was translated into an actual design.

Figure 3-3. Tweeb Summary tab

Balsamiq Mockups for Desktop

Balsamiq's Mockups for Desktop (a.k.a. Mockups) is probably the best tool for those just getting started with wireframing. I've seen people who have never created wireframes produce very well-thought-out concepts using Mockups. This is because Balsamiq has distilled the key iPhone and iPad components into its tool, including only what's necessary to create a concept app. It also makes its wireframes appear like hand-drawn sketches, even though they are digital. This helps those creating the wireframes and those looking at the concepts to focus on ideas and not on design.

Mockups also offers a nice way to link wireframes together, which is useful once your concept has matured. Putting Mockups into presentation mode for a customer allows the customer to navigate the app through these links by clicking elements on the screen. Balsamiq's CEO, Peldi Guilizzoni, discusses this feature, and more generally, the purpose of wireframing, in an interview at the end of this chapter.

For more information, see *http://www.balsamiq.com/products/mockups/desktop*.

iMockups for iPad

iMockups for iPad, by Endloop (*http://endloop.ca/*; shown in Figure 3-4), is similar to Mockups. It initially launched with the opening of the iPad App Store and only exists on the iPad (at the time of this writing). Creating a wireframe on the iPad (whether it's for the iPad or the iPhone) is a unique experience because everything is controlled by touch. I find that paradigm allows me to much more quickly draft a wireframe at the expense of it being less detailed. Because of that, it is a good place for you to draft your wireframe, since it won't allow you to obsess over details. iMockups can also export files for use in Balsamiq's Mockup tool.

For more information, see *http://itunes.apple.com/app/imockups/id364885913*.

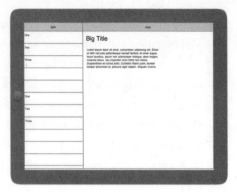

Figure 3-4. An iMockups wireframe I created in less than a minute on my iPad

OmniGraffle

OmniGraffle is a full-featured Mac and iPad app used by many information architecture and user experience professionals. It can do much more than wireframing, which results in it requiring a little more patience to learn. This also results in it being the most expensive option to use on your Mac or iPad.

The stencils you'll need to wireframe for the iPhone or iPad aren't bundled with OmniGraffle. Because of its popularity, however, they are easily downloaded for the Mac from sites such as Graffletopia (*http:// graffletopia.com/stencils/tags/iphone*).

It's not fair to say that you should "graduate" to OmniGraffle, because the other tools are extremely capable of helping you get your job done. My recommendation, however, is to start with the other tools and then expand your horizons based on needs. For example, I use all of these tools together, and sometimes will start a wireframe in Balsamiq's Mockups and then revisit it in OmniGraffle. If you are creating wireframes for a client, you may also consider using OmniGraffle to create a more polished wireframe.

For more information, see *http://www.omnigroup.com/products/ OmniGraffle/*.

Other tools to watch in this space include Interface, Stencils, Review Sync, Live View, and Screenport. Interface (*http://lesscode.co.nz/interface*) and Stencils (*http://www.stencilsapp.com*) are iOS apps that allow you to link together the mockups you create, showing how they progress from one screen to another (similar to Balsamiq Mockups, but on the device itself). There's also a growing trend to wireframe in Apple's Keynote, which most Mac users have installed on their computers (e.g., *http://keynotekungfu.com/* and *http://keynotopia.com/*).

Review Sync (*http://getreviewapp.com/*), LiveView (*http://www.zambetti.com/projects/liveview/*), and Screenport (*http://tapmates.com/screenport/*) aren't wireframing tools, but instead allow you to easily display your wireframes or design assets on your devices.

Reengaging Customers

I don't want to make this process seem as sequential as I wrote it in this chapter. You may, for example, need to have subsequent discussions with customers to receive confirmation of your assumptions. That is, you should not necessarily begin drafting a wireframe until your ideas have been validated and you have identified and understand your customers' problems.

With wireframes, you need to be careful about which customers to show them to and at what point. Don't use your first attempt at wireframes to get reactions from customers. You'll want to revise your ideas, and possibly get some immediate comments from friends, family, or colleagues. You should solicit feedback from customers once you have two or three screens that have gone through some amount of revision and feel complete to you. Make sure they communicate the direction in which you are trying to take the app.

When you do present wireframes to customers, ensure that they understand why you used wireframes. Be selective with the number of customers who see your wireframes, because even with the context you provide, they might not understand their purpose and be turned off by how basic they look. Although the wireframes will allow you to get additional customer insight, in many ways they will be more important to you and others that help you build your app.

Interviews

KISSmetrics: Cindy Alvarez

COMPANY: KISSmetrics

POSITION: Product manager

BACKGROUND: Cindy Alvarez is the product manager at KISSmetrics, where she is currently building two products (KISSmetrics and KISSinsights) using customer development and lean startup techniques.

LINKS: *http://www.cindyalvarez.com/; http://kissmetrics.com/*

Ken: *You are a leading voice in using "customer development" to build products. What is that and how does it help people build better products? More specifically, why was customer development conceived and what problems does it try to solve?*

Cindy: Customer development is a set of techniques to identify your market, understand their pain points and priorities, and validate that they're willing and able to solve those pain points—before you start building a solution.

It's the opposite of "if we build it, they will come" thinking—who can afford to take that kind of risk? By working closely with early customers, you are not only learning about the market, but also building your leads list. The people you interview will become your beta testers, the first people to give you their credit cards, and hopefully, the people who recommend you to their peers.

Customer development also forces you into ruthless prioritization. In a traditional product development roadmap, developers want the first release to be perfect and include all of their pet features. When you have engaged early customers, you know what the most critical features are and you feel the pressure to release them as quickly as possible. You can often omit features that you internally thought were critical but your customers just don't need.

Ken: *A big part of customer development is about validation. When you talk with customers, what specifically are you learning from these interviews and how do you ensure that you are learning the right things?*

Cindy: For one thing—and this should encourage anyone looking to start customer development—people are incredibly willing to talk and share details about their behaviors. The trick is to focus on that person, on his or her experiences. Your customers should never feel like they have to "study" in advance of your interview.

Some of the questions to explore in interviews include:

- How many people are required to get a task completed? What are the bottlenecks that prevent the task from being done better/more frequently/faster/cheaper?

- How much time/money/thinking is this person willing to invest in solving the problem?

- What's the frequency and severity of this problem/pain? (Occasional, mild but constant irritation, or rare potential catastrophe?)

- How long do certain tasks take, and what preparation or cleanup work happens before and after them?

Fundamentally, your product needs to maximize rewards and minimize barriers to adoption for your target market. What does this customer find motivating and exciting? What does this customer find off-putting or intimidating? You need to understand those levers and align your product with them.

Ken: *How early is too early to begin the customer interaction and interview process? That is, what should be a baseline before interacting with potential customers? Is some sort of visual required?*

Cindy: The biggest mistake most people make is waiting too long for customer interaction. The more mature your idea is, the harder it is to collect raw customer feedback. It affects the way you frame your questions as well as the way you filter their responses—tending to magnify comments that agree with your idea and minimize those that don't.

It's certainly not impossible to do customer development with a well-developed idea or prototype, but it can be a challenge. If you have a visual to show customers, wait until the end of the interview to do so. Get as much raw input as possible first, because once customers see something they will subconsciously tailor their answers based on what they've seen.

Ken: *What do you do with customer feedback and how quickly do you go back to them once you've digested and potentially implemented anything they suggested? How do you ensure that you aren't fatiguing customers and are properly respecting their time?*

Cindy: I send out "what we've learned" updates about once every six weeks to all beta customers. If certain people helped bring an issue to light, I'll usually follow up twice—once to confirm that this is a priority for us, and again when it's implemented.

I think people worry too much about overcommunication—when you take customers' input seriously, they feel a sense of ownership. They want to hear back from you! Just remember to do more updating/thanking than asking. I try to maintain a 2:1 gratification to "ask" ratio.

Ken: *Who are the other voices that help influence the evolution of a product besides customers? How do you balance or include the perspectives of advisors, bosses, analysts, and other stakeholders?*

Cindy: Customers are the experts in what their problems and priorities are, not how to solve them. They don't care about you building long-term sustainable competitive advantage or developing new technologies, and they don't know where social or technology trends are heading.

Ken: *Are there any tools you use regularly to help coordinate or facilitate customer development? What do you use to keep track of everything you are learning and for interacting individually or corporately with customers?*

Cindy: I use surveys to identify the best candidates to contact—it's actually an internal tool that I use, but Wufoo is a great service for that. I track notes on our internal wiki and send out summaries via email to my team. With customers, almost all of my communications are via manually composed emails. It takes longer to write, but my response rate is close to 50%. You never get that kind of response rate to mass emails or surveys. It's not very scalable, but that's kind of the point—this is a hands-on, intense activity.

Balsamiq Studios: Peldi Guilizzoni

COMPANY: Balsamiq Studios

POSITION: CEO

BACKGROUND: Launched in June 2008, Balsamiq Mockups helps people build great software by letting them easily sketch out their ideas, then quickly collaborate and iterate over them.

LINK: *http://www.balsamiq.com/products/mockups*

Ken: *What is Balsamiq Mockups and why did you create it? Where does it fit in the process of building a product or application?*

Peldi: Balsamiq Mockups is a simple little wireframing tool. It tries to replicate the experience of sketching in a notebook or on a whiteboard, but on the computer. It's digital but still looks like a hand-drawn sketch, to encourage honest feedback and to help everyone focus on the structure of the application instead of graphic details, which can be dealt with at a later stage.

Our sweet spot is the early stage of the application design process, when you want to jot down your rough ideas and refine them with input from other stakeholders. It's designed to be easy enough for nontechnical people to use, and powerful enough to be embraced by developers and designers.

Ken: *For someone with no creative or software development experience, what are some of the biggest challenges to building a wireframe or mockup? What pitfalls should these types of people look to avoid?*

Peldi: When I first started designing software, I remember having the tendency to want to add lots of buttons, options, and bells and whistles to my interface. With experience—reading a lot of user experience books and conducting a number of usability tests—I have learned that designing truly enjoyable software is about figuring out ways to solve problems in a way that's as close to invisible as you can [make it]. It's all about resisting the urge to add anything at all to the user interface.

Ken: *Some might say your iPhone controls are too limited. Do you have a certain philosophy in what is or is not there for the iPhone specifically?*

Peldi: We chose the main controls, which together with the rest of the UI controls included in Mockups should allow you to prototype about 80% of your applications. Once again, it's about doing the 20% that covers 80% of the use cases.

We only provide the core to help you focus, but our users have been sharing other, more complex controls if you need them: *http://mockupstogo.net/tag/ apple*.

Ken: *What are some of the ways your customers are using Balsamiq Mockups to test out iPhone and iPad app concepts? Are there any best practices for putting a mockup in front of a potential user to get feedback?*

Peldi: I have seen people create a row of iPhone interfaces, one screen after the other. Then to run through them you just scroll horizontally from left to right. If all of your screens don't fit on one row, make another!

If instead you are using Mockups for usability testing, we suggest having one screen per file, linking them together, and showing them in presentation mode with the linking hints disabled. This way, your testers will click around and explore the prototype while you watch and learn in painful yet enlightening silence.

Most of all, don't fall in love with your first or second wireframe. Sleep on it and come back to it. I bet you'll be able to simplify it more and more.

Ken: *Can you point to the best or most extensive examples of mockups you've seen created through Balsamiq? What is the easiest way for people to get started creating their first wireframe or mockup?*

Peldi: There are people who create prototypes with hundreds of screens. We actually don't encourage that with Mockups. In fact, if you're creating hundreds of screens, maybe you should rethink your application design to simplify it!

To get started, I would just download the demo from *http://www.balsamiq. com/products/mockups/download* and start dragging things around. Maybe try to reproduce an application you already know out of memory—I usually do iTunes. Or start from one of the many examples posted on our community-powered website, *http://www.mockupstogo.net*. There's lots of good stuff there.

Recap

Here's what you learned in this chapter:

- Customers are important, and you should start talking with them now instead of much further along in the development process.

- Not all customers are created equally. You want to find "earlyvangelists" who represent the right type of customer to talk with at this stage of your app's existence.

- There are many ways to find customers. Referrals are the best way to get introduced, but there are also many opportunities to take advantage of social media sites and use surveys to capture customer information.

- Customer interviews provide you the first opportunity to begin validating the assumptions about your app. The best thing you can do in customer interviews is to listen. Let the customer explain problems and solutions and don't try to convince the customer about the validity of your ideas.

- Wireframing will provide you a way to visually conceptualize your app without concerning yourself with design details. Using software designed specifically for wireframing will allow you to fully concentrate on creating a vision of your app, which later will be transformed into an actual design.

Development

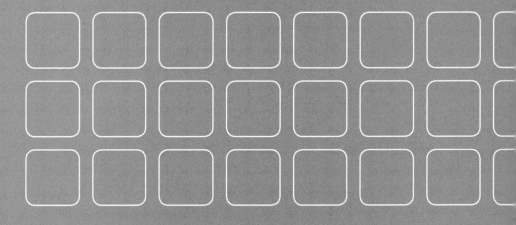

For Hire: Identifying Help

DON'T BE ASHAMED if you are creatively or technically challenged. Because you've focused on the ideas and concept of your app, you'll be in a much better position if you need to hire or outsource its design or development. Because the app market is booming, there will be no shortage of people and companies ready to "help" you. Your job will be to separate those who are merely following the app gold rush from those who can successfully bring your concept into the App Store.

In this chapter, you'll explore:

- Skills needed to bring an app into the App Store

- Your role in the development process

- How to estimate costs to develop your app

- Places to look for help and how to evaluate resources

Your App Team

Although some people reading this book have the creative or technical abilities to build an app without help, others do not; this chapter is focused on those in the second category. If you fall into this second category, you are already in a much better situation because of what you've been doing, including becoming a connoisseur of apps and engaging the iOS development community (part of Phase 1 of your marketing crescendo from Chapter 8). Your next step is to find those with the expertise you are lacking.

If you are developing your app yourself or you already have resources to build it, you don't necessarily need to read this entire chapter. The interviews, however, are particularly insightful, and I encourage you to read them. Also, the chapter contains some good nuggets about scheduling and where not to cut corners with your team members.

Before I start pointing you to places to look for software developers or designers—in the form of independent contractors, small app development firms, or agencies—to help you build your team, I want to equip you with three pieces of information:

1. The types of skills that are required to build apps

2. How to vet those who claim they can help you

3. An understanding of the costs involved to build apps

In terms of the third point, although you won't receive any cost estimates until you begin interacting with designers or developers, it's important to go into these conversations with the right expectations and background on the talent market.

Skills

Because building an app is fundamentally a software development effort, the same types of skills are required. I'll break these skills down into three broad categories: product management, design, and software development.

Product management

Product management is what you've been doing and will continue to do throughout the remainder of your app's existence. It entails a number of responsibilities, including strategizing, managing customer interactions, testing, and marketing. The product manager is the person who owns the product, not in the sense of legal ownership (although that could be the case), but in terms of ensuring that the app's vision becomes its reality.

Third-Party Frameworks: Build Once, Run Everywhere

If you are a do-it-yourself person or want to launch your app on multiple mobile platforms, you may want to look at PhoneGap (*http://www.phonegap.com/*), Appcelerator (*http://www.appcelerator.com/*), or other third-party frameworks that help those with little or no knowledge of programming to build and launch apps. In particular, PhoneGap allows apps to be built in HTML and JavaScript, which significantly widens the pool of people available to help with your app.

I generally don't recommend these options, for two reasons. First, Apple recently began cracking down on these types of frameworks, indicating that certain ones take an approach that is not permissible for use on the App Store (i.e., Apple will reject apps that use them). Although PhoneGap and Appcelerator appear to be OK in Apple's eyes, you should be aware of the company's broader stance on third-party frameworks.

Second, I do not feel that these frameworks embrace the philosophy of what it means to build an app "the Apple way." Apple wants apps built using its development tools, implementing custom and not templated designs. To some extent, these frameworks are shortcuts and this usually shows in the apps that are produced by them. As a result, apps using these frameworks are usually not the ones featured by Apple. That's not always the fault of the framework used, but rather the types of people it attracts.

The bottom line: investigate and use PhoneGap, Appcelerator, or other options because of the benefits they offer and not as a workaround or way to save you money. A great resource for those who want to explore PhoneGap in particular is *Building iPhone Apps with HTML, CSS, and JavaScript* (*http://oreilly. com/catalog/9780596805791/*) by Jonathan Stark (O'Reilly).

This last point is worth spending a moment to explore further. By being the visionary of your app, you will be the product (app) expert. This expertise derives from your understanding of the App Store and what you are learning from your customers. The firmer you are with the strategy and direction the app should take, the fewer questions your team members will have.

With more details, especially details that are documented (rather than just floating around in your head), you'll have a larger pool of talent you can choose to work with and will, in most cases, reduce what it costs you to build your app. Consider the difference between giving a detailed written description of the house you'd want a builder to create for you and just loosely describing it. Even though the builder knows how to build homes, he won't necessarily create one you like without clear input and direction from you. The same is true in the development process for your app.

More tactically, the product manager acts as a project manager, tester for quality assurance (QA), marketer, and customer support representative. These responsibilities can include scheduling meetings, taking notes, ensuring that tasks are being completed on time, keeping a team talking, writing marketing copy, rigorously testing the in-progress app, and regularly interacting with customers through all marketing and support channels. Since your other team members may have little interaction with customers (although you should do your best to directly expose the team to them), you will need to aggressively represent your customers and be a proxy for them internally.

I wrote most of this book to help you perform the functions of the product manager. So, in a sense, you can view not having to hire a product manager and executing these duties yourself as a way to save money. I do, however, want to offer you a word of caution about operating under this mindset. These responsibilities are extremely important, and if you decide to assume them, you need to consider yourself a full-time member of your team. Failing to do so can result in your app getting off-schedule, miscommunication (or no communication) among team members, and launching an app that has no real chance of success. If you have the financial resources, or if your strengths are in design or development, you should consider having an actual product manager oversee your app for you.

The interviews at the end of this chapter also provide some helpful perspectives on the various roles required in developing an iPhone app.

Design

The designer for your app will lead all its creative direction. This includes choosing the colors and fonts and creating the logo, app icon, any required artwork, and actual screens. The product manager will collaborate with the designer to ensure that these elements match the app's vision and strategy. As the designer completes the design assets, she will give them to the developer to incorporate into the app.

Although you will want a designer with app experience, it's good to work with designers who are comfortable with other forms of media. For example, as part of the marketing process, you'll need to build a website. The branding aspects of your app (colors, typography, and logo) are also more general design tasks.

Great design is extremely important in the App Store. In the next chapter, you'll also learn that great design does not focus on visuals alone.

Software development

I've been using the word "development" to describe the entire process of building your app and "developer" to generally refer to those involved in creating an app. The software developer, however, is the person who will actually code and program the application and drive your app's development. Development, in this context, includes the technical architecture, programming, integration with any external data sources, and optimization for your app. I describe each of these items in detail in the next chapter. For now, it suffices for you to know that your developer is responsible for making your app functional, as well as integrating the design assets created by your designer.

Of all the roles on your team, the developer has the least leeway in terms of not having direct experience building Mac or iPhone apps. In the past, I've worked with designers who had not designed an iOS app and picked it up fairly quickly. But I've had disastrous results with people trying to learn iOS development on the fly. That's somewhat dependent on the talent of the person you use, but let my experience be a lesson for you and go with someone who has at least basic (and demonstrable) Mac or iPhone programming knowledge.

Compared to your designer, your developer is going to be doing more work and be more heavily involved in your app's progress, especially in the long term. Once an app is launched, unless there's a major redesign—which does not occur very often, and sometimes does not occur at all—most of the ongoing effort will be development-related. In most cases, after your app is in the App Store, your developer will probably be able to use the existing design assets in future versions of the app.

Vetting Help

Due to how hot the market is for building apps, and especially iPhone and iPad apps, there will be no shortage of people willing to "help" you. You can avoid those types of inquiries by beginning your search the right way and then knowing how to better vet potential team members. Trust your instincts and judgment throughout this process. If you have a bad feeling about a person or a company, don't proceed.

Referrals and client references

If possible, try to work with people you know or who are in your larger network. Making that happen may include asking friends or family to make introductions for you, or hitting LinkedIn and Twitter to ask your colleagues and peers to do the same. It's better to work with people you have done business with in the past or who come with a referral from a contact. Getting a referral can help you avoid this search entirely.

With referrals or with people you find outside your immediate network, always ask for client references. Talk with these references about their apps and App Store experiences. If someone doesn't have any client references because he is just starting out, don't be completely scared away. If he can demonstrate a reasonable amount of competency, use his lack of references as a negotiating point to lower costs.

Portfolios

Portfolios are a great means to understand a designer's or developer's skills. A portfolio showcases the apps or the parts of the apps that someone previously built.

At first glance, a portfolio may seem relevant only to a designer, since it's easy to visually inspect the work. The nice thing about the App Store, however, is that you can download any portfolio app (see Figure 4-1) and try it yourself. That allows you to experience a developer's work too by seeing how responsive an app is and whether it seems stable or crashes.

Figure 4-1. Portfolio example from Toffeenut Design

The other use of the portfolio is that you can discuss the apps with the designer or developer. Ask why her app looks or functions the way it does, what some of the tough decisions were, and what she considers the best and worst parts of the app (especially what she believes needs to be improved). I find the best way to do that is to focus on two or three screens. Try to really dig into the details beyond what's obvious. Another reason this step is important—and you might be surprised by this fact—is that some people will misrepresent apps as part of their portfolio when they really are not. That won't be possible if you have these types of discussions.

If their apps are fairly different from what you want to build, ask them how they'll approach designing or developing your app. Guide them to be more specific and ask what they see as the big challenges with your app compared to what they previously built. A good approach is to point them to one or two apps that are similar to yours and then follow the same exercise as with their portfolio apps by focusing on two or three screens and then discussing with them.

Agreements and protection

Aside from making sure your team members have the right skills and talent, you will want to make sure you find people who are willing to agree to some basic rules regarding confidentiality and protection of your idea and application. This includes maintaining your rights to your idea and the assets your team develops for your app.

This protection is often accomplished through a nondisclosure agreement (NDA) and a standard contractor agreement between you and any of your team members. The purpose of the NDA is to define the terms under which you and your contractors will disclose confidential information to each other during the course of the engagement. It may provide protection of that information for some period of time (as specified in the agreement) so that it cannot be shared with third parties.

The main goal of the contractor agreement is to establish your rights to the assets your contractors develop. It may also include a description of what tasks or milestones your contractors must accomplish to receive payment.

These guidelines are for informational purposes only and should not be construed as legal advice. Although NDAs, contractor forms, and related resources are available for free on some websites, such as LegalZoom.com, Nolo.com, and Docstoc (*http://www.docstoc.com/*), they may not fit your specific situation. I strongly recommend that you consult an attorney to ensure that your agreements are accurately drafted and enforceable.

Costs

In Chapter 1, I mentioned that $10,000 was a fair number to use for the cost of a well-built app. Sure, it is possible to pay less than that (and much more!), but in general, as that price goes down, so will the quality of the app. To quote Davide Di Cillo, an iPhone app developer and the founder of GetAppsDone.com, who is interviewed at the end of this chapter:

…keep in mind that a $20 per hour developer isn't always cheaper than a $100 per hour developer. I've worked with developers that even if more expensive, were saving me money by being faster and more responsive.

For some background on why that number is in some ways a conservative estimate, note that many apps will take between four and eight weeks to build, with the average being six weeks. With a full-time developer (40 hours per week) and a part-time designer (20 hours per week), the average man-hours per week is around 60. Six weeks multiplied by 60 hours per week equals 360 hours. Solid designers and developers will charge around $100 per hour, with top talent peaking at around $150 per hour and lower-end U.S.-based contractors charging around $65 per hour. Using the $100-per-hour rate yields a total of $36,000 (360 hours × $100 per hour). That number can quickly fluctuate: if your app took four weeks to build (240 hours) and the average was instead $75 per hour, the total would be $18,000 (240 hours × $75 per hour).

For games, the number of total hours is much higher, and ranges between 700 and 2,000 hours. This equates to three to six months of work, depending on the number of developers working on the game simultaneously.

It may astound you to know that depending on complexity, the cost of developing an app can range from less than $5,000 to more than $100,000. That lower boundary typically involves working with offshore or independent developers, whereas the higher number is from hiring professional companies or agencies. Looking at the median cost from TheyMakeApps.com (see Figure 4-2), a resource for finding app developers, you can see that development cost lies within the $10,000 to $15,000 range. Contractors have also requested that TheyMakeApps.com add a $50,000+ category to assign to their listing.

Figure 4-2. A TheyMakeApps.com fee breakdown based on contractors self-reporting what they charge to build apps

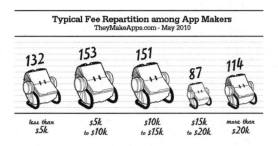

Typical Fee Repartition among App Makers
TheyMakeApps.com - May 2010

less than s5k	s5k to s10k	s10k to s15k	s15k to s20k	more than s20k
132	153	151	87	114

One last note about these costs: on the lower end, they largely assume that you are acting as the product manager for your app, performing the roles described earlier. This implies that your "services" are free. To perform a more rigorous cost analysis, you might consider including your hours in these estimates. Assign yourself an hourly rate—perhaps what you could make if you were consulting, based on what you make at your job, or by actually paying yourself some sort of salary—and multiply that by the number of hours you plan to spend on your app per week. Add that to the previous numbers to get another perspective on costs.

Reconciling costs

Hopefully, you didn't damage this book or your screen too badly after reading the preceding paragraphs. The reality of the situation is that you are in a hot market in which people with the skills to build apps are scarce resources. You'll find that the best designers and developers won't haggle with cost estimates or their rates because others will gladly pay them.

To reconcile these costs, start with the quantification of your app as performed in Chapter 1. You should understand the larger purpose of this effort (e.g., it's the start of a long-term investment in the mobile space) and, if you are pursuing a paid app, have some sense of what the financial returns should be.

Although I'll show you some practical ways to lower costs, you need to be able to reconcile them with the motivation behind your app. Mentally you must be "all in" with your app, equally committed to it and prepared to lose anything you've invested. That's a telling yet truthful statement about the nature of the App Store.

Remember that if you continue to update your app once it is launched, each update will also come with a cost. Depending on what the updates include, they typically will equate to a fraction of what it costs to build the entire app. Not accounting for them, however, can give you a false sense of out-of-pocket costs.

Ways to save

Ensuring that your product assets (e.g., initial research and wireframes) are as detailed as possible is a smart way to reduce your costs. If you have little or no experience building software, some of these items will not be more fully completed until your team is in place. Even before then, however, do your best to think through the biggest challenges of your app. Bringing more information to your potential resources will help them better estimate costs and build your app more efficiently. Both of these will impact the bottom line of what it costs to build your app.

Second, try to keep the first version of your app as simple as possible. That means scaling the app back to its key features, choosing what has proven to be most important to your customers. This approach not only is helpful from a cost perspective, but also is a strategic decision for your app. Many apps try to do many things at once, and as a result, they do nothing well. Thus, by focusing your first release in this way, you'll reduce the risk of overinvestment while also developing a better app.

The experience, quality, and location of those you contract can drastically impact costs, but not necessarily the way you'd think. For example, working with offshore or less experienced resources (such as students or recent graduates) can put your app cost more in the range of several thousand dollars. Yet, this usually can be accomplished successfully only by people who know how to collaborate with these types of designers and developers to achieve the results they want. Those who are less seasoned or have no experience in this area often choose the cheaper option, only to spend thousands of dollars with an unsatisfactory outcome, or worse, with nothing to show for it. The investment, in this case, becomes considerably higher than initially agreeing to a more costly estimate or hourly rate from more experienced or proven resources.

There are additional challenges with offshore or overseas resources, including language barriers and adjusting for time zone differences. Again, it's possible to overcome these problems, but few have gotten the formula just right; the benefits are numerous to those who have.

A lesser-known way to reduce the cost of building your app is to find developers who are willing to reuse code from their other apps or client projects. The reason is that the actual development usually represents the largest portion of the cost. You might even consider working with a developer who has developed an app that is similar to your idea.

The caution for this approach is that you'll need to ensure that you have the full rights to these assets—through a written agreement—in case you sever your relationship with the developer or your app is acquired. In the first case, you wouldn't want the developer to keep the code if he is no longer involved in the app. In the second case, you wouldn't want the developer to claim that your app couldn't be sold or that a portion of the proceeds were owed to him.

On this point, I want to conclude this section by addressing the use of partnerships and revenue sharing (referred to collectively as "partnerships") as a way to lower costs. It's possible that instead of paying for help, you might convince people to lend their skills or assets for free in exchange for partial ownership of your app, a share of the app's proceeds, or recognition (if you have a free app).

In most cases, I find that one or more parties in partnerships become disillusioned by the perception that another party is not as committed or is not doing as much work as other members. This causes frustration, distrust, and often a dissolving of the partnership before the app even makes it to the App Store.

One remedy to this situation, which does not make a partnership foolproof, is to have a written agreement that stipulates how the equity is divided beforehand. This solution also has its problems, because it may not be clear what each effort is worth. For instance, since the main value you might bring to your team is your idea and your understanding of your app's landscape, doing "less work" in terms of building your app shouldn't necessarily imply that your share of the app should be lower than others'.

Another major issue with partnerships is that disappointment and frustration can occur if the app does not immediately meet expectations when launched into the App Store. Part of the underpinnings of a partnership is the promise of the app. If it appears to have no promise through its download count or sales numbers, your partners may be unwilling to continue to invest their time in it. This can leave you in an unsettling predicament.

If you are absolutely determined to build your app using a partnership, at least do so with people you've worked with in the past or have known for some time. And still be sure to put the terms of your partnership in a written, signed document. My overall recommendation is that if your idea is worth pursuing, consider some of the options to reduce your costs, but be willing to invest money in it. Doing so will simplify legal paperwork, and ultimately will allow you to drive and own the direction of your app.

Visit *http://kenyarmosh.com/appsavvy* to help estimate the cost to build your app. You'll also find information about how to create a reusable template to solicit contractors, as discussed in the next section.

Finding Resources

Now that you understand the types of skills needed to build your app, know ways you can vet your team members, and have some sort of expectation regarding costs, you are ready to begin engaging those who can help you. You can find these people through several outlets, and your choice will be based on your needs and preferences. Since most of these will be online, however, it's helpful to have a reusable template to solicit inquiries. You'll collect standard information from these contractors so that you can judge them against each other. I'll cover how to do that first, and then I'll highlight some of the places you can look for your potential team members.

Streamlining Solicitations

To expedite the process of soliciting contractors, you'll create a reusable template focused on getting the same information from all interested parties. After you receive this information, you'll share more details and any app assets you have as you learn more about each contractor. Depending on how unique you consider your idea to be, few to no substantial details about your app need to be shared until you feel comfortable or have received a signed NDA (or comparable documentation).

The best way to think about the template you create is that each part of it should require some response from a potential contractor. By approaching it in this way, you will ensure that it is kept concise and actionable, while screening those who might not be right for you.

The template should include a brief description of what the app is about, the skills required, a request for the contractor's portfolio (preferably links to the App Store), additional information about the contractor (e.g., other creative or technology skills), when you are looking to start and complete the project, your plans for compensation (e.g., paid or partnership), and how to get in touch with you. This last item is often dictated by the outlet you are using to post your solicitation.

Don't worry about including the budget for the app at this point, unless it is required wherever you are advertising. Those who see an actual budget number for your app will be motivated by that number alone, meaning they will be motivated for the wrong reason. Any smart contractor should evaluate your solicitation based on the information you provided. It will communicate that you are serious and thoughtful.

Where to Look

After you have completed your recruiting template, you are ready to find help. The outlets you choose to target will be based in part on your budget and time constraints. Pursue as many or as few of these outlets as you want, but don't settle until you are satisfied with the number of options you have to sort through to help you build your app.

Tweeb Developer Recruitment

Instead of including all the details in each place you advertise, you might consider creating a single questionnaire for your contractors to complete, using one of the survey tools mentioned in Chapter 3.

I find the questionnaire useful, for a couple of reasons. First, whether you're advertising online or emailing someone, the initial correspondence or introduction will be short, since the survey has all of the questions. Second, the survey tool will organize all of your responses neatly into a single location. You can then compare all options more easily.

For Tweeb, I took the questionnaire approach (see Figure 4-3) when recruiting a developer, posting an advertisement on Craigslist and getting referrals from several people. In both cases, I asked contractors to complete my survey and followed up with those who best matched my requirements.

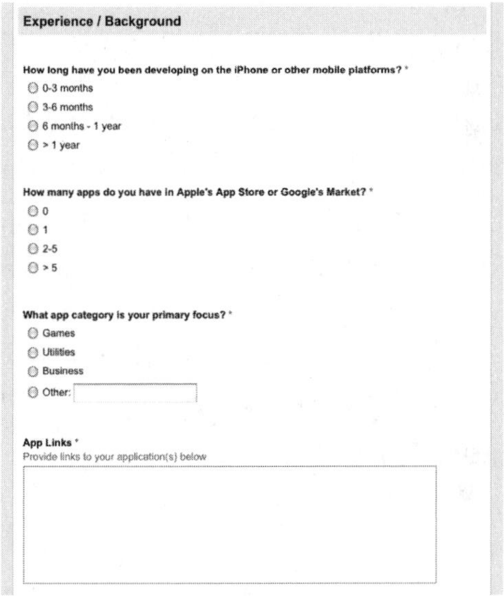

Figure 4-3. A portion of my Tweeb questionnaire when recruiting prospective developers

Experience / Background

How long have you been developing on the iPhone or other mobile platforms? *
- 0-3 months
- 3-6 months
- 6 months - 1 year
- > 1 year

How many apps do you have in Apple's App Store or Google's Market? *
- 0
- 1
- 2-5
- > 5

What app category is your primary focus? *
- Games
- Utilities
- Business
- Other:

App Links *
Provide links to your application(s) below

Independent contractors

Those who are slightly more cash-strapped will need to be more proactive and creative in their search. In these cases, independent contractors (also referred to as "indie developers" or "freelancers") are the best options. Independent contractors are people who moonlight their services, create their own apps but use contracting to supplement their income, or have a very small development firm (one to three people). Offshore or overseas options also fall into this category.

There are a handful of great ways to find this type of help. The first is to get involved in the local tech community. NSCoder Night (*http://nscodernight.com/*) and CocoaHeads (*http://cocoaheads.org/*) provide extremely targeted options. You can also check out Meetup.com and find mobile or app-focused groups. Attend these groups and meetups or post to the message boards inquiring for help. In these situations, it's best to initially introduce yourself and ask those who are interested to get in touch with you before sharing your template or questionnaire.

You can also use Craigslist to stay local by posting a "gig" that solicits contractors (e.g., *http://washingtondc.craigslist.org/cpg/*). In this case, it's fine to make your advertisement short and link to your questionnaire (if you created one) or simply use your template. If you do have a questionnaire, you need not include a "reply to" address when creating the listing. Although I firmly believe in the ability to work with remote resources, it is nice to be able to occasionally get together with your team. That makes Meetup.com and Craigslist especially valuable outlets, since they are geographically targeted.

It's likely that many of the apps you either admire on the App Store or think have functionality that could be useful to yours have been built by indie developers. As mentioned earlier, consider reaching out to these people, because you will be able to evaluate their skills and experience. Remember that the App Store listing shows the website link for all developers.

These developers also may offer the best opportunity to help you reduce costs by leveraging their existing code assets. Besides checking out the App Store, you can browse sites such as the Behance Network (*http://www.behance.net/*), Ember (*http://emberapp.com/*), Dribbble (*http://dribbble.com/*; see Figure 4-4), or Forrst (*http://forrst.com/*) to find inspiration and potential resources through the portfolios of designers, in particular.

A great app-specific resource to use is GetAppsDone.com (its founder is interviewed at the end of this chapter). GetAppsDone.com provides a targeted outlet for you to advertise your opportunity. Once your listing is created, it can automatically be shared on Twitter and Facebook.

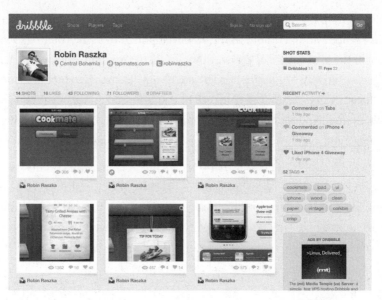

Figure 4-4. Dribbble portfolio page for Robin Raszka of tapmates

Although I caution you against doing this—unless you have previous software development experience—you can also pursue low-cost offshore resources. In fact, it's likely that your Craigslist posting will generate some of these inquiries. To find these types of options, browse to oDesk (*http://www.odesk.com/*), Elance (*http://www.elance.com/*), or vWorker (*http://www.vworker.com/*).

Agencies

If your app is fairly complex or you have a budget of more than $10,000, you might want to consider working with an agency rather than an independent contractor. The first benefit of an agency is that it typically will have all the resources you need to build your app, including a product manager, along with well-defined processes and tools (e.g., automated development builds). Second, an agency usually, but not always, can build an app more quickly because it has more resources at its disposal. These advantages will generally cost you significantly more, but you should feel the difference in the service you receive and the quality of the app (depending on the agency!).

One warning I want to provide you on this front is that many creative and web agencies added iPhone and iPad development to their roster of services only in the past couple of years. Although there are some crossover skills, as you've already begun to see, there are unique elements to building apps for these devices. Thus, my guidance to you is to find an agency that is dedicated to mobile development or that has a group that is focused in this area.

Finding mobile agencies is considerably easier since TheyMakeApps.com opened. Although you can also find independent contractors on this site, TheyMakeApps.com (see Figure 4-5) is probably the closest thing there is to a mobile agency directory. After designating that you want to build an app on the Apple platform, you can specify a location for your vendor/agency as well as the budget range for your app. The results will show you the available agencies, along with their websites and portfolios.

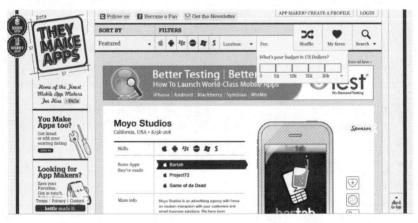

Figure 4-5. TheyMakeApps.com budget criteria selection

Make Your Decision

As you begin receiving replies from interested parties, be sure to follow the advice in this chapter on how to vet these resources. You should already have the portfolio from their initial response. For those you follow up with, you'll want to ask questions about the apps in the portfolio, talk with client references, and execute any legal documentation.

Once you have evaluated a contractor's work, verified that she can meet your timetable, signed any needed legal documentation, and had at least two substantial email exchanges or phone conversations, you should request a cost estimate in writing. To give yourself some options, try to get cost estimates from at least two contractors for each skill type (i.e., designer or developer) you need.

Ensure that you understand their process and workflow and how they came to their cost estimate. Clarify whether their estimate is a fixed bid or is based on the number of hours they think it will take; be sure to find out what happens if they go over these hours. Ask if they see any other ways to reduce costs. Don't forget to inquire about what it typically costs to perform app updates and what, if any, updates are included as part of the estimate (e.g., bug fixes).

When you've finally decided whom you want to work with, execute your contractor agreement (see the "Agreements and protection" section), ensuring that it includes a description of services and stipulates the payment terms. The description of services will flow directly from the contractor solicitation template and product assets. For the payment terms, some contractors will let you know what they require while others are flexible. Most contractor agreements include "exhibits" at the end of them to address each item specifically.

Be fair, but don't pay more than half of the cost estimate up front. If your contractors are working on an hourly basis, require them to provide you weekly updates on their hours and written confirmation from you for them to exceed their original cost estimate. Make sure additional payments are based on major accomplishments, such as submitting the app to the App Store, or better yet, having the app approved into the App Store.

As part of your agreement, request that your contractors provide you real-time access to the assets they create or have in progress. If the relationship dissolves (not desirable, but possible), you want to ensure that you can take any creative or code assets with you.

Interviews

GetAppsDone.com: Davide Di Cillo

COMPANY: GetAppsDone.com

POSITION: Founder

BACKGROUND: Over the past two years, Davide's company, 39 inc., has been continually contacted by those needing assistance in building their iPhone applications. Realizing there wasn't a streamlined process for connecting iPhone developers with potential clients, Davide created GetAppsDone.com, a place where companies and iPhone developers can connect with each other.

LINKS: *http://www.getappsdone.com/; http://39inc.com/*

Ken: *Once someone has an iPhone app idea and has validated it's a good idea to pursue, what do you consider to be the next steps in building the app?*

Davide: They should write down on a piece of paper (that white thing some people still use) all the features they came up with for their application, and cross out at least half of them because I'm sure they won't need them. People still confuse iPhone applications with desktop applications. For instance, for the Get Apps Done iPhone application, it could make sense to send out a resume, but the question is, would you send out the resume that could help you find your next job from a phone, or would you rather do it from a desktop or laptop where you could make sure everything is perfect?

Once you nail down the list of features you need, then it's time to find the right developer for it. I talk about *developer*, but in my opinion, working with teams (designer plus developer) is always better than working with a single person. The designer will help you create the right user experience while the developer can help you refine the features of your app.

Ken: *Some individuals and companies don't have access to those who know how to build iPhone apps. Where are the best places to start looking for help? How does GetAppsDone.com assist with that and how does this differ from other options available?*

Davide: Posting a (free) ad on GetAppsDone.com is a good way to start, but there are many other ways, like looking for a local developer group on sites like Meetup.com or openly asking on Twitter.

GetAppsDone.com differs from all those "rent-a-coder" sites because we don't have a bidding system. In our case, not having that feature adds a lot of value, because we don't create a race to the bottom for the prices that usually favor lower-quality work. Often, whoever is looking for resources doesn't understand how it is possible to receive bids from $1,000 to $10,000 for the same project, so they just go for the cheapest. With GetAppsDone.com, we let the developer contact the solicitor directly, giving them the opportunity to present themselves as they desire.

Ken: *Since iPhone design and development is a hot space, these skills are now listed on everyone's resume. How do you filter and vet those who are accomplished versus those who are just looking to monetize on someone's inexperience?*

Davide: A good idea is to ask for work examples and previous clients' references. Other than that, it is really hard to judge the real knowledge of a developer without being technical.

A trick that I have is never to hire "yes" people. You want your developer to be honest with you and you want them to say "no" when they see something wrong in your idea. Starting with the assumption that there's always something wrong or not cost-effective in an idea, your developer should help point out some problematic feature request at least once.

Ken: *From what you've seen, how long does it usually take to build an iPhone app once the right resources are in place? What areas do first-time app publishers under- or overestimate?*

Davide: Time frames are all over the place. Usually, those looking for help underestimate the number of changes they will request during the process. No matter how little and simple they look from the outside, sometimes they require a lot of work "under the hood." I always try to underpromise so that I have room for those changes, and no client will ever complain if we deliver an application earlier than estimated.

People also underestimate everything that comes after the application development: marketing, PR, and customer service. Those are key elements for the success of an application.

Ken: *What aspects of creating an app can be done in parallel? What can't? Are there ways to get apps done faster besides having more resources available?*

Davide: Design and development. We usually prepare a wireframe of how the application should work, including areas and spaces for different elements, so that we can work on the development and the polished design elements at the same time. Then, we just need to swap the less-finished elements with the final ones.

As far as the best way to get apps done faster and in a cost-effective way, my suggestion can be condensed to three words: keep it simple. Don't try to squeeze every feature you see in your favorite apps; just pick the one or two features your application really needs and try to make those perfect.

Ken: *Although it can vary greatly, what guidance or framework can you provide to those trying to evaluate the cost of developing an app? What ranges are you seeing in the market? How can costs be reduced? Where should costs not be reduced?*

Davide: Again, costs are all over the place. If we look at the U.S. market, I would say for an application that uses custom design and a few API calls, the range could be between $5,000 and $10,000.

My suggestion is to try to use developers who already built apps similar to yours and ask them if they can reuse any of the code they already wrote. I always try to help our clients to save money, not undervaluing our service but offering smarter solutions. And keep in mind that a $20-per-hour developer isn't always cheaper than a $100-per-hour developer. I've worked with developers who, even though they are more expensive, were saving me money by being faster and more responsive.

AppStoreHQ: Chris DeVore

COMPANY: Mobilmeme, Inc., which operates AppStoreHQ and iPhoneDevSDK

POSITION: Executive chairman

BACKGROUND: AppStoreHQ is a leading smartphone discovery platform.

LINK: *http://www.appstorehq.com/*

Ken: *What sorts of skills are needed to build an app? What does an ideal team look like?*

Chris: Apart from platform-specific knowledge about the unique capabilities of the device (e.g., using the camera or accelerometer, or delivering push messages), the core skills are the same as for any software development project. The following are skill areas, not head-count requirements, but on bigger projects they often fall to specialists with experience in each discipline:

Product leadership

> Understanding customer needs, defining user scenarios, keeping the team on track

User experience/user interface design

> Creating logical and concise user flows, integrating visual and other creative assets (artwork, audio, video, animation) to create an engaging experience

Software development

> Creating the logic and process layers required to deliver the envisioned experience: authenticating users; capturing, accessing, and presenting data; performing logic functions; integrating with other phone- and web-based systems, and so on

Testing

> Systematically performing all the intended functions of the applications to identify any software or design errors; testing supporting infrastructure for scalability, load, and potential errors caused by dependencies on third-party systems

Ken: *Some individuals and companies don't have access to those who know how to build apps. What are the best places to start looking for help?*

Chris: Literally thousands of firms are scattered around the world that develop apps for hire, but the capabilities of these firms, and the [resultant] quality of the applications they develop, can vary widely. The best place to start your search is among developers who have already successfully published apps of the type and quality you have in mind. The best-known publishers of top-selling apps rarely work on contract, but there are hundreds of lesser-known but extremely skilled developers who do. Look for existing apps in the category you're focused on that deliver the quality of experience you'd like to achieve, and get in touch with the developers directly (a directory of published developers, with filters for category, number of published apps, and average rating, can be found at *http://www.appstorehq.com/developers*).

Ken: *From what you've seen, how long does it usually take to build an app once the right resources are in place? What areas do first-time app creators under- or overestimate?*

Chris: The answer obviously varies widely, based both on the complexity of the app and on the skills and capabilities of the team, but a typical project will take between two and three months from start to submission for approval, with that last step requiring another two weeks (if you're lucky) or longer (if you're not), or resulting in outright rejection (if you're pushing the boundaries of what Apple has decided to allow that week).

Ken: *What aspects of creating an app can be done in parallel? What can't? Are there ways to get apps done faster besides having more resources available?*

Chris: Projects don't often get bogged down at the handoffs between functions like design and development; the greatest enemies of on-time delivery are poor upfront planning and mid-project changes in direction. The best way to ensure a smooth and rapid development process is to come into the engagement with a clear set of goals for your application and provide key assets like content, artwork, and legal approvals well in advance. You can also remove friction from the development process along the way by providing clear and timely guidance on strategic decisions as the app development process unfolds (just make sure your mid-stream guidance is consistent with your original goals and vision).

Ken: *Although it can vary greatly, what guidance or framework can you provide to those trying to evaluate the cost of developing an app? What ranges are you seeing in the market? How can costs be reduced? Where should costs not be reduced?*

Chris: App development is like any other complex project: time, cost, and quality are fundamental constraints, and making changes on any one of these vectors will necessarily impact the other two. Want your app built in a hurry? Expect to pay more and get less functionality and polish than you would if you allowed more time. Working with a tight budget? Plan to limit scope and allow extra time if you'd still like to deliver a quality experience. Based on recent market data, $5,000 is the minimum you should expect to pay for a basic app delivered with reasonable quality, but it's not uncommon for budgets to run an order of magnitude higher.

Ken: *On the flip side, how should app designers and developers think about pricing their services? Where do they typically under- or overestimate costs? How can they best promote themselves in a hot but increasingly competitive market?*

Chris: The best way for app development firms to command a premium price is to consistently deliver great work for clients with recognizable brand names. This is even more effective if you specialize in a particular domain, whether it's games or utilities. Deliver a great shopping app for a well-known brand and every product manager that competes with or aspires to emulate that brand will come knocking, asking you to do the same for them. If you haven't yet built a noteworthy app, consider building one at reduced rates for a marquee client. If the app you deliver is good, the lost revenue from that project will pay for itself several times over in referrals and new-client inquiries. And if you constantly find yourself going over budget, look hardest at your customer communication and project management practices—the root cause is most often here (and not in functional disciplines like design or development).

Recap

Here's what you learned in this chapter:

- Your team will consist of a product manager, designer, and developer. Most likely you will take on the critical role of product manager, overseeing the vision for your app, being the primary point of contact for your customers, ensuring that your app is bug-free, and performing the marketing responsibilities.

- Understanding how to vet help will make you more effective when you actually begin interacting with interested parties. Use client references, portfolios, and a willingness to execute legal documents as ways to filter your options.

- Coming to terms with the costs for your app should help you realize the seriousness of your investment in it. Although there are some ways to reduce those costs, as with any venture, pursuing your app is a risk and you should be mentally prepared to lose your entire investment in the app.

- Partnerships are an especially complicated approach to building apps. In theory, they seem like good options, but in practice, even the best partnerships require exceptional trust, additional paperwork, and ongoing reevaluation.

- Depending on your budget and time constraints, you can work with independent contractors or an agency. The trade-offs will usually include cost, speed of development, and sometimes quality.

5

Getting a Working App

YOU MAY BE FRUSTRATED that you *still* don't know what your app is going to look like or how it's going to function. Not to fear: with an initial validated concept defined and the right people now in place, getting a working app will be a smoother process. You'll work with your team to break down how you are going to build the app, further refine your concept, and determine what the first version of the app you submit to Apple will include.

In this chapter, you'll explore:

- Understanding your app's roadmap

- Breaking down the features for the first version of your app

- An overview of the design and development process

- Managing the progress of your app

The Development Process

My purpose for waiting until now to describe the development process in detail is that many people who build apps are extremely anxious to "get started," without really understanding what it means to get started. In particular, those who have the design and development skills to build an app without help often forgo the processes of researching competition, understanding what's going to make their app different, and sketching the key screens of their app, and instead start building it right away. The result is a misinformed app that is doomed to fail before it even hits the App Store.

Here's a secret you're going to be very happy to know: you've actually already begun the development process…the right way. Most people associate "development" only with designing or programming. But the entire development process—at least when building apps intelligently—includes your efforts to outline your app assumptions, your initial wireframes, and the validation of those ideas and assets with your customers. Of course, there's more to your app than what you've done up to this point, and even more than the actual programming that is soon to start. Although those in the software industry divide the various parts of the development process differently, here's how I'll refer to them in this book (noting what's been accomplished and what will be accomplished in later chapters):

Strategy

- Initial research (Chapter 1)

- Development of the assumptions about your app (Chapter 2)

- Customer outreach, validation, and initial wireframes (Chapter 3)

Design and development

  Design (this chapter):

  — Colors

  — Typography

  — Apple's Human Interface Guidelines (HIG)

  — User experience

  — App name, icon, and screens (including splash screen)

  Development (this chapter):

  — Technical architecture

  — Programming

  — Integration with external data sources

  — Optimization/performance tuning

Quality assurance

- Testing your app and interacting with beta testers (Chapter 6)

- Building an app onto a device using Xcode (Appendix)

Launch

- Submitting your app to the App Store (Chapter 7)

- Preparing for the availability of your app in the App Store (the "Launching Your App (Phase 5)" section in Chapter 8)

As a reminder, from Chapters 1 and 3, you know that marketing is an ongoing process you're following in conjunction with developing your app. I'll continue to point you to Chapter 8 to help you keep building your marketing crescendo.

Your App's Roadmap

To bring the initial version of your app into the App Store, and to keep making progress on it beyond that point, you need a plan. In the technology world, this plan is often referred to as a *roadmap*. There are many different philosophies and approaches to creating a roadmap; I'm going to distill what I consider the core of that for you by sharing how I develop an app roadmap.

Before I do that, though, I want you to understand that you should always consider your roadmap as only a guide. Building an app that is driven by customer feedback means your roadmap needs to be fluid and flexible, constantly influenced and adjusted by what you hear from customers. Readjusting your roadmap based on feedback matches the same paradigm you are using to initially build your app; you'll continue to start with your own assumptions (i.e., the features for a release from your roadmap) and then validate them against customer input and the data you have at your disposal.

Releases, Features, and Updates

The roadmap of your app consists of your app's releases. A *release* consists of a distinct set of features for your app, where a *feature* is a specific function your app performs. A release is also commonly referred to as a *version* of your app. Most often, the first release or version of your app that you submit to Apple will be "1.0." After the initial release of your app, Apple refers to the subsequent versions you submit as *updates*. Thus, in most cases, "release," "version," and "update" can be used interchangeably.

Verbiage aside, there are three key aspects of a roadmap:

1. Outlining the initial universe of features for your app

2. Breaking down these features into specific tasks

3. Appropriately prioritizing these features, and subsequently the tasks related to the features, into their respective releases

Compared to the third item, you'll find the first two are much more operational in nature.

Get features out of your head

Before you can strategically assess what features should be assigned to a specific release of your app, you need to outline all the features that have been rolling around in your head. You probably wrote some of them down somewhere, but they are still likely not fully defined. You can infer features from the competing factors from your strategy canvas, assumptions you've validated with customers, and any wireframes you created. So, your first job is to use those materials and whatever else you've been thinking about but never verbalized to create a list of what you consider to be the features of your app.

At this stage, you don't need to get fancy about where you capture your "features," but I recommend that you use some sort of digital means instead of pen and paper so that you can more easily manipulate and share them. I write "features" because it doesn't matter if it really is a feature, a task or item that is related to a feature, or just some idea you have about your app. What's most important at this point is to get these items listed quickly and without worrying about how to structure or categorize them.

Here is the initial list of features I created with my team for AudioBookShelf. Note that I'm a little more experienced in this process, so I grouped these features into categories as part of this process. Once you've listed what you consider your features, try to do the same.

Initial feature list for AudioBookShelf

Orientation

- Landscape only

Bookshelf

- Discovery through scrolling across bookshelf and seeing spines
- Books show age (e.g., antique versus glossy) and width based on book length
- Typography on books varies
- Explore different styles (e.g., leather-bound); color important

Book Info

- Cover/Title
- Description
- Author
- Narrator
- Length

Book Player

- Chapter browser
- Play/pause/stop
- Rewind/fast forward (5s; 15s; 30s; 1 min; 5 min; etc.)
- Volume control
- Chapter forward/back
- Bookmark
- Speed x2

Another way to think about features is to consider the screens you might have in your app and develop your list based on what each screen requires.

Defining v1.0

For many reasons, associating features with a release—and in particular, your first release—is not a trivial exercise. Beyond the more obvious question of how to determine which features will go in which release, it will be extremely tempting to always try to squeeze in one more feature. For now, you need some guidance on how to begin thinking about what features should be included in the first version of the app you submit to the App Store.

Prioritizing features

Although other factors can influence the set of features you include in the first version of your app, here are a number of common elements, starting with the most important:

Customer feedback

You have a great starting point for knowing what customers consider the key features of your app. From your customer interviews, you discovered what problems or situations your customers are most frustrated with, as well as what they are hoping you can solve for them in your app. With your initial wireframes and feature list, you can use any of the channels you have available (e.g., email) to further discuss what your customers consider to be important.

Remember that anytime you discuss features with customers, don't focus on the feature itself. Instead, talk about their problems, wants, and needs and relate that back to your solutions (features) and the benefits you plan to offer them through your app.

Why they'll buy

One way to further distinguish the most critical features of your app is to determine which ones would compel your customers to purchase your app. Beyond pushing these features to the top of your list, those who are pursuing In App Purchases will begin to identify what features should be paid upgrades.

Core functions

Some number of basic features will be required for your app to function. If they are not present, your app will be inoperable. For instance, if you are connecting to an external web service, this may include logging in to it from your app with a username and password. For AudioBookShelf, at a minimum the playback controls of play, pause, and stop were required for the audiobook to work.

Complexity

Features vary in how easy or difficult they are to implement. A feature's level of complexity will impact how long it takes you to build it. Whoever is designing and developing your app will need to determine the time required to build features. Don't assume that design-intensive features are necessarily development-intensive, or vice versa.

At this point, you and your team may not have a sense of the exact effort required to build a particular feature, and that's fine. It's more important to get a general sense by categorizing the difficulty of features relative to each other. A useful metaphor commonly used in the wider software development community is the "t-shirt sizing" method, whereby you might label a feature as S, M, L, or XL depending on how difficult it will be to build. It will be unlikely, for example, for you to deliver four XL features in one release, unless you have a large number of development resources available.

These initial complexity estimates will be refined as your features are broken down into actual design and development tasks.

Cost

You're not building your app independent of costs. You can have a *monetary cost* of a budget you or your company has specified for your app, a *scheduling cost* of needing to get your app into the App Store by a certain date, or a combination of both. Obviously, the complexity of the features will have a direct impact on cost; pursue the most customer-important, simplest, and least costly features first.

Design and development tasks

Based on the aforementioned factors, the feature list for the first version of your app should be taking shape. To further understand what features will make it into the 1.0 release of your app, you need to get a better handle on the level of effort required to build each feature you've identified. That will occur by you and your team breaking down the features into tasks.

By breaking down a feature into a short, descriptive task, you'll have a more comprehensive understanding of whether it can be built in a couple of hours or a couple of days. The t-shirt sizing you did will help you get started. An S feature, for example, may have only one task associated with it, whereas an L feature could have five or more. Defining these tasks and subsequently understanding how long a particular feature might take to build will require close collaboration with your team members.

Cutting features

The motivation for the more detailed level-of-effort estimates you'll receive from defining these tasks is that time will be an overarching factor for every release you submit. As described earlier, time itself is a constraint, but it also will equate to dollars spent and dollars lost. The longer you don't submit the first version of your app to Apple, the more time competitors have to launch a similar app or improve an existing one. You'll risk losing downloads or sales, and potentially compromising the purpose of why you started building this app. That doesn't mean you should rush your app to Apple, but if your estimates are showing that your first app will take three months to build, it's time to remove some features from the first version.

> It's not uncommon for proven, experienced developers, especially of games or larger apps, to take three months to build and launch an app. Even in their case, it's a risky proposition to take that long to get an app to the App Store.

Be aggressive with pushing features out of your initial release during your roadmap planning. It's better to cut them now than it is to start building them, only to realize that they will prevent you from getting into the App Store in a timely manner.

Although it's a broad and sweeping recommendation, I'm going to urge you to ensure that your initial release requires no more than eight weeks of design and development time. If you can reduce the amount of time you spend on the first version, you minimize the risk of your app sinking into an abyss of never launching. So, consider those eight weeks as not a goal, but rather the absolute maximum amount of time you should allocate for that first release. This should hold true even if you are submitting your first app to the App Store. In fact, I'd argue that it's OK to spend up to eight weeks on an initial release only if it's your first app. More experienced developers should strive for two to four weeks.

Creating your initial roadmap

Now that you've identified the features for your first release and the remaining unassigned features for your app, and you've allocated time to build the first version of your app, you can begin to construct your roadmap. My preference for maintaining an app's roadmap is to use a table format in a spreadsheet or wiki. Wherever you maintain your roadmap, realize that it is distinct from the tools you will use to manage the progress of the app, and that it is focused on vision and not execution.

If you choose to maintain your roadmap in a spreadsheet, note that typically the columns of the spreadsheet are dedicated to the versions of the app planned, with the first row being the version number, the second being the Apple submission date, and the third being the tentative release date (see Chapter 7 for details regarding what Apple calls the "Availability Date"). At this point, you only need two columns. The first column will be labeled "1.0" (or whatever you choose as the initial version number for your app), and will include all the features you've identified for this release. The second column will be labeled "Backlog" and will include a prioritized list of the remaining features you've outlined for your app (see Figure 5-1).

☆ **TweebRoadmap**

last edited by KY   0 mins ago

Version	1.0	1.1	Backlog
Submit	01/16	02/16	
	Previously scoped Current Issues	Error Checking	Custom date range Graphs for followers and clicks Search for terms Following that aren't following back (following screen) Additional URL shorteneres (supr;owly) Additional settings for twitter client selection Link all user handles to "profile" screen Webkit for viewing links

Figure 5-1. An early Tweeb roadmap, maintained in a wiki powered by the online collaboration tool PBworks (*http://pbworks.com/*)

Going forward, you will add new columns for new releases (updates), transferring backlog features into them or creating new ones based on customer feedback and other factors ("scoping" updates is covered in Chapter 9). You can visit *http://kenyarmosh.com/appsavvy* to get a sample roadmap spreadsheet.

Your App's Description

Having outlined the features of your app, you should take this opportunity to create a better description of your app. Not only will this enable you to more clearly discuss your app with customers, contacts, friends, and family, but also, and more importantly, this description will become part of your marketing assets and will be used in such places as your website and the App Store.

The first part of your description should be a short tagline that quickly communicates the essence of your app. It doesn't have to be a complete sentence, and instead can be more of a blurb. Here are a handful of examples for you:

Tweeb – Twitter stats in the palm of your hand

AudioBookShelf – Listen to History's Treasured Masterpieces on Your iPhone

Outside – Reinventing the Weather Forecast

Digital Post – Newspaper for iPad

Grades – Roadmap to an A

As part of this step, you may also want to begin exploring some app names. As you can see from the preceding app samples, as well as from other top apps in the App Store, simple and straightforward names are better. Even Robocat's creatively named weather app, Outside, still communicates what it is about. The other benefit for simpler names is that they will be more memorable and searchable—through search engines, beyond the App Store.

Additional factors to consider when thinking about your app's name include checking the availability of website domains (use *http://instantdomainsearch. com/* and *http://www.bustaname.com/* to speed that process) and Twitter handles. A popular way to overcome the availability limitations is to append the word "app" to the end of the desired name. For example, here are the domains and Twitter handles for the apps mentioned earlier: *http://www. tweebapp.com* and @tweebapp, *http://outsideapp.com/* and @outsideapp, and *http://gradesapp.com/* and @gradesapp. You don't necessarily need an app-specific Twitter handle if you've decided to use your personal Twitter account to engage customers.

After you have the tagline, you'll want to expand it to a three- or four-sentence description. Prospective customers will read this information immediately after looking at your app's name and tag line. This description should capture your app's key differentiators. Here are descriptions for Tweeb and Digital Post:

> *Tweeb*
>
> *Tweeb is a Twitter analytics and Twitter follower management app for the iPhone and iPod touch. It's the only app that provides a simple, digestible, and comprehensive view of how you're doing on Twitter.*
>
> *Digital Post*
>
> *A variety of top news sources have been pre-selected & filtered including AP, Reuters, AFP, Christian Science Monitor, McClatchy, Politico and more. No need to add or manage RSS feeds, Digital Post always stays up-to-date with the top news stories!*

The final part of your description should detail five to seven specific features about your app. You don't need to list every feature. Just highlight the ones your customers have told you are the most significant and compelling. Here's what I included for Tweeb:

> *Tweeb*
>
> *On-demand stats that always includes fresh, up-to-date data.*
>
> *Clean, crisp, and intuitive "Summary" dashboard with trends for tweets, followers, buzz, and clicks.*
>
> *Quickly view your recent tweets, manage those you follow ("friends"), and post from your favorite Twitter client in the "Me" tab.*
>
> *See if what you are tweeting is creating any "Buzz" by checking out those who are mentioning or retweeting you. Tweeb supports Twitter retweets and will also show you who is retweeting you.*
>
> *Better understand follower engagement by viewing click data for tweets that include bit.ly or j.mp links in the "Clicks" tab.*

Since your app doesn't exist yet, make your tag line, description, and features aspiring. Spending a small amount of time detailing these items now will help you to focus on what you want the core of your app to be as you move through the rest of the design and development process.

Design and Development

Although detailed discussions of an app's design and development are beyond the scope of this book, I want to outline some of the primary elements of each. What I cover in this section will be a good starting point for you, but you should strive to deeply understand all aspects of bringing an app to the App Store. So, although you will possibly be relying on others to design and develop your app, knowing what is being worked on and being able to provide intelligent feedback regarding work in progress will make you a more useful member of your team. Ultimately, that will help deliver a better app to the App Store.

As alluded to previously, the more detailed the product assets you create—research, wireframes, feature and task list, and roadmap—the fewer questions, and consequently, the less upfront work there will be for your designer and developer. This not only speeds the progress of your app, but also reduces your bottom-line costs.

Design

You'll work closely with your designer to expand your concept app. Through that collaboration, you'll determine your app's color scheme, fonts, logo, app icon, and of course, the screens themselves. Be inspired as you undertake your app's design. Review with your team apps that reflect what you consider great design; it's a major distinction for Apple and for customers. Through these sessions, take time to not only study the actual designs, but also how you interacted with the app. In the following paragraphs, Josh Clark, the author of *Tapworthy: Designing Great iPhone Apps* (*http://oreilly. com/catalog/0636920001133/*; O'Reilly), provides some key points regarding the importance of visual design. Note that his tips for iPhone apps are equally applicable to the iPad.

> *As an app designer, your interface choices affect not only what your customers can do with their devices but how they feel about them, too. A well-designed interface has the power to charm and beguile. Don't dismiss this as touchy-feely hokum: an emotional connection is the basis for*

all marketing and storytelling, and make no mistake—your app is in fact a story. In this very personal context, people think about an app as content more than "software," an experience more than a tool, and entertainment more than a task. Here are some pointers for balancing style, efficiency, and usability in an iPhone interface—the ingredients of personal connection.

Choose a personality. *Just like people, apps are irresistible when their personalities are in tune with both audience and context (Figure 5-2).*

An efficient, just-the-facts design lends an air of confidence to a productivity app. Warm wood textures, meanwhile, give other apps an organic feeling that is both homey and luxurious. Don't let your app's personality emerge by accident. Before you start tinkering with color schemes, graphics, and navigation models, consider how you'd like people to perceive your app. Businesslike and authoritative? Comforting and familiar? Sleek and poised? Homespun and crafty? Fun and toy-like? Opulent and plush? By choosing a personality for your app before you start crafting its visual identity, you give yourself a framework for making consistent decisions based on the emotional vibe you're after.

Figure 5-2. Voices, which has a vaudeville personality appropriate to a funny-voices novelty app

Favor standard controls. *Because they're commonplace, the iOS's standard controls are sometimes dismissed as visually dull. Not so fast: commonplace means familiarity and ease for your audience. Conventions are critical to instant and effortless communication. That's why road signs around the world are standardized. Drivers hurtling down the freeway shouldn't have to do double takes to figure out what a sign means. When instant and effortless communication is critical, conventions are a designer's best friend. Buttons, icons, and toolbars are the road signs for your app, and iPhone screens that use standard controls have a no-nonsense seriousness that lends them a similar authority and don't-make-me-think understanding. Before creating a brand new interface metaphor or inventing your own custom controls, ask whether it might be done better with the built-in gadgetry.*

Add a fresh coat of paint. *Standard controls don't have to be dreary. Use custom colors and graphics to give them a fresh identity (Figure 5-3). This technique requires a light touch, however; don't distract from the content itself or drain the meaning from otherwise familiar controls.*

You stay classy. *Luxurious textures applied with taste (Figure 5-4) increase your app's perceived value. The same sumptuous materials of beloved personal totems—a leather-bound notebook, a glossy gadget, a retro timepiece—can likewise be put to good use in your interface to conjure the same attachment.*

Figure 5-3 (Left). Wine Steward, which adds a parchment graphic to the background of each table cell, making the entries appear to be written on an aged wine label

Figure 5-4 (Right). Organic textures, which add a sense of luxury to the Cross Fingers

Borrow interface metaphors from the physical world. *Lean on users' real-world experience to create intuitive experiences. People will try anything on a touchscreen, for example, that they'd logically try on a physical object or with a mouse-driven cursor. The card decks, spinning dials, push buttons, sliders, and light switches of the iPhone's standard toolkit require no learning; we already know how to use them thanks to our experience with their real-world counterparts. These physical look-alikes are most effortless when the interface is the same size as the gadget that inspired it. When iPhone apps mimic a real-world handheld device (Figure 5-5), for example, the iPhone actually seems to become that device, and you inherit the time-tested ergonomics of the original, too.*

Figure 5-5. Guitar Toolkit, which creates an intuitive interface by mimicking a guitar tuner

Don't be afraid to take risks. *Make sure your interfaces are intuitive, sure, but don't be afraid to try something completely new and different. Designers and developers are hatching fresh iPhone magic every day, and there's still much to explore and invent. While you should look hard at whether you might accomplish what you need to do with standard controls, it's also worth asking, am I going far enough? Allow yourself to explore the possibilities, and don't be afraid to experiment with offbeat concepts.*

The app icon is your business card. *The icon carries disproportionate weight in the marketing of your app, and it's important to give it disproportionate design attention, too. Think of the icon as a packaging label (Figure 5-6)—it's great if it's pretty, but it's even more important that it be descriptive and identifiable at a glance, for both branding and usability. Avoid cryptic or inscrutable imagery, and don't be overly clever with the visual metaphors. More commerce, less art. Make your app icon a literal description of your app's function, interface, name, or brand.*

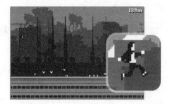

Figure 5-6. App icons for Canabalt, which borrow the colors, styles, and textures directly from the app interface to create recognition and fidelity

---

Two good resources on the process of designing an app's icon include Michael Flarup's "iPhone App Icon Design: Best Practises" (*http://pixelresort.com/blog/iphone-app-icon-design-best-practises/*) and Sebastiaan de With's "Here, Icon Icon!" (*http://blog.cocoia.com/2010/here-file-file/*). Point your designer to these links.

User experience design

Of course, there's more to designing an app than aesthetics alone. Beyond colors and typography, which are extremely important, the design process for the iPhone and iPad is especially unique because the interaction with these devices is centered on touch (i.e., Apple's Multi-Touch).

To give a little more context to the importance of the touch metaphor (besides what we covered in Chapter 2), an entire subspecialty of the larger design field is dedicated to user experience and interaction design. Those involved in this arena focus on designing products to be usable and easy to understand, instead of creating the visual aspects of them. Many designers take on both roles, with some doing so more successfully than others.

The importance of user experience, in particular, has grown tremendously in the digital age. And that attention increased back when the primary mode of interaction was through the mouse and keyboard on much larger screens. This should underscore how significant the user experience will be with your apps, where the screens are considerably smaller yet controlled with touch gestures.

Human Interface Guidelines

Apple heavily touts the Multi-Touch elements of its devices and the new standard it set with the iOS platform. The company has worked diligently to preserve the elegant experience it has enabled on its devices, both within its own apps and with those developing for the Apple platform. To do that, Apple has created a set of standardized design frameworks and extensive *Human Interface Guidelines* (HIG) for each of its devices.

If you've completely ignored all of Apple's documentation to this point, do yourself a favor and read the HIG for both the iPhone and the iPad (part of the iOS Reference Library). In doing so, you'll learn how Apple approached porting apps such as Mail and iPhoto to the iPhone, and subsequently, how it did the same from the iPhone to the iPad. You'll also become familiar with all the iPhone and iPad views and controls that Apple provides in its design frameworks and you'll learn how to properly implement each of them. In Figure 5-7, Macro Arment's popular Instapaper shows the split view in use for the iPad version of his app.

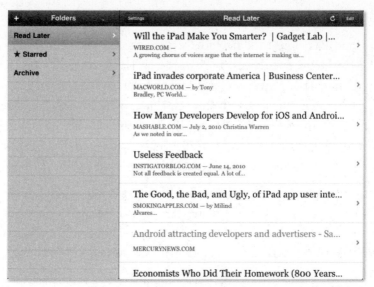

Figure 5-7. The "split view" in use for the iPad version of Instapaper

With the knowledge you will gain from the HIG, even if you are not a design expert, you'll help shape your app's user experience by ensuring that these elements are properly implemented. This particular point is critical, for two reasons:

- Apple is fairly stringent about its HIG, and failing to observe them, at least in the past, was one of the most common reasons for app rejection during the approval process.

- Apple favors applications that embrace the same simplicity of its applications; this partially follows from adhering to the HIG.

Through the HIG, I'm hoping you are now completely aware that your application will need great visual *and* user experience design to be considered a well-designed app.

iPhone versus iPad

As mentioned before, the differences between the iPhone and the iPad start with how you use the devices. The iPad display is more than 2.5 times larger than the iPhone display, so unlike the iPhone, the iPad is not extremely functional when you use it with only one hand; you need to use both hands or rest it on a surface. And where the iPhone and iPod touch are predisposed to being portrait-oriented, the iPad appears more natural and useful when in landscape mode.

For the iPad, however, there is a much higher expectation—almost a demand—that applications work in both modes. The change in orientation typically only alters the view and controls that are displayed. For example, when in portrait mode, the list of folders for Instapaper is moved from the master pane of the split view (shown in Figure 5-7) to a *popover* view (see Figure 5-8).

Figure 5-8. The list of folders for Instapaper in a popover view

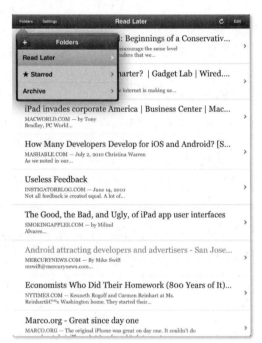

The proverbial elephant in the room, however, is the difference in display size between the two devices. Although a big design challenge with the iPhone is its limited screen real estate, the iPad has the exact opposite challenge, with considerably more screen to fill. To accommodate these differences, even though the iPhone and iPad share some common views and controls, Apple did release a number of iPad-specific ones with the launch of iOS 3.2. You probably already saw many of the iPhone or iPad views and controls in either your wireframing tool or Apple's HIG. You can also leverage Teehan+Lax's iPhone and iPad GUI Photoshop design templates to understand the different elements available:

- iPhone, *http://www.teehanlax.com/blog/2010/06/14/iphone-gui-psd-v4/*

- iPad, *http://www.teehanlax.com/blog/2010/02/01/ipad-gui-psd/*

The views and controls for each device facilitate the different use cases for the iPhone and iPad. As you might recall from the multitasking discussion in Chapter 2, the iPhone's focus is on discrete and short-lived, often time-filling tasks, flowing from its portability. Clearly the iPad is also portable, but unlike the iPhone, it is not pocket-sized. The resultant experience is that it is used more like a laptop than the iPhone is. Arguably, the iPad is a more portable laptop, and that's how many people treat it. The iPad's dimensions make it comfortable to use for much longer periods of time, especially for reading, browsing the Web, and managing email. Even though the iPhone 3GS and iPhone 4 can also be paired with a Bluetooth keyboard in iOS 4, the iPad is the obvious winner for this feature, with its considerably larger display.

You can see these differences most evidently in the popular apps on each device. The killer iPhone apps included to-do managers such as Things, flick games such as Flight Control, and streamlined mobile views for websites such as Mint.com. Comparatively, the earliest successes for the iPad included the document reader GoodReader, numerous newspaper and magazine apps, full-sized board games such as SCRABBLE for iPad, and Apple's own iPad-optimized iWork suite (Pages, Keynote, and Numbers).

Beyond the HIG distinctions, however, these iPad apps reveal considerably more custom visual design. With the iPhone's smaller real estate, many developers got away with using the native design elements provided by Apple for their iPhone apps. Not customizing the design becomes much more obvious on the iPad, however, and the best iPad apps take advantage of every pixel available, reinterpreting and reinvesting in their interfaces on this device. For example, compare Amazon.com's iPhone and iPad apps, in Figures 5-9 and 5-10, respectively, and notice the more custom design of the latter.

It's going to take some more time to truly understand how people experience and interact with the iPad. For some initial usability results, read Jakob Nielsen's first findings at *http://www.useit.com/alertbox/ipad.html*.

Translating wireframes to screens

The big task in the design phase will be to translate any wireframe assets you initially created into a refined, usable, and visually pleasing design. I recommend that your designer begin this part of the process once a first pass at the branding elements (colors, fonts, and logo) is completed, as you will need to use these branding assets in other places, such as your website, even before the app is released.

Of course, at this stage you likely haven't developed wireframes for your *entire* application. As you gain experience in wireframe development, I recommend that you have done so once you reach this stage in future projects. Assuming you haven't, though, have your designer start with what you *did* develop and work on that screen (or those screens) until you jointly agree that they properly reflect the look-and-feel (visual design) and layout (user experience design) that you want for your app. In other words, finish one or two screens and use them to help set the tone for the remaining screens. The features you outlined for the first release should inform how you identify the remaining screens and flow for your application.

It's time for your next marketing checkup. Once you have your branding assets ready, begin reading the "Phase 2" section of Chapter 8.

Devices and resolutions

With the introduction of the iPad, and subsequently the iPhone 4, designing for iOS apps has become increasingly more intensive. The reason relates to the differences in the sizes of these devices and their resolutions (see Table 2-1 in Chapter 2).

Depending on the devices you target, multiple versions of the same screen and icon will need to be created. In fact, if your app is to be released across all devices, it will require up to nine versions of its icon because of the screen sizes and resolutions of the iPhone (original, 3G, and 3GS), iPhone 4, and iPad (see Figure 5-11). You can point your designer to the following links, which provide more detail about this subject:

- *http://developer.apple.com/iphone/library/documentation/ UserExperience/Conceptual/MobileHIG/IconsImages/IconsImages.html*

- *http://mrgan.tumblr.com/post/708404794/ios-app-icon-sizes*

As described in the "iPhone versus iPad" section, some of these screens will not require a simple resizing, but rather will entail a fresh approach that caters to the device. The same is true for the icons. In particular, the iPhone 4's Retina display provides for the highest-quality design, with 326 pixels per inch (versus 163 for its predecessor or 132 for the iPad). This means icons can contain more detail and richer textures. It is very likely that the next-generation iPad will also have Retina display, which will require another variation of design assets.

Figure 5-11. Neven Mrgan's most common icons required across all iOS devices

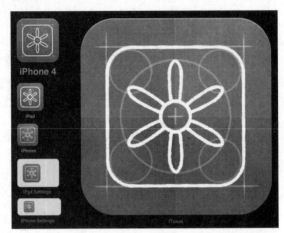

Finishing touches

Focusing on the user experience of your app will go a long way toward removing some of the confusion or questions your customers may have, but it won't eliminate all of them. That's why, as you finish your app's design, you should consider adding fun and interactive ways to guide and educate your customers about your app.

The best approach is to incorporate this guidance into the natural use of the app. There's usually a correlation between apps that include this type of detail and their level of success. One stellar example is the iPad app Penultimate, which is a notebook that allows a person to sketch and write notes. The first notebook included in Penultimate is a dedicated user guide detailing the various functions of the app. Figure 5-12 shows how Penultimate explains its eraser function.

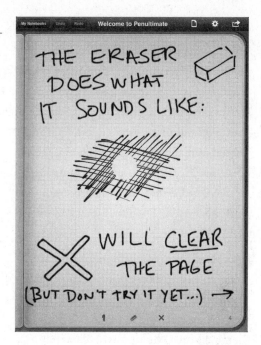

Figure 5-12. Penultimate's explanation of the eraser function in the first notebook

Other great examples include the initial introduction to Tapbots' Pastebot (see Figure 5-13) and the opening hint from Sophia Teutschler's Articles (see Figure 5-14).

Figure 5-13 (Left). Tapbots' Pastebot initial introduction

Figure 5-14 (Right). Articles' opening hint

Depending on your app, you may not have the opportunity to create such an engaging experience. In Tweeb, for example, I opted for a more content-focused implementation. Tweeb performed some fairly complex calculations, and so even though it received rave reviews about its design, some customers had questions about how their stats were calculated. Nearly all customer questions were addressed by directing them to the information button available for each screen—identified by the "i" shown in Figure 5-15—which, when tapped, displayed customized help text on the screen (see Figure 5-16).

Figure 5-15. The Tweeb information button—the "i" shown here—which, when tapped, reveals help text that is specific for each screen

As you explore more and more apps, take screenshots; press the Home + Power buttons at the same time and a screenshot will be saved to the device's Camera Roll. Over time, you'll have a nice collection of best practices, tips, and unique design elements that you'll be able to adopt and make your own. For additional inspiration, visit galleries such as *http://ipadappsthatdontsuck.com*, *http://www.tappgala.com/*, *http://wellplacedpixels.com/*, and *http://tapfancy.com/*. Regularly discuss with your team, and especially with your designer, apps that inspire you.

Figure 5-16. Directing users to the information button via the Tweeb Twitter account

Development

Getting into the details of programming may send chills through your body. Most people feel less comfortable with development than with design because development is typically a less familiar area and does not provide the same type of visual inspection that design does.

There are ways to check on the progress of development, though, and validate that it is on track and moving forward. Before I help you understand how to do that, I want to give you a brief overview of what will be happening in the development process.

Technical architecture

Your developer should spend some time thinking about how the various pieces of your application interact. In larger technical efforts, before a single line of code can be written, an architecture of the system is usually created. Some may consider this overkill for an iPhone or iPad app, but I recommend that you have your developer provide either a concise written description of your app's architecture or a visualization of it.

From personal experience, I can tell you that even developers who have taken the time to create a sketch of an app's technical architecture often run into situations they didn't expect. Taking the time to think through these aspects with your developer before any code is written greatly reduces the risk of the developer not accounting for a major piece of functionality or a scenario that can cause you to miss your initial release deadline.

Programming and integration

The majority of your developer's time will be spent programming the inner workings of your app. As with the design process, I recommend having your developer try to focus on one screen or feature at a time. This will allow you to fully test and experience a completely finished part of your application versus having random, unconnected pieces available.

Push your developer to identify and start on the hardest elements of the application first. This might mean no functionality is available for a longer period of time at the start of the development process. But this approach will avoid a situation in which you think you are coming to the end of the development phase, only to discover there's a serious problem with a complex and integral part of the app.

If your app integrates with external data sources through APIs or web services, the parts that handle this integration will likely be the most complex.

This could include connecting to social networking sites such as Facebook or downloading data from a server. These situations will require your application to check network connectivity and potentially cache or store data onto the device. The challenge with integrations is that your app will be dependent on something external to it and outside your control. Your developer will need plenty of error checking to make integrations work; your job will be to try to break them once they're available for testing.

Installing your app onto your device is covered in Chapter 6. You should, however, start installing and testing the app on your device(s) as soon as a feature or screen is ready.

Repositories and source code

In Chapter 4, I mentioned ensuring that you have access to your app's in-progress design and development assets. In that context, ensuring access was as a matter of safety and to protect you from relationships gone bad. Hopefully, however, you'll primarily use this access to successfully collaborate with your team members.

Although it is mostly a tool that your developer and designer will use, to facilitate this collaboration you'll want to use a hosted *repository* to house your app's assets. The repository should include the designer's creative designs or artwork, the developer's code, and possibly any strategic materials. The repository not only allows all team members to access these assets, but will also provide *version control*, ensuring that everyone is using the most current version of the assets and that they are able to recover and compare older versions of the assets. In reality, your developer is the only person who probably needs access to *all* of the assets.

Today, the most commonly used repositories are based on Subversion or Git. Developers will usually dictate what they prefer, so don't be concerned about which to choose. Some project management tools covered in the next section, such as Unfuddle, can act as both your hosted source control repository and your issue tracker, making them more appealing options. Here are a handful of repository options for you and your team to consider:

- Beanstalk (Subversion), *http://beanstalkapp.com/*

- GitHub (Git), *http://github.com/*

- Unfuddle (Subversion; Git), *http://www.unfuddle.com*

- Kiln (Mercurial), *http://www.fogcreek.com/Kiln/*

These repositories are also useful if you plan to open-source all or part of your app (e.g., *http://github.com/brow/leaves*) and make it publicly available. Although uncommon, it is worth noting that you will probably not want to open-source anything until you've submitted and released the app.

To make it easier to get the source code from your repository (e.g., Unfuddle or GitHub), I recommend using version control client software rather than just using a web or command-line interface. The software you use is dependent on the type of repository for your app (noted earlier). The following list includes options for each:

- Versions (Subversion), *http://versionsapp.com/*

- Cornerstone (Subversion), *http://www.zennaware.com/*

- Gitti (Git), *http://www.gittiapp.com/*

- Gity (Git), *http://macendeavor.com/gity*

- GitX (Git), *http://gitx.frim.nl/*

It's always good to try a couple of options until you feel comfortable. Once you've settled on one, ask your developer to help you connect to your repository. There will be a one-time setup, and after that you should only be refreshing ("update" in SVN or "pull" in Git) your source. The software you downloaded will make these updates easy going forward because there are buttons that initiate this process (see Figure 5-17). Unless you are also the designer and/or the developer, it's highly unlikely that you'll ever need to send anything back to your repository, so you'll mostly be bringing the updated assets down from the repository.

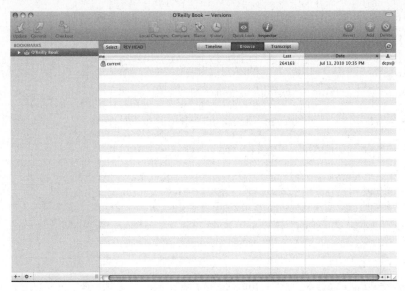

Figure 5-17. The Mac application Versions, which provides an Update button to retrieve the latest source code

At this point, the main benefits of having access to the repository will be to have physical possession of your app's assets, as well as to see how often your app is being updated (technically, how often *commits* with new or updated code are sent to the repository). There are other benefits, such as being able to build your app onto your device. This is a more technical process that is mentioned in Chapter 6 and detailed in the Appendix for those who are interested.

Tuning and optimization

Much further into the process, the development focus should shift from building new functionality to tuning and optimizing what exists. From a customer perspective, this means making the app snappier, smoother, and issue-free. More technically, your developer will be working on ensuring that your application is not leaking memory, overutilizing the device's CPU, or being submitted with poorly written code.

Managing Your App's Progress

Conceptually, you now understand the types of steps involved in building your app. It's time to get more tactical again, though, so that you can help guide your app into the hands of your testers and eventually into the App Store.

Staying Organized

Managing your app's progress requires good organization and collaborative, real-time access to the status of features and their tasks. As customers enter the picture more fully—while testing the app, and later, when it's live in the App Store—you'll also need a way to track their input.

You can try to develop your own solutions, but it's best to turn to any number of third-party tools built specifically to help you collaboratively manage your development progress or customer feedback. The tools available are plentiful and competitively priced. Before investing too heavily in any of them, ensure that they'll meet your needs.

Tasks and tickets

The tasks, from the breakdown of your features, are the smallest building blocks of your app. You'll input these tasks (also referred to as "issues" or "tickets") into an *issue tracking* tool, which will allow you to assign when they are due, their priority (e.g., highest, high, normal, or low), their owner, which release they are part of (in this case, probably the 1.0 release), their current status, and other information, depending on the tool you select. As you, your team members, and your customers uncover problems with your app, you will also log and track these problems (bugs) in this tool.

"Status" is an important field in any ticket, because it should inform you whether the ticket is not started, is in progress, or is completed. You and your team members should be very diligent about updating tickets with notes and editing fields such as "Status" or "Ownership" regularly. If tickets are kept up-to-date, you will know if you are staying on schedule in meeting your app's submission date or if you have fallen behind. Because the highest-priority tickets will be worked on and completed first, you will start moving the lower-priority ones to the next release or the backlog.

Here are some issue tracking options to consider:

- Unfuddle (see Figure 5-18), *http://www.unfuddle.com*

- Lighthouse, *http://lighthouseapp.com/* (integrates with Beanstalk and GitHub)

- FogBugz, *http://www.fogcreek.com/FogBugz/* (integrates with Kiln)

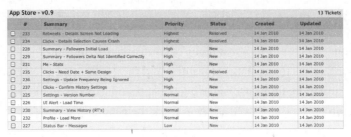

App Store - v0.9					13 Tickets
#	Summary	Priority	Status	Created	Updated
233	Retweets - Details Screen Not Loading	Highest	Resolved	14 Jan 2010	14 Jan 2010
234	Clicks - Details Selection Causes Crash	Highest	Resolved	14 Jan 2010	14 Jan 2010
228	Summary - Followers Initial Load	High	New	14 Jan 2010	14 Jan 2010
229	Summary - Followers Delta Not Identified Correctly	High	New	14 Jan 2010	14 Jan 2010
231	Me - Stats	High	New	14 Jan 2010	14 Jan 2010
235	Clicks - Need Date + Same Design	High	Resolved	14 Jan 2010	14 Jan 2010
236	Settings - Update Frequency Being Ignored	High	New	14 Jan 2010	14 Jan 2010
237	Clicks - Confirm History Settings	High	New	14 Jan 2010	14 Jan 2010
225	Settings - Version Number	Normal	New	14 Jan 2010	14 Jan 2010
226	UI Alert - Load Time	Normal	New	14 Jan 2010	14 Jan 2010
230	Summary - View History (RT's)	Normal	New	14 Jan 2010	14 Jan 2010
232	Profile - Load More	Normal	New	14 Jan 2010	14 Jan 2010
227	Status Bar - Messages	Low	New	14 Jan 2010	14 Jan 2010

Figure 5-18. Unfuddle tickets for Tweeb v0.9

Release Numbering

I decided to launch Tweeb into the App Store as version 0.9 to indicate that all the features for the official 1.0 release were not yet complete. I submitted version 0.9.1, which was a bug fix release, shortly after the initial version was approved.

Most developers in the App Store use this three-decimal software versioning convention, represented as "major version.minor version.bug fix." The general philosophy of this convention is as follows:

Major version

> Several major features added, new design, or significant functional changes; does not happen very often; example: 1.7.6 to 2.0

Minor version

> New feature added, some smaller design tweaks, and a number of bug fixes; happens regularly, but not every release; example: 4.0.5 to 4.1

Bug fix

> Focused on addressing critical bugs or high customer pain points that don't typically require new functionality; most frequent kind of release; example: 2.3.7 to 2.3.8

Customer feedback and support

If your app becomes very popular or even shows any signs of life, you'll begin to get overwhelmed with customer inquiries and feedback through a variety of channels (e.g., Twitter and email). As with your tickets, you'll need to stay organized, and the first step in doing that is to try to funnel as much of this information to one place as possible. Thus, your customer support tool will be comparable to your issue tracker, but externally (i.e., customer) focused.

Customer support tools present a couple of challenges, but don't let this devalue their importance. The first challenge is that you won't be able to capture a significant customer support channel—Twitter—through any automated fashion. The second challenge, which relates back to the first, is that customer support inquiries will often require that you create a ticket in your issue tracker. For example, if you receive a customer question—through Twitter, email, or your customer support tool—about a function of your app that you previously had not verified as broken, you'll need to create a ticket in your issue tracker for this bug. When the bug is fixed you'll need to update that ticket's status and let the customer know the issue has been resolved. The interconnectedness of these actions is why some customer support tools integrate with issue trackers.

Unfortunately, there's no perfect solution to this, and you'll have to evaluate, publicize, and then be firm about how customers should contact you regarding support or feature requests. You may, for example, indicate that you don't offer support through Twitter, or opt to use a shared support email inbox (e.g., *support@tweebapp.com*) instead of a third-party support tool.

Here are some customer support tools worth considering:

- Zendesk, *http://www.zendesk.com/*

- Tender, *http://tenderapp.com/* (integrates with Lighthouse)

- Get Satisfaction, *http://getsatisfaction.com/*

- CoTweet, *http://cotweet.com/*

Screens and Prototypes

Be demanding yet reasonable throughout the design and development process. Your team should be iterating quickly, delivering new or updated assets every day. On the design side, these assets should be screens or artwork for the app. On the development side, this should be a working prototype of the latest app that incorporates the existing design assets. Speed and consistency are more important than polish and the risk of missing deadlines during the earliest stages of this process.

The value of a fully functioning prototype of your app—installed on an actual device—should not be underestimated. Your developer will demo your app in a tool called the iPhone Simulator. This tool only mimics an actual device and will not uncover certain bugs or include full support for capabilities such as Multi-Touch (although it can do so using a third-party tool called iSimulate; see *http://www.vimov.com/isimulate/*).

In general, the earlier your app gets on a device, the better. So, even early in this process, you should push your developer to always test the app by building it onto the device. Developers often won't want to test the app this way because it takes slightly longer to load it onto the device compared to the iPhone Simulator. At the very least, however, it must be tested on the device itself before it is sent to you.

Your next marketing checkup should occur when the design of a screen from your app is near completion. This screen will be used on its own, so it does not need to be integrated into your app yet. When that is the case, go to the "Phase 3" section in Chapter 8. Figure 5-19 represents the evolution of the wireframe I showed you back in Chapter 3.

Figure 5-19. The evolution of Tweeb, from wireframe to design

Interviews

Tapbots: Paul Haddad and Mark Jardine

COMPANY: Tapbots

POSITIONS: Founders; programmer (Paul) and designer (Mark)

BACKGROUND: Tapbots are "utility robot" apps designed and engineered for the iPod touch, iPhone, and iPad. These applications are easy to use, focused, and fun.

LINK: *http://www.tapbots.com*

Ken: *Assume you have an app you feel good about pursuing. How do you map out building it? Do you break the app down into screens, features, or stories? Do you create a development schedule?*

Mark: The first thing we do is figure out what the core purpose of the app is. It's usually described in one or two sentences. Then we write down all the features and tasks that are needed to fulfill that core purpose. The most important features usually [become] version 1.0.

We try to keep an app from doing too much. Pastebot is almost an exception, but we did our best to stay on focus. We felt strongly that it was intended to be a clipboard manager, and its features should be focused around that task. It can be tough to say no to potentially good ideas, but in the end, we need our apps to stay focused.

Once the core features have been established, I start sketching wireframes and Paul usually begins the low-level groundwork for the app. We usually have about 90% of the artwork done before Paul starts coding anything on the interface level. The missing 10% usually consists of minor things like settings, dialog boxes, and other things not essential to the core functionality of the app. Once the app is in somewhat of a working condition, we iterate on what's not working, which includes design, functionality, and the user interaction experience.

We don't make a development schedule until we see the end of the road. Being a small team has its advantages. We don't have the pressure to meet deadlines. We work until we feel the app is good and not to a time limit. Once we are at the end of the road, we do need to plan for testing, localization, and marketing, so that's when we start making schedules.

Ken: *Whether it's the iPhone or some other platform, something typically goes wrong or not according to plan when developing software. What sort of time do you allocate (if any) to potential problems and bug fixing?*

Mark: For the most part, [we allocate] whatever time is needed to fix the issue. And that means solving the issue or finding a suitable workaround. It really depends on the size of the issue. Some bugs can wait, while others demand immediate and full attention.

Ken: *Related to these issues, do you do any rapid prototyping to identify potential roadblocks in the development of an app, or do you move immediately into full development once you have your plan in place?*

Paul: [We do] very little [rapid prototyping]. I might check if something is possible given the current hardware limitations (speed/memory), but for the most part, it's full speed ahead with development. Our apps tend to be simple enough from a concept standpoint that it doesn't make sense to spend a ton of time prototyping things. For the most part, the majority of the time I spend is in getting the UI to look and work just right.

Ken: *How do you—and how can developers—reduce development time without cheating in the process? What aspects of creating an app can be done in parallel? What can't? Are there ways to get apps done faster besides having more resources available?*

Paul: I'm a big fan of creating reusable classes/components. It won't save you much/any time on your first iPhone application, but if done correctly, it'll save time in future applications. Every app we create adds more classes to our library, which means we don't have to duplicate efforts and we can also get a consistent look-and-feel to our apps. Another great benefit with using reusable classes is that often features for new apps can be quickly added to existing apps, which makes for happy users.

Ken: *Tapbots is known for its incredibly polished interfaces. What do you do to ensure that they are not only polished, but also functional and easy to use?*

Mark: We use them. And [we] have other people use them. We tend to take design risks with our apps, and they don't always work out. What looks good onscreen doesn't always translate well when the user is interacting with it on the iPhone. We aren't afraid to design/code something and then start over if it doesn't feel right. The biggest part about our apps is the over-all feel of them when using them. We put a lot of effort into making sure that WOW factor is there. If we, the developers, are excited with how it works, then we can be pretty sure that customers who haven't spent hours upon hours with the app will enjoy it.

Ken: *Discuss what you consider the key differences of designing for the iPhone versus the iPad.*

Mark: I can't speak too much about the differences, as I have yet to design for the iPad. My instinct, though, is that it's not a matter of just making everything bigger. The limitations and constraints of the iPhone made things simple. Now, there's a lot more pixels to worry about. Then there's the device orientation. Despite these concerns, I think it's safe to say we are going to love designing and developing for it.

Ken: *Overall, what is the key part of the development of your shiny apps?*

Mark: Having clear goals for the app from the beginning and sticking to them. For us, our goal for all of our apps [is that they] are fun, focused, and easy to use. We really try to build around [that] goal.

Agile Web Solutions: Roustem Karimov

COMPANY: Agile Web Solutions

POSITION: CEO and co-founder

BACKGROUND: Started in 2006 by Dave Teare and Roustem Karimov, Agile Web Solutions is the company behind 1Password, the most popular password manager for Mac OS X, iPhone, and iPad, with more than 1 million users worldwide.

LINK: *http://agile.ws/onepassword*

Ken: *Since you had an existing product, how did you initially map out 1Password for the iPhone? Did you break the app down into screens, features, or stories? Did you create a development schedule?*

Roustem: The development of the iPhone and iPad applications was driven by screens. Dan Peterson, our lead designer, mocked up most of the application screens in Photoshop before any coding started.

For the iPad version, once Dan completed the initial mockups, the whole team reviewed them and tried to imagine using the application on a real iPad. Things like being able to switch sections without moving your hand, left- versus righthand usage, and what portion of the screen is covered when interacting with it were considered. Basically, the screens were used as "target practice" and to help brainstorm additional ideas.

After the mockups were redesigned to incorporate the team's feedback, the development team started implementing the design. It was an iterative process, and the layout and contents of each screen were revised as we worked through the implementation.

As for the schedule, we didn't really have a formal schedule, but the goal was to be in the App Store by the launch of the iPad App Store. This forced us to limit the scope of the first version, and we removed features such as syncing with MobileMe and attachments.

Ken: *What makes developing for the iPhone and iPad unique? Please also discuss what you consider to be the key differences between designing for the iPhone versus the iPad.*

Roustem: There are a lot of similarities in designing [for the] iPhone and iPad. The main difference is that the amount of real estate on the iPad requires a lot more effort during design. This is magnified by the fact that Apple encourages a custom user interface specific to the iPad.

Developing for the iPhone and iPad is a dream in many ways. There are amazing development tools, polished frameworks, and APIs. Also, the App Store helps developers to not worry about running their own online store.

It comes with its own challenges as well. For example, developing on one platform and testing on another can be tricky, because the iPhone Simulator is not 100% identical to the real device.

The biggest difference is that iterative development is much harder on the iPhone platform. This is because it could take several days for the application to be reviewed by Apple and accepted into the store. Apple also makes a large beta program impossible. On the Mac, we currently have thousands of beta testers, whereas on the iPhone, we cannot have more than about 50. As a result, we submit new versions much less frequently.

Ken: *Whether it's the iPhone or some other platform, something typically goes wrong or not according to plan when developing software. What sort of time do you allocate (if any) to potential problems and bug fixing?*

Roustem: At first glance, building "slack time" into the schedule to plan for the unknown seems like a good idea. The problem is Parkinson's Law: work expands so as to fill the time available for its completion. If the schedule was expanded by 20% in an attempt to plan for the unknown, the feature set would increase by 20% as well.

Not only that, but Apple is constantly creating new "magical and revolutionary" devices and adding new features. It is hard to plan far into the future when new "game changers" appear so frequently.

Instead of spending time on detailed schedules, we prefer taking a more agile approach and do not plan far into the future. There is always something important waiting for the next version of 1Password, and the priorities of these features are constantly changing. If something important pops up, like a new platform or a critical problem, then we simply drop everything else until it is finished.

Ken: *How did you decide what features went into 1Password and 1Password Pro? Specifically, how did you determine what paid features would compel customers to choose 1Password Pro?*

Roustem: I am not sure we did it right in the beginning. Some of the premium features, like folders or additional syncing options, weren't ready when the Pro edition was launched, and we decided to start with a lower introductory price. Today, this could be done much easier with the In App Purchase option.

Ken: *Do you have any guidance for developers on thinking about how to break up major (e.g., v3.0) and minor (e.g., v2.1.1) updates? Do you work on major and minor updates in parallel? When is an update complete and ready to be shipped?*

Roustem: It is a fairly straightforward process on the Mac where we make all major upgrades paid, include new features into the point (3.1, 3.2) updates, and mostly provide bug fixes in the point-point (3.1.1, 3.1.2) updates. There is no paid upgrade option for iPhone or iPad apps, and we simply try to keep the major version in sync with the desktop application and use point and point-point updates in a similar fashion.

Ken: *You launched the iPad version of 1Password Pro as a Universal app. What went into that thought process?*

Roustem: This was an easy decision. It helped to differentiate between the regular and Pro editions and also created a certain symmetry where the Pro edition combines all features of 1Password for iPhone and 1Password for iPad.

Recap

Here's what you learned in this chapter:

- Although you didn't realize it, you already started the development process through the work you've done up to this chapter. That work gave you the foundation to start actually building your app the right way.

- Outlining the features of your app will help you develop your app's roadmap. Your roadmap will be your guide to bringing the first version of your app to the App Store and will serve as a starting point for what features may go in future releases.

- Developing your app's description now will help you better communicate what your app is about in your customer interactions. This description will also inform your website content, and eventually, your App Store description.

- Understanding some of the aspects of the design and development process, at least at a high level, will make you a more useful team member. You will need to continue to expand your knowledge of iPhone app design and development to truly be able to guide an app successfully into the App Store.

- Leveraging third-party web-based tools to manage the features, tasks, and feedback of your app will keep you organized. You and your team will use these tools to better collaborate with one another and have a real-time view into the progress of your app.

6

Making Your App Better Before It Reaches the App Store

TO FURTHER VERIFY that your app resonates with your customers and to reduce software issues in your app, you are going to want to install it onto your device and your customers' devices before Apple even sees it.

In this chapter, you'll explore:

- Installing the app on your device

- Understanding "beta" and working with your beta testers

- Performing quality assurance by collecting feedback

- Working with your developer to resolve bugs

Installing Your App

Testing your app before it reaches the App Store will likely be one of the most difficult and frustrating tasks you'll encounter. It will also be one of the most important things you'll do.

The difficulty of this process is that Apple wants your app in its store and not "in the wild." So, although Apple provides a means for distributing your app directly to customers, it's tedious and limiting. The tedious part is that you need to grab some unique information from each customer's device, called a *UDID* (unique device identifier); the limiting part is that Apple only provides 100 testing slots per year in the standard developer program (which is probably what you initially signed up for during registration).

Although registering for the iOS Developer Program is covered in the Appendix, it is worth noting here that Apple also has an iOS Developer Enterprise Program, which costs $299 instead of $99. Though you will still need to register for the standard program to distribute applications on the App Store, the enterprise program streamlines internal distribution and allows unlimited slots to test applications in-house. To qualify for this program, you need to verify to Apple that your company has at least 500 employees. More information is available at *http://developer.apple.com/programs/iphone/enterprise/*.

To have your app installed onto your and your customers' devices, you'll collect UDIDs, register them with Apple, subsequently download a mobile provisioning file, and then use that file along with your app to get it working on the device. This process probably appears confusing, so I'll walk you through each step.

UDID

"UDID" stands for "unique device identifier." A UDID is a 40-character alphanumeric identification number that's unique to every single iPhone, iPad, and iPod touch. You and your testers need the UDID of each device onto which you plan to install your app for testing.

There are several ways to collect the UDID, and I'll cover two now. The simplest method is to use one of the dozens of apps on the App Store that will both pull the UDID from the device and quickly send it to you via email. Simply search for "UDID" in the App Store. The apps that appear at the top of the resultant list are your best options (see Figure 6-1). Some apps, such as Info – UDID, provide other device information, including OS version and device features.

Another method for obtaining the UDID is through iTunes. Plug in your device, select it in iTunes, and visit the Summary tab. Click the words "Serial Number" in the top section (they won't appear clickable), and they will transform to "Identifier (UDID)." Select Edit from the menu and choose Copy (see Figure 6-2). The UDID will then be placed on the clipboard.

Figure 6-1. UDID apps on the App Store

Figure 6-2. UDID in iTunes

Registering a Device with the Provisioning Portal

Before you read this section, keep in mind that I won't be dissecting Apple's *iOS Provisioning Portal* (*http://developer.apple.com/ios/manage/overview/index. action*), which is part of the *iOS Dev Center* (*http://developer.apple.com/ios/*). The reasons are to protect you from being overwhelmed and to continue to equip you with only what you need to know to get your job done.

This section assumes that your developer has set up your App ID and iOS Distribution Certificate, and that you have the appropriate permissions to register devices into the iOS Provisioning Portal (*http://developer.apple.com/ membercenter/help.action?programType=iphone*).

You may deem what I'm about to detail for you as too technical. The truth is, you really never have to visit the iOS Provisioning Portal and can pass this task to your developer. But if you want to free yourself from always relying on your developer and help keep him focused on more important and less logistical tasks, keep reading.

The iOS Provisioning Portal is a critical part of the iOS Dev Center that provides you the resources to distribute your application both outside and on the App Store. You are currently in the "outside" state, which Apple calls *ad hoc distribution*, and to use this method of distribution you need to register the UDID of any devices that will run the current version of your app.

Once you have those UDIDs, browse to the iOS Provisioning Portal and visit the Manage tab of the Devices section (*http://developer.apple.com/ios/ manage/devices/index.action*). This area is where you'll be submitting the UDIDs to Apple. You can add each UDID individually or upload them all in a *.txt* or *.deviceids* file via the Add Devices or Upload Devices button. Each UDID must be accompanied by a Device Name, which helps you distinguish the UDIDs from each other. More significantly, the Device Name will replace the use of the UDID (which is a long alphanumeric string) and become the main way to reference a device. For these reasons, make this name descriptive (such as "First-name Last-initial Device-type"). For example, aside from my iPhone 4, I have a 3G and 3GS iPhone, second-generation iPod touch, and 3G iPad. So, I'd name them "Ken Y iPhone 3G," "Ken Y iPhone 3GS," "Ken Y iPod touch 2nd Gen," and "Ken Y 3G iPad," respectively.

Be careful and somewhat selective with the UDIDs that are added. Even if you remove one of the devices and then add it back later, it will still count toward the 100-devices-per-year regulation that Apple stipulates. Apple does this so that you don't try to use this method as a permanent alternative to the App Store.

Once you add one or more UDIDs, you'll see them added as registered devices. Notice that they will show as "0" in the Profiles column (see Figure 6-3). That will change once you complete the next step.

Figure 6-3. The Devices section in the iOS Provisioning Portal; notice the Profiles column shows 0

Mobile Provisioning File

To install an app outside the App Store through ad hoc distribution, Apple requires that a *provisioning profile* be present on the device. There's more to a provisioning profile than what I'll discuss here, but for now just note that it essentially informs a device that an app not approved by Apple can be installed.

Click down to the Provisioning section of the iOS Provisioning Portal and select the Distribution tab to associate the devices added in the previous section to the provisioning profile for your app. Although this step depends on how your developer set up the provisioning profile, it will probably be specific to your app and the type of distribution you'll be doing. Although there are compelling reasons to have one profile per distribution type (including requiring that you and your testers install only one provisioning file for all your apps), you'll probably want to have a quick chat with your developer if you see a generic provisioning profile name that doesn't inform you of its contents (e.g., "mobile provision" versus "App Name Ad Hoc").

To associate device names with the appropriate provisioning profile, click the Edit link in the last column. You'll then be brought to the Modify iOS Distribution Provisioning Profile page, where you'll see the distribution method of the profile, along with some other developer-centric information such as the App ID. Since the distribution method in this case is Ad Hoc, the bottom section is where you'll be able to select the devices you want to run your app. Choose Select All if you're adding all the device names, or use the checkboxes to select a subset of them (see Figure 6-4).

Figure 6-4. The Modify iPhone Distribution Provisioning Profile page

The madness is almost done. Click the Submit button when you've added all the appropriate devices. You'll find yourself back on the Distribution Provisioning Profile page, with the Status of the provisioning profile (the one you just added devices to) changed to Pending. Refresh the page and it will soon read Active again. Click the Download button to finally receive your prized mobile provisioning file (which will be named according to the provisioning profile and will end with *.mobileprovision*). Put this file in a safe place. You and your customers will use the provisioning profile, along with your actual app, to install the app onto your device.

Anytime you add a new device for testing, you'll need to add it to the provisioning profile and subsequently download this file again.

Development App

Up to now, you've likely only seen your app run in the iPhone Simulator. With all the work you've just done, you are close to finally seeing it on your device.

The last ingredient you need in order to install your app is the "ad hoc distribution" development version of it. Your developer should provide this file to you, which will end with *.app* or *.ipa*. If your developer doesn't name the file descriptively enough, you may want to add the version number or date to it (e.g., "App-Dev-v091.app"). As you continue the testing process, you might need to revert to one particular version, and a standard naming convention will help you locate the right one.

Installing through iTunes

Take both the mobile provisioning and app files and drag them into iTunes under the Library area. You don't need to drag them into any particular category; iTunes will know what to do with them. Connect your device, select it, and then go to the Applications tab. You should see your application available under Sync Applications. Select it and then click the Sync button.

In theory, the development version of your app should now be installed. From my experience, however, installing an ad hoc app through iTunes almost never works properly the first time a sync occurs, even if everything was done correctly.

The most common error for the app not being installed relates to a "signer not valid" error (see Figure 6-5). This message usually occurs when the developer's credentials were not configured properly in building the app for distribution. Try syncing again first. If the same message reappears, your developer will need to send you a new mobile provision, new app, or new versions of both files.

Figure 6-5. "Signer not valid," the most common error for ad hoc distribution installations

During development, it's a good practice for you to completely remove the app from your device before installing the next version of it. So, if you tested one part of the app's functionality and then a new feature is completed and available to test, delete the app from your device and remove the existing app in iTunes (go to the Applications section under the Library area, find the app, right-click it, and select Delete; then select Move to Trash when prompted). A good practice—although definitely playing it safe—is to sync your device at that point to make sure both the device and iTunes agree that the app is gone. You should then drag the latest version of the app back into the Library and follow the aforementioned steps to install it.

Although not as conservative or thorough, you may also just want to ask your developer to update the *build number*, which should prompt the ad hoc app to "upgrade," rather than following the process described in this section.

Installing through the iPhone Configuration Utility

You'll quickly find that using iTunes to manage your app is slow and frustrating. One of my favorite tools, which speeds up the installation considerably, is the iPhone Configuration Utility (*http://support.apple.com/kb/DL851*, shown in Figure 6-6). This tool does not require syncing and will allow you to install the profile and the app directly onto your device.

Drop the provisioning profile and application under the Library area. Then, attach and select your device and install the appropriate provisioning profile in the Provisioning Profiles tab. Once those steps are completed, you can install the app under the Applications tab.

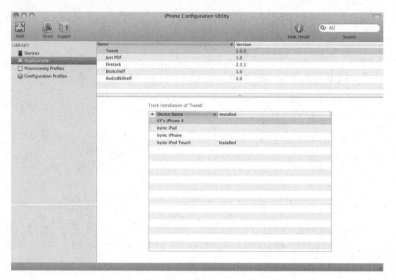

Figure 6-6. iPhone Configuration Utility

More generally, as you become comfortable with this process, you may not want to wait for your developer to send you versions of your app to test. If you are willing to get more into the technical details, have your developer set you up so that you can build your app directly onto your device through Xcode. This setup will allow you to access the latest version of your app without your developer's assistance. You'll start by accessing your app's repository, as described in Chapter 5. If you'd like to learn more, check out "Building onto a device" in this book's Appendix.

Going Beta

No, "beta" is not the name of a fraternity of iPhone app developers. When software is labeled as "beta," developers are communicating to customers that they may encounter problems and should use the software at their own risk. Over the past several years, the latter warning has largely become meaningless because of how long software has remained as "beta" software.

For the purposes of this book, "beta" will mean the app you distribute to customers prior to it being on the App Store.

Don't think about beta as being your opportunity to release a half-completed app. Instead, consider it a continuation of building the best product and further developing relationships with those who will eventually help you market your app. By releasing a beta app outside the App Store, you'll continue to validate assumptions, hone product features, and find out what's broken (yes, something will be broken). In general, you'll be doing yourself and your customers a huge favor.

It's time for your next marketing checkup. Revisit the "Phase 3" section of Chapter 8, as it will help you recruit customers for beta testing (in particular, see the "Recruit beta testers" section of that chapter).

Cultivating Beta Testers

To test your app with others who are not on your team, you'll need a key ingredient besides your app: customers. At this point in the development process, you should already have a pool of customers who are willing to be beta testers. You shouldn't be wondering who these customers are or whether they have iPod touches, iPhones, or iPads. If you don't understand who your customers are, revisit Chapter 3 because you have bigger problems than what will be uncovered in beta testing.

Even though you should know who is interested in testing your app, there are still some basic criteria for identifying who qualifies as a beta tester. If your app takes advantage of any device-related features—for example, video—this will limit your beta testing pool. A slightly less obvious item is related to the device's operating system. Your testers may be running older versions of iOS that could prevent them from installing your app. Although you will need to qualify testers, don't be too limiting because you will want to have your app tested across many different device and iOS combinations, provided that they meet the minimum requirements.

Both the device and the iOS requirements are straightforward items to communicate and subsequently filter potential testers. What's more difficult is putting the app into your testers' hands and then incorporating their feedback into the development process. Collect their UDIDs if you haven't done so already, and upload them into the iOS Provisioning Portal. Refer to the previous section to learn how to do that; you can use the instructions for installing the app on the device to guide your testers through the rest of the steps to install your app (see Figure 6-7). My recommendation is to have them use the iPhone Configuration Utility; it requires some additional steps, but it will make the actual installation process smoother.

Figure 6-7. Release notes and installation instructions email for the Tweeb beta testers

Due to the high number of logistics involved in ad hoc distribution, make sure you've tested your app internally before you start distributing it. In fact, you and your team should be using the app extensively before customers receive it. It's important to respect your beta testers' time. They shouldn't be identifying basic errors or problems with the app. You should.

Quality Assurance and Feedback

With some amount of patience, you should now have a development version of your app that is installed on your device and the devices of your beta testers. Installing the app was not an end unto itself, but rather the beginning of testing, refining, and improving the app.

Make Testing "Real"

Depending on the size of your team and the resources you have available, you might have one or more persons dedicated to performing quality assurance (QA). Regardless of whether that is the case (and it probably won't be for many of you reading this book), I want to challenge you to really *own* the responsibility of having the right features that work properly. This means you should be the most ardent beta tester of your app, discovering obvious bugs before others do and influencing how best to improve features from your actual use of it. That's the same way your beta testers should be experiencing the app—in conditions that reflect the real-world environment of your App Store customers.

I'm emphasizing this point so strongly because you won't discover issues by just seeing the app in the iPhone Simulator or through formal QA by testing the app through a series of predefined steps. What makes developing for the iOS unique is that hardware heavily influences the testing process. In addition, aside from device-related features and iOS versions, these devices also have various states for network connectivity. For instance, it's possible to have no cellular network, an EDGE or 3G connection, or WiFi present at various signal strengths. You should test, for example, the process of opening your app in Airplane Mode—available in your device's Settings app— where no network connectivity is present and see if it works.

Many apps crash because these types of scenarios are not initially accounted for during development. To precisely state the larger takeaway, everyday conditions are hard to simulate in a formal QA process (which you should still use) and often will only be encountered by using the app outside of a testing environment. Even Apple tests its devices and apps this way, requiring its engineers to experience them in regular use outside of the Apple campus.

Feedback and Bugs

Through whatever channels you are using, keep the lines of communication open with your beta testers. When you provide them the latest development version of your app, be sure they know if you want them to test anything specific, and let them know of any changes that have been made since the last time they tested the app by including a *changelog* or release notes outlining what is new, updated, fixed, or outstanding. Also, remind them how to properly install the new app (refer back to Figure 6-7).

You may want to take advantage of the open source framework known as Hockey, which allows you to update your beta app remotely. Using it will remove the need to send out the latest development version. Instead, the beta app will update automatically, when a new version is available. See *http://github.com/TheRealKerni/Hockey* and *http://buzzworks.de/blog/announcing-developer-framework-hockey* for more details. Note that you should rely on Hockey for updating the app only. You still should stay in touch with your beta testers and distribute release notes and related materials.

Here is the information I included in the release notes for Tweeb:

Tweeb Release Notes

For this version of the app, please check out the new retweet features located in the "Buzz" tab. The following are the items that have changed since the last version you tested:

Fix

- Special characters in passwords

- Issues with counters showing "0's" when device uses non-U.S. region format

- Summary screen counter not showing lost/gained followers

Update

- Better performance when multiple accounts loaded

Be aggressive about getting feedback from your beta testers. If possible, meet with your testers and watch them use the app. Request to record their usage of the app, ask them questions, listen, and absorb as much as possible. Although you want to find bugs throughout this process, it's more important to understand how your customers are using your app.

You should provide guidance regarding what you need from your testers when they submit bugs. A statement that reads "It crashed when I pressed a button" won't help you much. When customers send you bugs via email during testing, they should include what device and OS they have, what type of network connection was present, what tab or screen they were on, and what specific steps caused the issue. If applicable, also ask for a screenshot.

As mentioned before, Apple made it very easy to take screenshots on its devices. To do so, simply press the Home and Power buttons at the same time. You'll hear a camera shutter sound and the screenshot will be placed into the device's Camera Roll.

Going Deeper with Nasty Bugs

Sometimes your developer won't be able to reproduce a bug found by you or one of your beta testers. Thankfully, there are a couple of Apple and third-party tools that can help with this situation by retrieving crash logs and other diagnostics data to help resolve these types of bugs.

iPhone Backup Extractor

An extremely handy piece of software that your beta testers can use is a third-party tool called the iPhone/iPod touch Backup Extractor (found at the uniquely named domain *http://supercrazyawesome.com/*).

This app runs only on the Mac, but it is one of the easiest tools to use to get all the relevant files to your developer. The iPhone Backup Extractor (see Figure 6-8) will interact with your tester's device backup files. If your tester uses it, she'll need to first sync her device so that the appropriate files will be present in the backup.

Figure 6-8. iPhone Backup Extractor

Organizer

Apple's Xcode, which is bundled with the iOS SDK (see the "Tools" section in this book's Appendix), has a tool that you will come to not only appreciate, but also use regularly: Organizer. As an aside, Organizer is another place you can grab the UDID for your device.

Once Xcode is open, you can access Organizer via the Window→Organizer menu item. Connect your device and you'll see it appear in the Devices area of Organizer. In the main screen, click the Use for Development button (see Figure 6-9) and you'll see the indicator change from gray to yellow to green, and two new tabs will appear, one of which is the Device Logs tab.

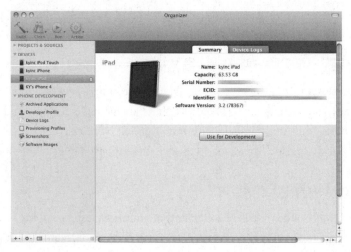

Figure 6-9. Clicking the Use for Development button in Organizer to access additional features

The Device Logs tab (see Figure 6-10) will allow you to search for your app and then pull some critical diagnostics data for your developer to use. Most of these logs will be listed as "Crash" in the Type column. You can drag and drop any of these files, which will end in .crash, from Organizer to your computer, but look for the latest based on the Date/Time column.

Another file type—a *.plist* file—can be useful to your developer. A majority of the time the information in the crash log will suffice to identify and resolve the issue. The next section explains where to find a *.plist* file.

Another time-saving function of Organizer is the ability to take screenshots that you can immediately drag to your computer. An annoyance with using your device to accomplish this task is that email, iTunes sync, or an app is required to transfer the screenshots. With Organizer, visit the Screenshots tab, have the screen you want captured open on your device, click the Capture button, and then drag the screenshot to your computer.

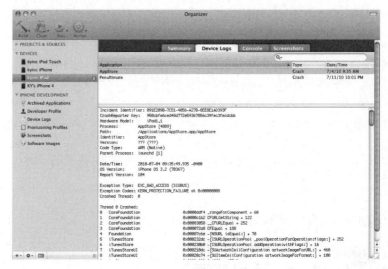

Figure 6-10. Organizer's crash logs

Finding crash logs on your computer

A device's diagnostics data (*.crash* and *.plist* files) can also be directly accessed from a computer. The prerequisite to accessing it, or at least to having the latest data, is to sync the device with iTunes.

Here are the locations where you can access these files on several operating systems. Once you navigate to the location, look for the filenames that resemble your app name.

Mac

   ~/Library/Logs/CrashReporter/MobileDevice/<device name>

Windows Vista/Windows 7

   C:\Users\<Windows username>\AppData\Roaming\Apple computer
   Logs\CrashReporter\MobileDevice\<device name>

Windows XP

   C:\Documents and Settings\<Windows username>\Application Data
   Apple computer\Logs\CrashReporter\MobileDevice\<device name>

Funneling Feedback

Use whatever tools you implemented in Chapter 5 to track all of the feedback, bugs, screenshots, and diagnostics files collected during your beta testing. Input, prioritize, track, and resolve both feedback and bugs. If your tool provides for it, give your beta testers direct access to log their feedback and bugs and then prioritize those items internally in order of importance.

Interviews

Hog Bay Software: Jesse Grosjean

COMPANY: Hog Bay Software

POSITION: Founder

BACKGROUND: Jesse Grosjean is the one-man show behind Bangor, Maine–based Hog Bay Software. His software includes the popular distraction-free writing tool WriteRoom and the simple "paper-like" to-do list application TaskPaper, both of which exist on the Mac and iPhone.

LINK: *http://www.hogbaysoftware.com/*

Ken: *What's the most important step when designing a new application?*

Jesse: I always start each product idea with a positioning statement following Geoffrey A. Moore's format:

   For [target end user] who wants/needs [compelling reason to buy].
   [Product name] is a [product category] that provides [key benefit].
   Unlike [main competitor], [Product name] [key differentiation].

This sets a foundation for the app that I use throughout the development process, and it provides the basis for marketing the app after release. Here are the positioning statements for TaskPaper and WriteRoom as examples:

TaskPaper: For Mac & iPhone users to make lists and stay organized. TaskPaper is a simple to-do list that's surprisingly adept. Unlike standard organizers, TaskPaper gets out of your way so that you can get things done.

WriteRoom: For Mac & iPhone users to write without distractions. WriteRoom is a full-screen writing environment. Unlike the cluttered word processors you're used to, WriteRoom lets you focus on writing.

Ken: *You now have an active community of people willing to test your software and apps, but "back in the early days" when that wasn't the case, how did you go about getting customer feedback? How would you suggest developers do that when dealing with iPhone apps and Apple's App Store?*

Jesse: Make sure that you start with an interesting idea that you can describe (positioning statement). Once you have that, then it shouldn't be hard to get feedback. You don't need lots of users, just three or four different conversations going on about the app as you build it. A good positioning statement is important at this stage so that you stay focused on the goal for 1.0 instead of just adding feature upon feature suggested by your early testers.

Ken: *What guidance do you provide your customers when they test beta software? Do you script them in any way about what they should be testing or just let them have at it?*

Jesse: I just let them have at it. Generally, I include a few notes of changes to look for in each new beta, but that's about it. I do it this way because I don't think that I personally would be organized enough, or have enough time, to create and maintain any more structure in the testing process.

Ken: *How do you interact with your testers and community? Are there tools you use to manage those interactions? Do you use different tools internally for yourself versus externally for testers?*

Jesse: Conversations can happen in my user forums, blog comments, or email. Recently (for iPhone beta testing) I've tried to stick more to email with all testers Bcc'd.

Ken: *When dealing with bugs in particular, what do you request your testers provide you in order to more quickly resolve them? What types of bugs do your testers usually find that you miss in your own QA?*

Jesse: Bugs need a reproducible case. I'll look for bugs that are not reproducible, but that's almost always a losing battle. In general, testers find bugs of all sorts, but for me I think a more useful part of the beta process is the feedback that I get about how the application actually works. Most of the conversation is about features to add/remove/change as opposed to bugs to fix.

Ken: *Once you have feedback from your customers, how do you determine what features get added, removed, or changed in the first version of the App Store release? In particular with the gated App Store approval process, how do you determine what goes into the first release versus an update?*

Jesse: I think a good rule of thumb is to release 1.0 as soon as the app's functionality fulfills the app's positioning statement. For subsequent updates, I just release when it seems right…balancing the desire to implement everything on my to-do list with the desire to get the release out as soon as possible. Generally, my release pattern is to do a big release with lots of changes, followed by a number of quick releases that fix bugs or polish behavior. Then not much [is released] until the next big release.

Mariner Software: Michael Wray

COMPANY: Mariner Software

POSITION: President

BACKGROUND: Michael Wray began his career in the Macintosh software industry by co-founding Power On Software in the early 1990s. In 2002, he took over the helm of Mariner Software. More recently, he brought Mariner into the iPhone and, ultimately, the iPad markets with offerings on the App Store.

LINK: *http://www.marinersoftware.com/*

Ken: *You now have an active community of people willing to test your software and apps, but "back in the early days" when that wasn't the case, how did you go about getting customer feedback? How would you suggest developers do that when dealing with iPhone apps and Apple's App Store?*

Michael: Name any era in Macintosh computing and one thing remains consistent: Mac users love to volunteer to test software. In our case, whether it was early on in System 7 days, the release of Mac OS X, to today, with the iPhone and iPad generation, Apple die-hards are eager to test new technology. Many users reached out to us years ago and have remained faithful testers even today.

Here at Mariner we make it real easy to apply to be a tester: we put a blurb on our home page on our website, post a notification in our forum, and send out newsletters reminding users they can "steer the Mariner ship" by participation in testing new products. With iPhone testing, as odd as it sounds, we literally have to be picky on who we can accept as a volunteer tester. Since Apple limits the amount of participants in ad hoc testing, we need to make sure whoever is participating is actually serious about testing.

Ken: *What guidance do you provide your customers when they test beta software? Do you script them in any way about what they should be testing or just let them have at it?*

Michael: When an app is in the early stage of testing, we try to set the expectations for the user. We are fortunate to have hundreds of testers to choose from that have strong beta testing experience, and thus, know what to expect. Obviously the words "PLEASE MAKE SURE YOU HAVE A BACKUP SYSTEM IN PLACE" are littered all over the documentation. The last thing we want is to be responsible for losing a user's data (fortunately, it hasn't happened to us). In terms of a script or path for users to follow, we rarely give them that direction. Having users use our software in their own environments and workflow is incredibly crucial for us. We have a pretty good testing lab, but there's no way we would ever be able to duplicate what users see on an everyday basis.

Ken: *How do you interact with your testers and community? Are there tools you use to manage those interactions? Do you use different tools internally for yourself than the ones you use externally for testers?*

Michael: We have a private (password-protected) forum where we communicate with our testers (and they with us and other testers). We have also implemented a support/knowledge base solution called Tender that is really helping with communication.

Ken: *When dealing with bugs in particular, what do you request your testers provide you in order to more quickly resolve them? What types of bugs do your testers usually find that you miss in your own QA?*

Michael: We encourage them to provide us with a bug report, so we can see exactly what was happening at the time of a crash. Providing in-depth background info for our QA folks is so critical to reproducing a problem. When we need to go back and forth with a few emails to get that information, the solution is usually delayed. Our testers usually find oddball bugs that happen in small quantities. That being said, there have been occasions where we missed something that I'm sure our users were scratching their heads over.

Ken: *Once you have feedback from your customers, how do you determine what features get added, removed, or changed in the first version of the App Store release? In particular with the gated App Store approval process, how do you determine what goes into the first release and what goes into an update?*

Michael: For every first-version app in the App Store, we have been able to draw from a close group of power users (as well as internally). Honestly, a lot of it comes down to supply and demand. If we get enough "demand" for a feature from several power users we poll (and it doesn't take a year to implement!), we usually "supply" it. In terms of what makes the cut in version 1.0 of an app, many times it's bandwidth-driven. If at that time, we have development bandwidth available, we usually can add more features in version 1.0. If our development team is juggling several different products and they are under major deadlines, the reality is that sometimes features will slip to a later release. It's not ideal, but we do the best we can with the resources we have.

Recap

Here's what you learned in this chapter:

- The process of installing an app outside the App Store requires your and your testers' UDIDs. You discovered several different ways for pulling the UDID off a device.

- Although you may decide you want your developer to handle the iOS Provisioning Portal, you became familiar with the aspects relevant to you and can add new testing devices to your ad hoc development mobile provisioning file.

- Cultivating a group of beta testers is going to vastly improve your app before it hits the App Store. You should be the best beta tester and constantly use the app in "real-world" conditions.

- Using Apple's Organizer, using other available tools, and being familiar with the diagnostic logs will get you, and ultimately, your developer, the information needed to troubleshoot and resolve the major bugs in your app.

- All of the feedback and bugs discovered through your testing process should be funneled into one location where you can prioritize, assign, and track them.

Launch

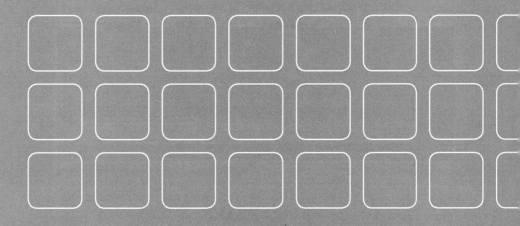

Preparing for the App Store Submission

YOUR APP IS NOTHING MORE than a pet project until it's in Apple's App Store. So, once you are confident about turning that pet project into an app that people around the world can download, you are going to fire up your browser and head over to Apple's iTunes Connect (*http://itunesconnect.apple. com*) to submit your application. Before that can happen, though, there are some final development tasks to complete as well as a checklist you'll want to cover to make submitting to the App Store a painless process.

In this chapter, you'll explore:

- Finishing up development items before submitting your app

- A checklist of what you'll need to submit to Apple in iTunes Connect

- Understanding the approval process and checking on the status of the app

- Dealing with app rejections and resubmission

Finishing Development

Analytics

If you are familiar with website management or online marketing, chances are you've heard the word "analytics" before. As is the case with websites, user activities within apps can be tracked.

Why is this important? Although Apple will provide you with some basic information about your application (mostly sales-focused), it won't be able to help you understand what your users are *doing* with your app. Analytics will enable you to see what features your users find most useful, and can help influence what you add or remove from the app later.

A handful of analytics packages are available. Choosing the right one will largely depend on what best fits your needs. For example, you may want to track custom *events*, such as when a customer touches a particular button in your app. You may also want to have the analytics from your app integrate with your existing web analytics. The last major differentiator that I'll mention is that some of the analytics platforms offer you the ability to view analytics, sales, and diagnostics information such as crash reports, all in one location. The following list includes some of the more popular options for you to evaluate based on what's most important for your app:

- Flurry, *http://www.flurry.com/*

- Heartbeat, *http://www.heartbeatapp.com* (a service of Mobclix)

- TapMetrics, *http://tapmetrics.com/* (a service of Millennial Media)

- Google Analytics, *http://code.google.com/apis/analytics/docs/tracking/ mobileAppsTracking.html*

- Omniture, *http://www.omniture.com/* (through SiteCatalyst)

Apple's latest policies indicate that analytics are to be used solely for the purposes of measuring advertising. Although Apple does not appear to be strictly enforcing this policy, note that what the analytics providers are able to collect and how they operate depends exclusively on Apple and is subject to change. Additionally, with the release of iOS 4, Apple has suggested that developers begin notifying customers if analytics data is collected and how it is used. Review Section 3.3.9 of the iOS Developer Program License Agreement to learn more about Apple's restrictions and requirements in this area.

You'll likely want to discuss these packages with your developer. Be sure to work with him to set up any particular events you want tracked in the application. Of course, it's critical to verify that the analytics are tracking properly before submitting the app. Even if your developer installed analytics during your QA and testing, have him double-check that they are installed when preparing the App Store version of the app.

Chris Brown, the founder of TapMetrics (now a service of Millennial Media), is interviewed at the end of this chapter. He discusses some details about properly launching an app and testing and installing analytics. Chapter 9 covers how to leverage analytics and events to inform you how customers are using your app.

Other tools for feedback

Other tools are available that let you gain insight into your app. You can also integrate these tools in some of your team's final development tasks.

In App Support

In the "Finishing touches" section in Chapter 5, I discussed providing a guided user experience for your customers. Sometimes, despite all your best efforts, customers will still have questions. To help with this situation, you might consider having a dedicated help or support area in your app. Many developers typically place this in a More tab or Settings area.

Some items to list in this area can include a help manual (much less interactive and fun than what we covered in "Finishing touches"), in-app email for customers to send support questions or feature requests, and even surveys (e.g., *http://haveasec.com*). The emails will be more explicit in communicating what your customers want. However, the help manual can also give you insight into what customers want. The manual is usually served through a web view (i.e., HTML that gets loaded into the app), and if you add web analytics to those pages, you can see what customers are looking at the most (see Figure 7-1). This should clue you in to areas you need to improve or make clearer in your app.

Figure 7-1. myPhoneDesktop settings

Prompt for ratings and reviews

Although you will reach out to your most engaged customers to ask for some initial ratings and reviews (detailed in Chapter 8) when your app launches, it's also a smart strategy to prompt customers to rate your app. Customers who may like your app often will not take the time to give feedback in the App Store simply because they are too busy.

It's especially easy to include this functionality in your app and prompt customers for ratings, thanks to some handiwork from Arash Payan, who created the open source project Appirater (*http://github.com/ arashpayan/appirater/*, shown in Figure 7-2). By default, Appirater will see if a customer has used your app for 30 days and launched it at least 15 times, and if so, it will ask the customer to rate the app. Using these criteria will ensure that satisfied customers are rating your app. If you want to be a little less conservative and get ratings more quickly, you can change these values (e.g., drop the number of days down to five).

Figure 7-2. Appirater in Icebird and Outside

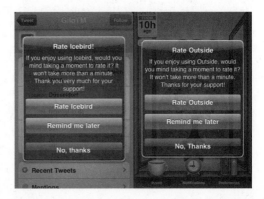

Your App Store App "Binary"

Recall that the app you've been using to refine and fix features is *not* an App Store version of your app; it's a development version. The final task for your developer to perform before the app can be submitted to the App Store is to prepare an App Store version of it.

An explanation of how to create an App Store build of your app will put you to sleep. It's unlikely that your developer got you this far and doesn't know how to create the app for App Store distribution. To be fair, though, many developers struggle with creating the App Store version of their app the first time they try it. Whether your developer is a newbie or a seasoned pro, a good resource for help in this task is *Learning iPhone Programming* (*http:// oreilly.com/catalog/9780596806446/*) by Alasdair Allan (O'Reilly).

Once the developer has the App Store version of the app ready, you'll receive either a *.zip* or an *.ipa* file (e.g., *<AppName>.zip* or *<AppName>.ipa*). These are the only two formats that Apple accepts, and each must be 2 GB or less. This file—what Apple calls the *binary*—will contain everything Apple needs for someone to install your application on a device, including the actual app and the app icons required for your app. Recall from earlier discussions (see "App type" in Chapter 1 and "Devices and resolutions" in Chapter 5) that various sizes of the creative assets are required depending on the devices targeted.

Your next marketing checkup, for the "Phase 4" section of Chapter 8, will begin prepping you for the launch of your app. With the approval of your app by the end of this chapter, you'll move into the final phase of the marketing crescendo. If you have been diligent with your marketing checkups throughout the book, you will have already consumed the majority of Chapter 8.

---

iTunes Connect

Checklist for App Store Submission

You may have a basic understanding of iTunes Connect if you were the one who registered for the iOS Developer Program. In any case, this section assumes you have an Apple ID that provides you access to iTunes Connect and allows you to add a new application. For related information, see this book's Appendix.

There is, of course, more to the submission process than just having the App Store binary. Potential users of your application need to be convinced that your app is worthy of being installed on their device (i.e., that they are willing to ante up less than the price of a cup of coffee for your blood, sweat, and tears). You will try to convince them through words and through images, which is what the App Store listing for your app contains. Table 7-1 lists the items you'll need as you proceed with the submission process.

Table 7-1. App Store checklist

Item	Type	Description	Limitations
Application name	Text	The name of the application.	None, but it will be shortened on the springboard and in various places in the App Store
Application description	Text	The content displayed in the App Store listing. Keep the description succinct. Browse the App Store's top apps to find good examples of application descriptions.	4,000 characters max
Keywords	Text	The words, features, and functions used to describe your application. Apple will use these words to associate your app with user searches in the App Store.	100 characters max; separated by commas

Application	Binary	The App Store version of your application (iPhone, iPad, or Universal).	Must be .zip or .ipa; size should be 2 GB or less for customers to download over WiFi, or 20 MB or less for customers to download over the cellular network
Large 512 x 512 icon	Image	The large version of the app icon that will be used in the App Store when users are browsing through the iTunes App Store.	At least 512 x 512 pixels; at least 72 dpi
iPhone and iPod touch screenshots	Image	Only one of the five available screenshot files is required for your app, but all are recommended. Make the primary screenshot the best one.	Must be a .jpeg, .jpg, .tif, .tiff, or .png file; sizes allowed are 320 × 480, 480 × 320, 320 × 460, or 480 × 300 pixels for all devices except the iPhone 4; high-resolution screenshots of 960 × 640, 960 × 600, 640 × 960, or 640 × 920 if the app is designed for the iPhone 4's Retina display
iPad screenshots	Image	Only one of the five available screenshot files is required for your app, but all are recommended. Make the primary screenshot the best one.	Must be a .jpeg, .jpg, .tif, .tiff, or .png file; sizes allowed are 768 × 1024, 1024 × 768, 748 × 1024, or 1004 × 768 pixels

Although there are other elements to submitting the app (which I'll cover in a moment), having these sorts of materials queued up will make the process easier and faster.

App Store Submission

Now the big moment…time to get your app submitted to Apple! Browse to iTunes Connect (*http://itunesconnect.apple.com*) and log in using the appropriate Apple ID. Assuming you have the appropriate permissions, you should see the Manage Your Applications link on the home screen (see Figure 7-3). Click it and then click the Add New Application button on the next screen. At this point, you are officially at the beginning of the submission process. By having your checklist assets close at hand, you should be less than five minutes away from submitting your app.

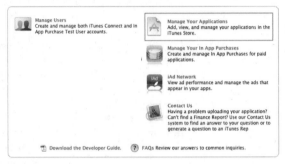

Figure 7-3. Clicking the Manage Your Applications link in iTunes Connect to begin the application submission process

App Information

Aside from the application name and SKU number (a unique number you assign to your app) the App Information screen focuses on slightly more developer-centric information (see Figure 7-4). In particular, you'll want to work with your developer to complete all the bundle-related fields.

Figure 7-4. The App Information screen, which has several key bundle fields that your developer will need to provide to you

From your checklist, you should already have your application name and should be able to easily fill that in to the App Name field. The SKU Number field is more for your benefit than anyone else's. This number, among other uses, will help you differentiate the sales for this app from others. Try to use some logic in creating it, such as incorporating the app name initials and year, but don't overthink it.

Rights and Pricing

Apple doesn't allow you to enter a price for an app. Instead, it uses a Price Tier, with Tier 1 representing $0.99 and Tier 85 representing $999.99. The tiers generally increment by $1, but in the upper tiers they increase by $5, $10, $50, and eventually $100. By selecting a different tier, you'll see the Customer Price in other regions in the Pricing Matrix, as well as Your Proceeds, which is the amount you'll receive after Apple takes its 30%.

The Rights and Pricing screen looks different and is less functional during an initial submission of your application. For example, you'll have to click See Pricing Matrix to view the Customer Price and Your Proceeds. More important is that during the initial submission, you will not see the Price Tier Effective Date and Price Tier End Date (described shortly). Come back to the Rights and Pricing screen either after you submit your application or after you submitted it without the binary to edit these options.

The Rights and Pricing screen contains three additional key elements: the Availability Date, price tier change dates, and stores where you want the application available. The Availability Date is deceivingly tricky. It provides you with an opportunity to set a date in the future for your app, but does not guarantee it will be available by that time. So, if you are trying to plan a marketing event around the launch of your app, don't base it on what you enter in the Availability Date section, unless that date is far enough in the future that you can guarantee it will be approved (usually three or more weeks into the future should suffice).

If you want to be available to support the app once it is launched, you may also want to avoid choosing a weekend date, though there may be some advantage to this approach, in that there would be less competition at that time (but you'd need to be available off normal business hours). There's also some advantage to launching an app at the end of the week, since sales are normally higher then and it's the time when Apple refreshes its Featured apps.

If your Availability Date passes and the app is still not approved, it will be made available in the App Store as soon as it is approved—that is, unless you edit the date before this occurs. To have better control of your marketing efforts, you will want to come back to change this date if that's the situation you find yourself experiencing. Apple provides a somewhat frequently updated App Store Review Status (see Figure 7-5) in the App Store Resource Center of the iOS Dev Center. It provides high-level information regarding how quickly new and updated apps are being approved. You may want to use this information as guidance for influencing your Availability Date (*https://developer.apple.com/iphone/appstore/approval.html*).

Figure 7-5. The App Store Review Status, available in the App Store Resource Center, which shows the number of submissions reviewed within the past seven days

Availability Date and When Your App Appears in the Store

There's a distinction between Apple approving an app and the app showing in the App Store, which is where the Availability Date is relevant. If Apple approves your app today but the Availability Date is set to tomorrow, the app will not appear in the App Store until tomorrow.

Developers generally set the Availability Date far enough into the future that it becomes a nonissue. Their strategy is to ensure that the app never has a chance of showing in the App Store after it is approved. When it is approved, developers will then edit the Availability Date based on when they actually want the app to start showing in the store.

Two items that won't show on this screen when you first submit your app are the Price Tier Effective Date and Price Tier End Date. They are related and can be used to create periods of time where you either drop or increase the price of your app. Apple included this feature because many developers will offer promotional pricing for an app for a specified period of time. Previously, you would have to log in to iTunes Connect to drop and subsequently increase the price, but that's no longer the case with Price Tier Effective Date and Price Tier End Date (shown in Figure 7-6). If you don't have any promotions planned yet, don't concern yourself with these items. As with everything in iTunes Connect, you can make edits and updates later.

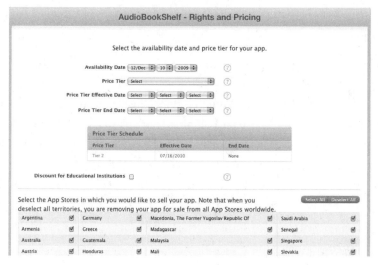

Figure 7-6. The Price Tier Effective Date and Price Tier End Date, which will initially not show on the Rights and Pricing screen

By default, Apple will make your app available to App Stores worldwide to increase the app's exposure and revenue potential. The distribution of your app can definitely be a strategic decision. There can be issues with how the app functions internationally, such as date formats impacting functionality or language barriers if the app description is not localized. You'll likely have assessed those issues before coming into iTunes Connect. To change the geographic availability, you'll need to click the "here" link in the text that reads "Or, you can select specific stores here" at the bottom of the Rights and Pricing screen. Deselect the App Stores where you do not want your app published.

There's a trend among more sophisticated developers to launch an app into a smaller comparable market before launching it globally. For example, many game developers focused on the U.S. market are first launching in Canada, improving the app, and then releasing it to the rest of the stores. This strategy is addressed more fully in the TapMetrics interview at the end of the chapter.

Version Information

The Version Information screen is arguably the most important of the submission process and is broken down into four sections: Metadata, Rating, EULA, and Images. The first and last sections will mostly be completed by having your App Store checklist assets handy. It's extremely uncommon to alter the EULA, so I will not be addressing that section at this time.

For the Metadata section (see Figure 7-7), you'll use the text portions of your App Store checklist. You'll be using your application description and keywords in this section and should be able to just copy and paste them into the relevant fields. You'll also be assigning your app to its primary and secondary categories (see Chapter 1 and the TapMetrics interview at the end of this chapter for information about choosing your category).

Figure 7-7. The Metadata section on the Version Information screen, which contains most of the textual content for your application

There are two Apple-centric fields in the Metadata section: Version and Copyright. The version number can be whatever you want, but it is exposed to your users and is unique to a specific version of your application. It's typical to number your first version of the app as "1.0," and then increment that number with each app update (e.g., "1.1.2" or "2.0"). As described in Chapter 5, most developers use version systems that include three digits (see the "Release Numbering" sidebar in Chapter 5). For the Copyright entry, add the individual or entity that owns the copyrights to the application. Apple prefers the format to be the year followed by the individual or entity (e.g., 2010 Ken Yarmosh).

Apple has made the Rating section easier for you by creating the app rating through a combination of selections for different categories. The ratings include 4+, 9+, 12+, and 17+. As you toggle the radio buttons for each category, you'll see the rating update.

Along with the Metadata section, the Images section is another place where you'll be happy to have all the App Store checklist items ready. You should be able to quickly match your checklist assets with the app icon and screenshots. Although it's not required, you'll definitely want to use all the screenshots available to you. As needed, be sure to reorder them to have some logical flow and focus. After completing the image-related fields, you can click the Save Changes button.

Common Reasons for App Store Rejections

Although App Store rejections occur less frequently now compared to the early days, you should still know the common reasons for rejections and be sure to avoid them. During Apple's WWDC 2010, Steve Jobs stated in his keynote that apps are rejected for three main reasons: the application doesn't function as advertised, it uses private APIs (generally, this means creating programming functions in your app that are not available in the iOS SDK), and the app crashes frequently.

Here are some other good resources that will help you avoid having your app rejected:

- *http://appreview.tumblr.com/*
- *http://apprejections.com/*
- *http://www.mobileorchard.com/avoiding-iphone-app-rejection-from-apple/*
- *http://www.mobileorchard.com/avoiding-iphone-app-rejection-part-2/*

App Summary and binary upload

Upon saving the details for your app, you will be taken to the App Summary screen. This screen represents the area you will visit for each of your submitted or approved applications. It will allow you to access and edit the details of your application going forward.

While you are at the App Summary screen, you are still not quite done with submitting your application to Apple. For starters, if you are enabling In App Purchases or iAds for this particular app, you will need to click either the Manage In App Purchases or the Set Up iAd Network button on the App Summary screen. A button for enabling Game Center is also present in the same area. At a more basic level, though, you will need to revisit the Version Information screen to add any desired localizations and submit your application binary.

Access the Version Information screen again by clicking the View Details button under Versions on the App Summary screen. This screen will look different than it did previously. Among other differences, in the top right-hand corner, you'll see two buttons, Ready to Upload Binary and Manage Localizations. I'll address the second button first.

Most apps are launched worldwide without localizing the App Store content. If you have a specific target market, however, you may want to add a new language through the Manage Localizations button. Once in the localizations area, you can reuse much of the information from the Version Information screen, but you will now have the opportunity to create the metadata content in an alternative language.

Assuming you have completed all other required items, click the Ready to Upload Binary button on the Version Information screen. Provide an answer for the Export Compliance question regarding encryption, which in all likelihood should be "No." Note that you will need to upload your binary through the Application Loader tool (Mac only, shown in Figure 7-8). Beginning in iOS SDK 3.2, the Application Loader comes bundled with the software (see the "iOS SDK" section in this book's Appendix). Apple will surface a direct download of this tool after the Export Compliance question is answered. You can also find a download link at the bottom of the Manage Your Applications page, which reads Download Application Loader.

Figure 7-8. The Application Loader tool, which you'll use to submit your binary

Once you have completed the binary upload, your application will move into its first phase of the App Store approval process: Waiting for Review. The next section will help you understand the approval process a bit more. Although it's important to understand this process, it's vital to use the approval waiting time for other activities that will help you make your app more successful. See Chapter 8 to get started on some of those items, if you haven't done so already.

App Store Approval Process

In the short existence of the App Store, Apple has taken a tremendous amount of criticism about its approval process. Developers complained about the lack of transparency into and consistency of the process. More broadly, their concerns centered on the fact that approving apps affected their ability to keep their software updated and functioning properly.

Today, Apple has not solved all of these problems, but is has significantly lessened the uproar. The biggest areas of improvement have been providing greater visibility into the approval process and reducing the time it takes to approve an app.

Status and status history

Your app can be in one of 11 statuses at any one time. These statuses vary from your needing to wait for Apple to Apple waiting for you. The most common statuses are as follows:

Waiting for Upload
> This status indicates that Apple is ready to receive your app's binary through the Application Loader.

Waiting for Review
> As mentioned previously, this state will occur upon your submission of a fully completed app. Once in this state, you will await Apple's review of your app.

In Review
> This status indicates that Apple has begun reviewing your application.

Rejected
> Not fun; this status indicates that your application has been rejected and requires you to address one or more items and resubmit your app to Apple.

Ready for Sale
> Your app has been approved by Apple; depending on what you selected for your app's Availability Date, it can be eligible to begin appearing in the App Store shortly.

A full listing of all 11 statuses is available from Apple in the App Store Resource Center of the iOS Dev Center (*http://developer.apple.com/ios/ appstore/approval.html*).

If you have opted to receive notifications (iTunes Connect→Manage Users→Edit Profile→Notifications) you will get an email whenever your app changes status. You can also see the current status and status history of an app by clicking on the Status History link (see Figure 7-9) from the

Version Information screen. The Status History page will include an audit trail of when the app was submitted, when it went into review, when it was ready for sale, and any other status changes.

Figure 7-9. AudioBookShelf's status history

I want to make two final comments regarding statuses. First, remain calm if your app gets rejected. Second, when your app becomes Ready for Sale and you choose for it to start appearing in the App Store (see the Availability Date discussion earlier in this chapter), it will likely take some time—possibly several hours or more—before it begins appearing in the App Store. Although you'll be eager to see it start showing, use this time wisely. Whether it's prepping your final marketing push or readying support channels, there are better things to do than constantly look for your app in the App Store (these "better things" are covered in the "Launching Your App (Phase 5)" section in Chapter 8). Your app will show in the App Store… eventually.

Rejections and resubmissions

Thankfully, you are joining the App Store at a time when rejections are both less common and easier to resolve. Although there was no official change in policy or announcement from Apple, anecdotally the approval process has seemed less stringent and faster since the beginning of 2010.

Rejection emails have also generally been more helpful. Members of the App Review Team from the iOS Developer Program often will give specific scenarios that cause crashes and may even include crash logs your developer can use to identify issues. The bottom line is that unless your application was rejected for more ideological reasons, such as Apple deeming it to have duplicated similar functionality to its own apps (e.g., the iPod app) or due to questionable content, having an app rejected is just part of your App Store journey.

If your app gets rejected more than once, you might consider using one of your Technical Support Incidents (TSIs) by sending an email to *idp-dts@apple.com*. Most memberships include two TSIs, but more can be purchased. You can access information about your TSIs from the Technical Support section of the Programs & Add-ons tab, which is part of the Member Center of the Apple Developer program portal (*http://developer.apple.com/membercenter/index.action#techSupport*).

Once your developer has resolved the issue and you've tested it (particularly in relation to why the iOS Developer Program stated it was rejected), use the Application Loader to replace the app's binary.

Approved and Ready for Sale

If you've followed your marketing checkups to this point, once your app has attained the Ready for Sale status, you'll have the option to launch it into the App Store. Or, if your Availability Date has already lapsed, your app will be published to the App Store shortly. In either case, go directly to the "Launching Your App (Phase 5)" section of Chapter 8.

Interviews

TapMetrics: Christopher Brown

COMPANY: Millennial Media

POSITION: Engineer

BACKGROUND: Christopher Brown is the co-founder of TapMetrics, which was acquired by Millennial Media in early 2010. He has also served as the CEO for Bitfire Systems, an iPhone application development and consulting company.

LINKS: *http://www.millennialmedia.com/; http://tapmetrics. com/*

Ken: *Discuss the importance of choosing the right category for an app. How does Apple use the secondary category, and will an app show up in it?*

Christopher: An app will be listed under the primary category in the App Store. The secondary category, however, provides an additional search term, allowing customers to use the search bar to browse for your app. Although the secondary category is optional, it is easy to select and costs nothing, gaining additional ways for your app to be noticed. The difficulty lies in choosing which category "best describes your application," as Apple says to do. While most people can easily pick two or three categories their app falls into, it is more difficult to pick a primary category for an app that most likely does multiple things. The most ambiguous categories usually fall between the Utilities/Productivity/Travel categories and the Games/Entertainment categories as well. I think the best course is to pick a category that best describes the key "pain point" your app solves.

Ken: *During the App Store submission process, many developers don't think carefully enough about their Availability Date. What sort of lead time is recommended between submitting the app and having it available on the App Store?*

Christopher: I recommend submitting an app to the store three to four weeks out. This creates the freedom to do two things. First, it gets you past the review gates of the iTunes Store. By shifting your launch date to the future, you can give Apple sufficient time to review your app, and you will have ample time to fix issues if they reject it. The average approval time has varied from a couple of days to more than two weeks, depending on the review load they have at the time. If you plan events and start telling everyone your app will be in the store in three days, only to find out you violated a rule in the Human Interface Guidelines, you may experience large delays that severely hamper the typical sales bump on initial launch.

Second, this forces you to create a marketing plan. You have time to get the app to bloggers that like to preview apps. You can create an ad campaign that starts a couple days before launch. You can tell the media when your app will be available. It means taking control back from Apple; you control the release, not them.

Ken: *Recently, developers (especially of games) seem to be launching their apps exclusively into smaller markets first (like Canada) before distributing them globally. Is that a smart strategy, and does such an approach make sense for all apps or only a particular type of app? How would you caution developers about proceeding this way?*

Christopher: I think this could be beneficial if you are releasing into a specific market that is known to appreciate the characteristics of your app(s). Games or entertainment apps come to mind here in particular. Certain applications may be loved in France or Japan but are simply not understood in the U.S. or the UK. Releasing an app in a market that is unfamiliar with the nature or culture of your app may earn you poor reviews. Giving it time to gain momentum in a market that is more likely to accept it may help it catch on later in other countries.

In markets where cultures are similar and popular content tends to spread more quickly, such as Canada and the U.S., it doesn't make much sense to me to "test" or "delay" the release. Get the app out there, take feedback from users, and make it better.

Ken: *What are some of the biggest issues developers have with installing analytics and what can be done to avoid them? How is TapMetrics' tool being built to address these problems?*

Christopher: What we are hearing about now is rejection of apps that use location simply for analytics or advertising and not for any utility within the actual application. The TapMetrics library allows a developer to release an application with or without location-based analytics simply by setting a parameter to "YES" or "NO" in one line of code.

Ken: *How can developers test that analytics are installed properly before going into the App Store? Specifically, can or should that be done during ad hoc distribution and beta testing? If so, what are the benefits?*

Christopher: We've seen success from developers who install analytics and then give the app out to beta testers. In addition to verifying that the analytics are functioning properly before release, they can measure usage and get feedback. This approach reveals problems you might not be aware of after focusing on the app for a long period of time.

PoweryBase: Dominik Balogh

COMPANY: PoweryBase

POSITION: President

BACKGROUND: PoweryBase, Inc., was founded in 2009 by Dominik Balogh and his colleague Pavel Serbajlo. They are the creators of, among other software endeavors, the successful iPhone applications NotifyMe and Bills.

LINK: *http://www.powerybase.com/*

Ken: *It's more than a fair statement that PoweryBase is an expert on push notifications, as seen through your NotifyMe application. For a new developer, what are the biggest challenges with push notifications and what advice would you give for getting started with them?*

Dominik: PoweryBase was among the first developers to start benefiting from push notifications as soon as Apple provided this technology. Therefore, it's fair to say that we've gained expert skills with it over time. Nowadays, it's not as difficult to implement push notifications into any application as long as the developer owns a highly reliable server. No special advice is needed if the developers follow Apple's implementation guidelines. At least in the past, some of the biggest challenges have been automated repeating notifications and support for time zones and daylight saving time.

Ken: *NotifyMe seemed to be a pretty successful application. At least from an outsider's perspective, the second app you launched—Bills—appeared to narrow down the scope of NotifyMe and yet it became even more popular. Describe how your Bills app got started and why you eventually launched it even though an existing app basically already had the same functionality.*

Dominik: Bills (full name: Bills ~ On your table) was specially designed to manage bills, bill amounts, and their due dates. Comparatively, NotifyMe is a more versatile to-do reminder. Sure, NotifyMe can also be used to remind you to pay bills on their due dates, but it's not as convenient. The reason we developed Bills was that we saw a potential and found that we weren't satisfied with other bill management applications available. Apple really liked our effort and picked Bills as a featured spotlight on the App Store.

Ken: *What are some good ways for developers to ensure that they are launching something unique and creative into the App Store?*

Dominik: With so many applications on the App Store, it's really hard to launch something unique. Recently, we've started asking ourselves whether the software has to be completely unique in order to gain success. There are many apps already available that can be made much better. Users are picky and mostly know how to determine the best one. If a developer is trying to figure out how to reinvent the wheel, maybe it's time to start thinking the other way around. Identify what is lacking on the App Store, add your innovations, and make it much better.

You could build a multibillion-dollar business this way. In fact, isn't that what Apple has been doing with their computers, phones, music players, and tablet device (the iPad)? Sometimes uniqueness and creativity means just making things that are already available better and more focused than your competitors.

Recap

Here's what you learned in this chapter:

- Although your application's features will be complete when you're ready to submit to the App Store, there are a handful of final development tasks to complete before the app can be submitted.

- Installing analytics in your application will later give you additional insight into how your customers understand and experience your application.

- Having the App Store version of your app—the app "binary"—and all of your other text and image content readily available will make submitting to the App Store much easier.

- The Availability Date of your application represents the date you want your app to start appearing on the App Store. Selecting a date far enough into the future will provide you the greatest control over when that will actually occur.

- A rejected app is no longer a major issue. Apple's operational improvements will help you better understand the nature of your problem and will give you greater visibility into when your app changes status.

8

Building Your Marketing Crescendo

AN AREA WHERE THE MAJORITY OF DEVELOPERS FAIL is either not marketing their app or believing that marketing doesn't begin until an app is approved for the App Store. In many ways, the reality is that getting your app approved by Apple should be a climax of your marketing efforts. To be more than just another developer on the App Store, you're going to need to embrace the idea that marketing evolves along with the development of your app.

In this chapter, you'll explore:

- The five phases of your marketing crescendo

- Developing your app communication channels (Phases 1–3)

- How to find and successfully engage bloggers and press outlets (Phase 4)

- Launching your app once it is approved (Phase 5)

Changing Your Marketing Mindset

Hopefully, you've been paying attention and you arrived here from Chapter 1 or Chapter 3 and not from the preceding chapter. I placed this topic near the end of the book because your marketing-related activities will hit one of their first peaks when your app finally launches—but this will occur only if you began your marketing efforts at the outset of your development process.

"Process" is a critical concept, and it's fair to apply it also to how you will approach marketing. This implies that marketing is not about one or two magical actions that will somehow shoot your app to the top of the App Store charts. Instead, it's an ongoing investment that parallels development; like the building of your app, marketing incorporates your customers.

Although I may be overgeneralizing, my instinct is that most of you don't have access to a massive marketing engine that you'll engage when your app is launched. Even if you do, trusting that engine to simply "will" your app to succeed is naïve and foolish. As first mentioned in Chapter 2, few companies can build products (not just apps) without the involvement of customers and not face negative consequences. The risk of an app failing is already high for developers who do not incorporate customers into the development process. That risk can be increased, however, by not including customers and then pursuing a huge marketing blitz once an app is approved.

The App Store contains examples of highly polished apps that were created by talented and hard-working developers but that ultimately floundered. The reasons were simple: the developers didn't validate their ideas with their customers and they proceeded with significant marketing launches. By not engaging customers early in the process and then relying on their brands and high-profile contacts to be successful, they ultimately wasted a significant amount of time and money.

If you are working within a larger organization that has a marketing department, I still encourage you to review this material. You should share the ideas in this chapter with your colleagues and work with them to keep your app's development and marketing in sync.

Obviously, attention for your app is a good thing. In fact, your goal will be to see a flurry of excitement when your app is finally approved. The difference is that the core of the excitement for your app should always be generated by customers. Even if your app is reviewed by bloggers and more traditional media outlets, the buzz from those sites will eventually decrease and more likely become nonexistent. Customers who are excited, engaged, and passionate about your app—because of their influence in the development of it—will be the ones who continue to help promote you well after the media is done with their "scoops."

The Best New Way to Market...Doesn't Exist

There's no shortage of people claiming new and "better" ways of marketing. A handful of fads over the past decade, in no particular order, include social media marketing, word-of-mouth marketing, integrated marketing communications (say that three times fast!), search engine marketing, guerrilla marketing, marketing as storytelling, and email marketing. I'll assume for the moment that those who promote these ideas actually believe in them and are not simply trying to profit off the marketing flavor of the month.

Operating under that assumption, what's evident is that practitioners continue to look for new methods of marketing because at some point marketing begins to lose its effectiveness. Consider, for example, the amount of money that has moved from print newspapers, radio, and television to online media such as search engine marketing. I won't provide you with the specific numbers, but as an example, think about all the stories you've heard about newspapers that have shut down, moved online, or cut back to weekly publishing schedules in the past two or three years.

The point is that in this 24/7, always-on world, consumers are more rapidly adapting to—and consequently ignoring—new and existing marketing innovations. Put simply, consumers don't want to be "marketed to" (do you?). They don't have the time or energy to be bothered with marketing...especially uninteresting, boring, or annoying marketing.

Now that you have that context, I'm not going to join in the marketing soup and outline a new theory or philosophy of marketing for you. I'm not even going to suggest that marketing your app is exceptionally different from marketing other types of new products. Instead, I'm going to focus on an extremely tactical marketing process that is proven in the App Store and beyond. As usual, it starts and ends with focusing on your customers.

How to Use This Chapter

This chapter is unique in that I reference it throughout the book. Depending on where you are in the development process, you will continue to revisit this chapter based on my guidance and undertake marketing efforts at the same time your app is being built.

I really want to encourage you not to think about development and marketing tasks as being distinct. Building an app that is driven by customer input will make marketing your app much easier. Conversely, marketing your app—the way it's laid out in this chapter—will give you insight into how to make your app better.

Throughout the book, I specifically direct you to individual phases of the marketing process outlined in this chapter. Still, I recommend that you peruse the remainder of the chapter to be completely familiar with all the elements involved in this process.

Your Marketing Crescendo

It's time for you to get musical. OK, not really. But I want you to grab on to the idea that your marketing efforts should be a *crescendo*. "Crescendo" is a term used in music that indicates a gradual increase in sound and intensity; the music starts soft and then slowly but surely gets significantly louder. The approach you follow for your marketing will be similar. You don't want to start your marketing with a big bang (or people will run away!); rather, you want it to peak in conjunction with your app's progress toward the App Store. Your initial marketing climax should occur when your app finally gets launched into the App Store.

Depending on your goals and the type of app you've built, that initial push may be all you need to achieve your goals. This is especially true if you are building timely or seasonal apps (e.g., a holiday-related app), or if you're pursuing simpler or gimmicky apps. These types of apps have shorter life spans and it's much more important to capitalize on all the buzz possible when the app is first launched. If you're building a more complex app or an app that has long-term value, the initial attention garnered by the launch of your app into the App Store is just the start of the journey. This case, in particular, requires a higher dependence on customers' goodwill post-App Store launch. Customers, and not bloggers or the press, will act as the gatekeepers for whether your app will be sustainable over the long haul.

In the following subsections, I outline the five phases of the marketing process, which correlate to ongoing development tasks. The final two phases are focused on readying for the actual launch of your app. All are referenced from their respective chapters as "marketing checkups."

Phase 1

In Phase 1, you'll further explore using Twitter. Twitter will serve to keep a real-time channel of communication open with the customers you've already interacted with, as well as help you discover new people who could be interested in your app.

You should have visited this section once before, when you were done reading the section "Surveys and the 'social' web" in Chapter 3. You might want to quickly review that section if it's been a while since you read it.

Phase 1 will also ask you to begin tracking what's happening in the iOS development community. You'll develop a reading list of influential thought leaders and start following them on Twitter, while also forming peer relationships through Twitter and elsewhere.

Use Twitter

Marketing your app begins when you first start talking with your customers. One of the channels identified in Chapter 3 that provided your first customers to talk with was Twitter. The Twitter demographic is ideal because it represents a more cutting-edge, early-adopter crowd. As you will shortly see, the value of Twitter extends beyond solely finding customers.

Be useful

> Twitter will be a primary way to engage meaningfully with your customers and keep them informed about what's happening with your app. Even outside the App Store ecosystem, Twitter has become a popular means to answer customer questions, make announcements, and offer special Twitter-only deals (e.g., *http://twitter.com/VirginAmerica*).

Some amount of etiquette is involved in being successful on Twitter. I can summarize much of that for you with some simple advice from Laura Fitton, an author of *Twitter for Dummies* and founder of the Twitter app directory oneforty (*http://oneforty.com*): "Be useful." Don't make Twitter about yourself or your app. Make it about others. Make it about solving your customers' problems, linking to great resources, and sharing practical advice. Being useful will increase the likelihood of people following you on Twitter, which in turn expands your audience and reach.

On that note, you will need to determine the presence you will have on Twitter. Some developers use their personal identities to represent their apps, while others create separate accounts specifically for the app. If you are new to Twitter, I recommend just starting with one account because maintaining that alone will entail some amount of learning. If you go with two accounts, consider whether you will launch more apps in the future. In that case, it's better to make the Twitter username of the "app account" related to your iOS developer name.

Indie developer and college student Jeremy Olson, who created the app Grades, has his own personal Twitter account (*http://twitter.com/jerols/*) and one for his app (*http://twitter.com/gradesapp*). When discussing Grades on his personal account, he mainly uses it to interact with those in the iOS development community. The Grades account, which was created closer to the launch of Grades, is all about news related to Grades, including what other people are saying about it. Visit each account to better understand how they are used. In Jeremy's interview at the end of this chapter, he shares some insights about Twitter, as well as marketing and launching an app.

Twitter clients

Twitter can seem overwhelming if you haven't used it before. One way to deal with those challenges is to find a Twitter client. The benefit of Twitter clients is that they streamline access to Twitter functions such as following a new account, mentioning (also known as "replying to") an account, searching, and composing new tweets. oneforty, the Twitter directory mentioned earlier, has an extensive listing of Twitter clients at *http://oneforty.com/category/Clients*, but I'm also going to share my own preferences.

For my personal account (*http://twitter.com/kenyarmosh*), I use the app Echofon (*http://echofon.com/*) because it syncs my timeline (all of the tweets from the people I follow) across all devices (e.g., Mac, iPhone, and iPad). Like Jeremy and others, I use my personal account to interact with peers and track technology news.

Before my interests in Tweeb were acquired, I also maintained an account for it (*http://twitter.com/tweebapp*). To manage the app account, I used a column-based client called TweetDeck (*http://tweetdeck.com/*). Column-based clients—including TweetDeck, HootSuite, and Seesmic—let you view much more information at once, allowing you to see what your customers are talking about while also keeping an eye on competitors and potential new customers (see Figure 8-1).

Figure 8-1. TweetDeck's columns, which allow you to see much more information at once

Follow your customers

Whether you are using Twitter.com or a Twitter client, you should follow the customers you previously found on Twitter (see Chapter 3). If you decided to have an app-specific account, use that account to follow them. Don't feel bad or stop following them if they don't follow you back. Feel free to reply to them from this account if you have something relevant to contribute.

Follow influencers and peers

Twitter can also be used to track iPhone-related news and interact with peers. By following influencers in the iPhone and mobile community (see Figure 8-2), you'll begin seeing tweets in your timeline that will provide helpful information to build your app and better understand the psyche of the iPhone community. You can usually—but not always—identify influencers by the number of followers they have. You can also check out their bios and timelines to see if their tweets contain information you find useful.

Figure 8-2. Viewing followers, bios, web links, and timelines to discover "influencers"

Beyond using Twitter search to find these types of people (e.g., searching for "iOS 4" and then perusing the accounts for the results returned), two tools I mentioned in Chapter 3 are again useful here: WeFollow and Twiangulate. For example, compare my account with Jeremy's on Twiangulate (*http://twiangulate.com/search/kenyarmosh-jerols/common_friends/table/my_friends-1/*) and you'll see the people in common that we each follow. Once you've found a couple of key influencers, plug them into Twiangulate and your job should become much easier.

You can find peers in pretty much the same way. Peers may not have very large follower counts. If you still consider their tweets interesting, follow them anyway. There's a higher likelihood that peers are going to interact with you on Twitter, so don't just try to cozy up to the "big dogs." You'll most likely want to add influencers and peers to your personal Twitter account (i.e., your nonapp account), to make those interactions less formal.

Keywords

You can save Twitter keyword searches to your account, which allows you to more easily reference them. You can easily import a saved keyword search into a tool such as TweetDeck as a column (you can also create a search column directly in TweetDeck). You'll then have a column dedicated to keywords that are relevant to your app.

For example, in the Tweeb account (@tweebapp), I had a search column for "tweeb" and "Twitter stats" (see Figure 8-1). These keyword searches are related to the features that customers of Tweeb considered important. With this setup, instead of prospecting for customers, they were pushed to me straight from Twitter. I then had the option of either interacting with these prospects right away or continuing to monitor them.

Lists and competitors

Although you will use Twitter to find new prospects and even track competitors, you should to be smart about how you do this. This is where Twitter's *list* feature, and specifically, a "private" list, will be applied.

The idea behind a list is essentially to group a number of Twitter accounts together. When you view this list, you will see all the tweets from those accounts. Again, a nice feature of a tool such as TweetDeck is that you can have an entire column dedicated to a list. By default, a list you create is public and others can see when their accounts are added to it. By marking it as private, that won't be the case. I recommend creating private lists consisting of your competitors and your competitors' most vocal customers. You can discover that latter group by seeing who your customers are mentioning in their tweets, as well as searching for mentions of your competitor (search the "@username" on Twitter or as a search column in your tool).

I also typically create lists to track the biggest advocates of my apps or client apps. Earlier in the process, such as where you are now, I use lists to add people that I'll want to engage later based on what they are tweeting about. So, if you are tracking a particular keyword and an account keeps surfacing, you might want to add that person to a list. Like with competitor lists, I usually keep these lists private. For a somewhat more progressive and public use of lists, check out Jeremy's account (@jerols).

Start reading

Link sharing is very common on Twitter, so with the peer and influencer accounts you are following, you'll receive pointers to lots of technology and iPhone articles. As you continue to visit those links, start either bookmarking the sites you find most informative or adding them to a feed reader such as Google Reader (*http://www.google.com/reader*). You can also visit sites such as Hacker News (*http://news.ycombinator.com/news*), Techmeme (*http://www.techmeme.com*), and Digg.com (*http://digg.com/technology*) to find the most popular community-driven tech articles of the day and subsequently discover new sites of interest. Spend 10 to 15 minutes a day tracking trends and digesting this information, whether from articles shared on Twitter or from your own favorite sources.

I've purposefully not given you Twitter accounts to follow or blogs to read in this section because I want you to find these people and sources yourself. Explore Twitter and the Web extensively and aggressively. Ultimately, you'll develop more natural relationships and learn much more by identifying these people and sources yourself.

Developing a reading list will show you who is important in the iPhone community. It will also identify the types of sites that might want to write about your app when it launches. Getting a sense of these outlets now will prepare you to pitch the most appropriate sites when the time comes.

Keep going

Phase 1 doesn't really "end." You'll continue to rely on Twitter to engage with your early customer community and peers, as well as keep tracking industry developments through your reading. What I've outlined in this section represents a baseline and starting point for you. Over time, you'll develop your own strategies and the best ways to leverage these resources for you and your app.

Phase 2

In Phase 2, you'll open another channel to communicate with customers and begin further enticing them with the vision behind your app. At this phase in the process, you still won't have a working app and will likely only have some branding and logo assets at your disposal. Despite these limitations, Phase 2 will help you lay the foundation for your email marketing efforts and web presence.

You should have visited this section once before, when you were done reading the "Translating wireframes to screens" section in Chapter 5. You might want to quickly review that section if it's been a while since you read it.

Email marketing

With my focus on Twitter, email marketing may feel a little dated. But it still represents one of the best ways to broadcast information very quickly to a large and diverse audience. This last part is important, because although Twitter is becoming prevalent, it still is used more heavily by early adopters than it is by the general public. Comparatively, most people online today have an email address, meaning that email marketing will be useful to a larger number of customers or at least a different type of customer.

Recall that early in your app's existence, interacting with "earlyvangelist" customers (see the "Traits of the right customer" section in Chapter 3) is preferable. These customers will endure the early hiccups of your app and stick with you because they'll believe your app is going to solve their problems better than anything else. These types of customers will get you only so far, though. Although they'll likely be your first paying customers, reaching *normals* will also be important.[1] These are the people who are potentially outside the reaches of Twitter, the blogosphere, and the tech community you've immersed yourself in up to now. If your customer discovery process produced many referrals for you, it's possible that these types of people consist more highly of normals than earlyvangelists. The point here is that email marketing will provide a more universal means to communicate with all types of customers.

You don't necessarily have to use an email marketing tool, but such a tool provides a number of advantages over email itself. Aside from basics, such as ensuring that your emails will get past spam filtering and helping manage your email list, one of the greatest advantages of email marketing tools is reporting. When sending an email, you'll be able to see the delivery and *open rates* (how often people actually open the email) of the email, monitor unsubscribes (i.e., when people decide they no longer want to be on your email list), and later, even track clicks to your website. This data will inform

---

1 See "Techies and normals," at *http://cdixon.org/2010/01/22/techies-and-normals/*.

you of the effectiveness of your outreach and what ideas and concepts are or are not resonating with your customers.

At a more fundamental level, however, your goal at this point will be to capture email addresses as you did with surveys. Most tools will provide you with a form to embed on your website (see Figure 8-3). This form will collect an email address from a visitor and allow you to later use it when you are ready to starting send email newsletters. Popular email marketing tools include MailChimp (*http://www.mailchimp.com/*), Campaign Monitor (*http://www.campaignmonitor.com/*), and Constant Contact (*http://www. constantcontact.com/*).

Figure 8-3. Email capture for Robocat's Rouse iPad app

"Splash" and landing pages

To place a form for visitors to fill out on a website or web page, you'll need to have a website or web page. At this point, however, this page really won't include much more than a basic graphic, some language that describes your app, and a form to capture emails.

These types of pages are often called *splash pages* or *landing pages* and their aim is to cast your app's vision and pique interest early in the development process (recall that a *splash screen* is the first screen in your app). They can also be used to test ideas about an app. For example, you might want to get a sense of what features are intriguing customers the most or even inquire about price points on the splash page through a poll. Overall, though, you'll want to focus the main action on capturing email addresses.

If you don't have any web experience, someone on your team likely does. You can also look for web designers in the same sorts of places you may have looked for designers to build your app (see Chapter 4). If you are more of a self-starter, you might want to try tools such as Unbounce (*http://unbounce. com/*), which provides visual editors to quickly build and publish splash or landing pages; in other words, you won't have to know HTML to use Unbounce. You can also take advantage of such tools' email capture functionality, which will allow you to easily access captured email addresses and import them into your email marketing platform. The splash page shown in Figure 8-4 is for Instagram, a life-sharing app for the iPhone. I'll show you my first splash page for Tweeb shortly.

It's best to publish your splash page on the same domain on which your website will exist. Doing this will help you in a number of ways, including getting your domain indexed earlier by search engines and keeping customers familiar with the website for your app. This approach will provide a good foundation for your eventual website.

Figure 8-4. Instagram splash page

Advertising your splash page

You're still not looking to draw the attention of the world to your app, but bringing some visibility to your splash page is going to be beneficial to you. First, you want to grow your list of email addresses. Second, you may want to infuse new perspectives into the development of your app. The email addresses you receive will likely include more normals, and you may want to contact them about what compelled them to learn more about your app.

The first way to bring attention to your splash page is to tweet the link to your followers on Twitter. Even if you have the email addresses of some of these people, unless you specifically received permission to keep them informed about your app, you should not automatically add them to your email list. After you tweet the link, those who visit your splash page will decide if they also want to sign up to receive emails about your app or continue to remain updated through Twitter.

> At the time of this writing, Twitter had just begun to explore its advertising model through what it calls "Promoted Tweets." Initially, this will allow advertisers to show up on the top of the search results page by buying related keywords. Watch Twitter in this space, as it could become another valuable advertising channel.

Chapter 3 also reviewed paid advertising through Google AdWords or Facebook. Both choices offer cost-effective ways to bring targeted traffic to your splash page. Depending on your app's focus, even a budget of $5 to $15 a day could help you get some traction for your splash page.

Phase 3

When you first begin Phase 3 of your marketing crescendo, you'll be in the midst of building your working app. At this point, you should have actual assets of your app, including screens for it. You'll use these assets to spur new interest, and will use them along with an eventually more complete version of your app to recruit beta testers (as discussed in Chapter 6).

You should have visited this section once before, when you were done reading the "Screens and Prototypes" section in Chapter 5. You might want to quickly review that section if it's been a while since you read it.

Splash Page Example

Since Tweeb is a Twitter app, I decided to focus exclusively on Twitter during Phase 2. Thus, I did not place an email sign-up form on the splash page when I launched it. Instead, I used my personal Twitter account to announce the splash page and Tweeb Twitter account (see Figure 8-5).

The initial splash page was placed on the Tweeb domain—*http://www.tweebapp. com*—and reflected the colors, font styles, and logo of the app. Even though the splash page was very basic, visitors got an initial sense of what the app was about and understood the attention to design detail through those elements. The background for the Twitter account was created to match the splash page (see Figure 8-6), which reinforced the app's branding.

Figure 8-5. Tweeb splash page with no email sign-up form

Figure 8-6. The background of the Tweeb Twitter account, which matched the splash page branding

Screenshot "sneak peeks"

The idea of teasers is not new. It happens often in the media, and most times it's done to help build frenzy about what is to come. The key about teasers is to keep people wanting more. You want to get them interested and excited, but not satisfied. They need to be kept curious, or you'll displace all of the anticipation that you are trying to create.

Since people are visual beings, when it comes to adapting teasers in the app world, text alone won't be particularly exhilarating. Instead, you'll want to focus on sharing pieces of the most finished designs of your app. In fact, keeping what you distribute almost entirely visual and not describing what it actually is will promote even more curiosity.

Mike Rundle (*http://flyosity.com*), a designer/developer and creator of the app Digital Post, did exactly that when he gave his followers a "sneak peek" (see Figure 8-7) of the iPad version of his app leading up to the launch of the iPad and the iPad App Store. As you can see, it was a simple yet captivating image, and he didn't provide many more details about it at that point.

Figure 8-7. Mike Rundle's sneak peek at Digital Post for his followers on Twitter

Start blogging

Twitter is a great place to share sneak peek designs from your in-progress app, but you'll want to start leveraging those assets in other places too. Up to now, you've only created a splash page for your app, and it's time to start expanding your web presence.

Blogs are another way to interact with existing and new customers. Obviously, whereas a sneak peek is focused on design, a blog is more about written content. The benefit of content is that search engines rely on it to index your site. So, when someone searches on a related keyword, aside from other important factors such as having your site linked to, your site absolutely cannot be shown as a search result (see Figure 8-8) if you don't have any quality content on your site.

There's no better way to start blogging than to start blogging. You'll pick up good tips along the way, but it's more important to get content published onto your blog than it is for you to know every blogging tip and trick in existence. If you have an existing blog or website and your app is going to have a separate page (or pages) on your site, you can use that blog to start discussing your app. Otherwise, consider using tools such as WordPress, Posterous, or Tumblr to get your blog started. If you want your blog to more seamlessly integrate with your splash page and website (which I recommend), take advantage of the custom domain options offered by some of these tools (e.g., *http://blog.<yourappdomain>.com*), have your blog reflect a design similar to that of your splash page, and possibly even use the self-hosted version of a tool such as WordPress (i.e., use *http://wordpress.org* instead of *http://wordpress.com*). A great first post on your blog can include some basic background about what your app will be about, incorporating the designs you just shared.

Don't proceed with the next section until your app is ready to be distributed to your customers for testing, which will occur by the time you get to Chapter 6. You'll be guided back here once that is the case.

Figure 8-8. Tweeb ranking highly in Google Search results due to the keywords associated with the site

Recruit beta testers

As with all customer interactions, recruiting those to beta-test your application is definitely a marketing activity. Beta testing will be the first time customers actually experience your application. You'll want to set the tone for the purpose of beta testing and guide them in how they can be most helpful.

By now, you should have a minimum of three channels to recruit beta testers: Twitter, your email newsletter list, and your blog. You should use all three sources to recruit beta testers. To reach those on Twitter, the best approach is to create a post on your blog and then link to it from a tweet. Your post should include the objective of your beta testing (e.g., testing a specific feature), the OS and device requirements (e.g., iPhone 3GS running iOS 4), some background on providing their UDID (see the section "UDID" and Figure 6-1 on page 184), how they should sign up (e.g., sending an email or filling out a form; see Figure 8-9), and how public you want this part of the beta testing to be.

Figure 8-9. Tweeb beta form to collect customer and device information

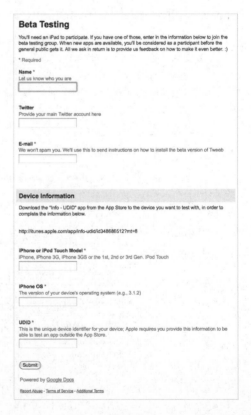

Depending on how far along you are in the development of your app, you may want to request that your beta testers not extensively discuss your app online. For example, you could ask that they not post screenshots of the app or write blog posts about it. Don't be overbearing, but definitely articulate what makes you most comfortable. You can become more flexible about what they share online the closer your app is to being submitted and approved into the App Store.

Initial email outreach

With the design assets from your sneak peeks and the written content from your blog completed, you should begin sending out updates regularly to your email newsletter list. Always try to repurpose content you create elsewhere. What you include in the email newsletter should derive from what you post on Twitter and your blog.

Although there may be some overlap among those who get your emails and follow your blog and Twitter account, recall that email is in many ways reaching a different audience. You can also make your emails act as summaries of what's happening elsewhere, with links back to blog posts, Twitter, or your website.

Don't use your email list to recruit your *earliest* beta testers. Again, although I'm generalizing, think about your email list customers as being slightly less tech savvy, with less patience for an app that's still not ready for prime time. As you near completion of the App Store version of your app and want some fresh perspectives, definitely consider including a request for beta testers through your email newsletter list; just don't make this the primary motivation for the email.

Phase 4

In Phase 4, you'll begin to transition to a "launch" mindset. Most of the development efforts for your app should be wrapping up and you either will have submitted or will be in the process of submitting your app to Apple for approval. Compared to other phases, the timing and execution of Phase 4 and Phase 5 marketing activities are much more critical. Be diligent with them so that you can maximize the buzz you generate around your app when it is approved.

You should have visited this section once before, when you were done reading the section "Your App Store App 'Binary'" in Chapter 7. You might want to quickly review that section if it's been a while since you read it.

Launch content

Write the launch content for when your app is approved. Starting with this content now—even though it's not needed yet—will put you in a launch mindset. It will also make it easier to focus on other critical tasks once your app is approved.

Your launch content includes your more significant blog post announcement and email newsletter, as well as the content for your website. Discuss what makes your app interesting, what features you are planning to add going forward, and how you are planning to incorporate customer feedback (e.g., point to your Twitter account and other designated feedback or support channels). I'll detail what you need for your website and what web content you need now.

Website

The website for your app has already evolved from being a splash page with an email sign-up form to include a blog. You are now going to prepare the remainder of your website assets, which will be used in both Phase 4 and Phase 5 of your marketing crescendo, as well as post-launch. As with your app, splash page, and blog, you might not be doing the design of the website yourself, but this information will help you guide its development.

Designing an app website has some unique elements to it. As with your app, it has to embody Apple-like design and attention to detail. The best app sites are also extensions of an app, almost giving a sense of being in the app itself. I'm including a couple of examples of well-designed app websites in Figures 8-10 and 8-11 and will subsequently review the common elements of them; refer back to these examples as needed.

Figure 8-10. The website for my app, AudioBookShelf

Figure 8-11. The Postman app website, another example showcasing common elements

Structure

Because you won't be unveiling your entire website at once, the most important aspect for you to address right now is its structure. You should build your site in such a way that it will be easy to roll out its new sections and features through Phase 4, Phase 5, and beyond. In fact, the smartest way to approach building your pre- and post-launch website is to build the post-launch website first and then remove elements from it until your app is approved into the App Store.

For example, in Figure 8-11, you can see an area of the page that's dedicated to press quotes. You won't have any quotes when your app website is in pre-launch mode. Similarly, you may not want to have any screenshots of your app available until after your app is approved.

To simplify thinking about the different stages of your website's existence, consider this progression:

1. Splash page
2. Splash page plus blog
3. Pre-launch website
4. Post-launch website

You've already implemented the first two stages. I'll cover the remaining elements of the last two stages of your app website in the order in which they'll be needed.

Pre-launch website

Device

App websites typically have an actual or close approximate of a device (i.e., iPhone or iPad) in a prominent place on the page. Later, the screen of the device will come to house your app in action (e.g., a video). In the early stages, however, it could just include the splash screen for your app or even a logo.

The device image is one of the first elements you'll want on the page because it immediately communicates that your website is about an app. It's possible your splash page already had a device image; if not, include one on your pre-launch website.

Teaser text

Include some crafty verbiage about your upcoming app that teases out its concept. For example, Tweeb's teaser text read, "Introducing a new way to track your Twitter account. Exclusively for the iPhone." You should provide some language that it's "coming soon." This text might represent the bulk of the content that you include on the pre-launch website. Consider replacing or adding text underneath it later with more background and description about your app.

Social media links

Link to your blog, Twitter, and other social media presences from your pre-launch site. I haven't covered Facebook in detail, but that is another outlet you may want to consider using (learn about Facebook Pages at *http://www.facebook.com/advertising/?pages*). Usually, these are placed in the header or footer (top or bottom) of the page. Make them easier to discover by using icons to represent the links.

Email sign-up

Your email sign-up form should still also be present on your pre-launch website. Compared to your splash page, it should not be as highly promoted (see Figure 8-12).

Figure 8-12. Tapbots' clever integration of the email sign-up form at the bottom of the site

About and contact pages

Make it easy for people to learn more about you or to get in touch. You can create separate "about" and "contact" pages to include this information, or for now, incorporate it on the same page. If your app or apps gain more prominence over time, you will likely want separate pages detailing this information. For example, your contact page might distinguish between questions about how your app works and feature requests.

Don't forget to include web analytics on your site so that you can understand traffic sources and how people are using the site. Install a solution such as Google Analytics (*http://www.google.com/analytics*), which is free, easy to use, and powerful.

Post-launch website

To reiterate, you won't be flipping the switch on your post-launch website until after your app is approved. Building the pre- and post-launch websites at the same time will streamline this process, though. As mentioned earlier, you should think about the pre-launch website as the skeleton of the post-launch website, meaning that it contains all aspects of the final site minus the more thorough post-launch details.

Device image revisited

Once your app is approved, your post-launch website should make your app feel "alive" by inserting more than just a static splash screen into the device image. The two most common ways to do that are either to cycle through the images in a slideshow fashion inside the device or to integrate a video. Keep the video short and with either concise dialogue or no narration and some catchy, upbeat music. Consider using a tool such as SimFinger to make it even better (*http://github.com/atebits/SimFinger*).

This may be confusing to you, but it won't be to a web designer. Creating a video takes a little more effort, but it can be of tremendous value when you begin pitching your app.

Features/description

At this point, you should know the most compelling features of your app and have your launch content and preliminary or final application description (for the App Store) at your disposal. Use these assets to include more details about your app on the website. Start with some brief narrative content, but err on the side of bulleting the key features of the app. You can usually place this type of content under your teaser text. It's also good to include the operating system and device requirements of your app at the bottom of this area.

Price tag

If you consider your price a key part of your strategy, or if your app is priced competitively, you might want to include a price tag on the page. You can always change this later. Regarding this point, since you will be looking for the optimal price of your app and may be adjusting your price often, be mindful that you'll want to update this element.

App Store button

If you've viewed any number of app websites, you've probably seen Apple's Available on the App Store buttons. Include one of those buttons, edited to match the color scheme of your app and the website, for branding purposes. In all likelihood, Apple's App Store will be better-known than your app when it first launches. Position this button close to where your app is located. Some developers also opt for a Buy Now button instead (see Figure 8-13).

Figure 8-13. App Store buttons for the apps Digital Post, Pastebot, and Outside, from standard to custom

Additional screenshots

Under your device image, place thumbnail images that, when clicked, expand to show an entire screen of your app. Although visitors to your site might view the image slideshow or video, they may want to explore these screens more thoroughly and at their own leisure.

Media and customer quotes

Designate an area for quotes from bloggers, the press, and customers. This last group is important, because even if your app is not initially reviewed by those in the media, it's possible that you'll receive App Store reviews or write-ups on customer blogs. Consider including two or three quotes and use well-known names and brands if you have them.

What's new

> Highlight the latest update (e.g., v1.0.1) and the release date (e.g., 10/30/10) of your app and any critical fixes or key new features added. Not only is this useful information, but it will also show visitors that you are maintaining the app.

FAQs/support

> Creating a page that is completely dedicated to frequently asked questions about your app will help you and your customers. You can initially launch this page with the questions customers asked you during beta testing or with questions you think will be common. Whether you have a FAQ page or not, be sure to highlight the best way for customers to get in touch with you about problems they are having with your app (this information could also be placed on the contact page). That might include a dedicated support email address, your app's Twitter account, a support tool you implemented in Chapter 5, or all three.

Remember that within your apps, you will have only a limited amount of space dedicated to helping customers with questions and engaging them more extensively. Take full advantage of Twitter, email, your blog, and your website to supplement this limitation.

Media outreach

Your media outreach is going to be the most time-sensitive part of getting your marketing crescendo to work. I can tell you from personal experience that beginning to do outreach too early, as well as too late, can very negatively impact your marketing plans. So, like Goldilocks, you've got to make your timing be "just right."

The purpose of media outreach is to find websites that could be interested in doing a review about you or your app. I include "you" because with the number of apps being pitched for review every day, having some interesting backstory about the app can help differentiate you from others. For example, in the earliest days of the App Store, the media loved Steve Demeter, creator of the highly successful game Trism, not only because of the game's sales numbers ($250,000 in two months) but also because he initially worked on the game at night while maintaining his day job. Backstories are a little more important for larger or more traditional media outlets such as newspapers, so don't overplay them. Here are some details of whom to pitch, how to pitch, and when to pitch:

Whom to pitch

With your Twitter community humming and the reading list you developed in the early marketing phases, you should have a pretty good handle on the types of outlets and people you'll want to pitch. Realize, however, that most people are probably pitching the same blogs and sites you are. That doesn't mean you should forgo those sites; instead, broaden your horizons to people, blogs, and sites outside the most typical ones. These may include smaller blogs that your peers or even customers have.

One way to find media outlets outside of those you are currently familiar with is to use search engines to identify those writing about features related to your app. More specifically, sites such as Google News are article-based and will return stories and blog posts rather than more generalized results. When you find a relevant article, look at the person who wrote it and track down an email address. If it's not listed there, you can also Google the person's name. Make sure you bookmark what this person wrote; I'll come back to how that's useful in a moment.

A good way to think about whom to pitch is to break down your list of outlets in two ways. The first is by likelihood of receiving a review (e.g., unlikely, probable, or definite). If you see that all of your sites are part of the "unlikely" category, you need to diversify. The second way to group your list is by reviewer type. You should not focus only on sites that review apps, but also on ones that are interested in what your app is about. For example, with Tweeb, my nonapp pitches were to people and sites who wrote about social media, Twitter, and analytics. That landed me three reviews on very reputable sites (SocialTimes, ReadWriteWeb, and Twitterrati), which are not extremely app-focused.

How to pitch

For your pitches, you are going to reuse many of the assets developed for your pre- and post-launch websites. This includes your teaser text, a brief description about features, screenshots, and a video, if you have one. If you are still sending pitches after your app is approved and in the store—which you should do—also include your iTunes URL and a promo code (promo codes and a useful promo code trick are discussed in "Launching Your App (Phase 5)"). If your app is not approved yet, which is the more likely scenario at this point, having a video will be particularly useful.

As with other types of outreach, I prefer to use templates for pitches. To be more effective, however, you will customize the first part of your template based on whom you are pitching. So, for example, use some context from an article or post someone wrote; that's where the bookmark to the person's writing comes into play.

Here's an email template I used while pitching Tweeb. It received a 60% success rate during my initial outreach. The customized part of the template is in **bold italics**, and although it's true, you can see it was fairly generic.

> ***Been reading your stuff for many years now***. I wanted to drop you a note about my latest iPhone app "Tweeb." It's focused exclusively on Twitter stats and includes click data from *bit.ly/j.mp* links shared in tweets.
>
> Would love for you to check it out. Feel free to drop me a line with any feedback.
>
> **Blog Post**
>
> *http://kenyarmosh.com/tweeb-twitter-analytics-for-the-iphone/*
>
> **Tweeb Links**
>
> *http://www.tweebapp.com*
>
> *@tweebapp*

The template is short and sweet. You may want to add attachments such as your screenshots or a link to your video. If your video is not live on your app website, you can either put it on a nonpublicized directory/URL or host it on YouTube or Vimeo. Arnold Kim, the proprietor of the largest iPhone game review site on the Web—TouchArcade.com—discusses the importance of videos and how best to pitch review sites in an interview at the end of this chapter.

When to pitch

There are different perspectives on how far in advance you should make your pitch. I recommend that you do so about one or two weeks before you hope for your app to be approved. This time frame is more important for larger sites, which are typically bombarded by review requests and often have editorial schedules to follow.

Making this timing "just right" is yet another example of the importance of intertwining your development and marketing efforts. You'll need to have a firm handle on how close your app is to being "App Store ready," when you plan to submit it to Apple, and how long the approval process is currently taking. Knowing this information will help you estimate when you are one to two weeks away from having your app in the store. Be careful, however, because your first time through the App Store approval process may result in a rejection.

Another tip on when to pitch is that you should stay away from making contact with the larger media outlets at the beginning of the week, and in particular, on Monday and Tuesday. Thursday and Friday have less volume; if you are a night owl or workaholic, try pitching on a Friday night or over the weekend. You may not receive a response as quickly, but I find that the response rates are higher.

Compared to many others who are pitching for reviews, you should have an immediate advantage given the approach you've taken to building your app. Your app should be considerably more useful and interesting than apps that weren't validated by customers. The media, in general, don't write scathing reviews unless they want to mock an app that is horribly embarrassing. That's not to imply that they won't have criticisms about your app, because they will. The point is that they want to write about apps that are unique, are creative, are well done, are supported by communities, and give them a story.

As for those who show interest in writing about your app, you will want to try to time their reviews, as well as all reviews, with the approval of your app into the App Store. You can let them know you'll follow up with them when the app is approved. If they are excited about it, however, don't hold them back if they want to write about it immediately. By receiving a review before your app is live, you'll be able to leverage it as confirmation of your efforts. You'll also be able to tweet a link to the review and select a quote from the review or article to use in your App Store description and on your website.

Launching Your App (Phase 5)

No, I didn't forget Phase 5. The actual launch of your app is significant enough that it deserves to be called out separately. The nice thing about Phase 5 is that with all the work you've done through the first four phases, the majority of what you'll be doing once your app is approved will mostly feel like quickly checking items off a to-do list. Yes, there's actually a method to the madness!

Promo Codes

If you have a paid app, you'll want to use promo codes to distribute promotional (i.e., free) copies of your app. Although many people don't realize this, promo codes are useful even if you have a free app, so keep reading.

I'm addressing promo codes outside of what I call the "launch checklist" because there's a little-known aspect of them that can help people preview your app before it's technically available on the App Store.

The iTunes Connect home page includes an area called Request Promotional Codes (see Figure 8-14). You'll visit this link to get up to 50 promo codes. In reality, that's not many, so be somewhat selective with who receives one of them. Also, reserve about 5 to 10 of these codes for your most loyal and helpful beta testers.

There are a number of stipulations about the use of promo codes, including that they can be redeemed only one time, are valid only in the U.S. App Store, and will expire after 28 days. You will, however, get another 50 codes for the app once an update is submitted.

Figure 8-14. Requesting promotional codes

Redeeming promo codes is a somewhat tedious process, but there's a nice trick—uncovered by tap tap tap—to make them easier to redeem and distribute. Give out a URL such as the following: *https://phobos.apple.com/ WebObjects/MZFinance.woa/wa/freeProductCodeWizard?code=REPLACE WITHPROMOCODE*, where "REPLACEWITHPROMOCODE" should be replaced with the actual promo code. When sharing promo codes, always use this method.

One final tip about promo codes, which makes them useful for paid as well as free apps, is that if your app has been approved but you have not yet made it available on the App Store, you can create promo codes and have people download your app using them. That's useful for reviewers who may have only seen a video or screenshot of your app but want to experience it firsthand before it's in the App Store (note that more technical reviewers may also be OK with the ad hoc distribution process described in Chapter 6).

There's another way to get paid apps in people's hands for free once your app is released: Gift This App, which I will cover in the next section.

Launch Checklist

As mentioned before (see the "App Store Approval Process" section in Chapter 7), once your app has reached the Ready for Sale status you'll have the option of launching it into the App Store. Or if your Availability Date has already lapsed, your app will automatically be published to the App Store shortly. In either case, when your app is set to be published into the App Store, it will likely take some time—usually several hours—before it begins appearing there. These first items are what you should complete during that time. I'll then detail a second set of tasks to finish once the app is actually showing in the store.

Notify key media contacts

Notify key media contacts who agreed to review or write about your app that the app has been approved. These contacts should receive promo copies of your app. So, send them the promo code link in your email.

Deploy post-launch website

> With your app's entry in the App Store imminent, you should push your post-launch website live. One piece of information that you were previously missing was the iTunes link to your app. You'll find this link in the approval email Apple sent you next to your Application Name. Copy this link and use it for your App Store or Buy Now button. If you really want to be savvy, sign up as an iTunes affiliate (*http://www.apple.com/itunes/affiliates/*)—powered by LinkShare—and use the URL generated to earn an additional 5% from any apps that are sold by clicking on that link.

Publish blog post

> Publish the announcement blog post about your app being approved. You won't publicize your post on Twitter or other channels until the app is showing in the App Store.

Some people advocate issuing a formal, paid press release. Although this varies according to the audience you're targeting, I find that they generally are not worth what they cost. Consider a "social media release" as an alternative. You can read "How to Write a Social Media Press Release" (*http://www.copyblogger.com/social-media-press-release/*) or try a nifty tool called PressDoc (*http://pressdoc.com/*).

After your app is available on the App Store, proceed with the remaining launch checklist items:

Notify other contacts

> Continue to reach out to other contacts (family, friends, colleagues, customers, reviewers, etc.) after your app is live in the App Store. Provide promo code links to your most engaged customers as a sign of thanks for their help.

Get ratings and reviews

> When you email your friendly contacts (including family, friends, and customers), ask them to rate and review your app on the App Store. They'll need to have downloaded or purchased the app to write a review. As a reminder, a review consists of both a star rating (from one to five stars) and a written description.

You'll need a combination of five ratings or reviews for your app before the Ratings will show any stars. People visiting your App Store listing will definitely look at this area, especially if your app is not free or is priced more aggressively. Getting friendly ratings and reviews in early will get you started in the right direction. If you are a purist and wonder if this move is "cheating," don't worry; if your app is bad or hurting, you'll hear about it.

Adjust App Store description and website

If there are any early favorable web or App Store reviews, snag quotes and highlight them on your website and in your App Store description. For the App Store description, place these quotes near the top, with the most popular names first.

Tweet it up

Tweet a link to your app's App Store listing and your initial blog post. If you really want people to read the blog post, ensure that it has a link to your app on the App Store and only tweet the link to your blog post.

Send email newsletter

Finally, once you've completed the preceding steps, announce the launch of your app to your email newsletter subscribers (see Figure 8-15). Try to reuse the content from your blog post or just introduce it and then link over to your blog. Be sure to include a link to your app on the App Store in your email newsletter.

Figure 8-15. Robocat's Outside 1.1 newsletter update

Additional Promotion

After the initial buzz for your app has settled, you should do some additional promotion. In fact, the first 30 days of being on the App Store are critical for the long-term viability of your app. There are a number of ways to keep people interested. For instance, you can and should continue to pitch bloggers and media outlets and get additional press for your app. Although I recommend that you come up with your own creative approaches, here are some proven ways to get additional promotion for your app:

App giveaways

> One way to make it more appealing for app review sites to take a look at your app is to offer to conduct an app giveaway for their readers. In this case, you're providing them promo codes, which they subsequently will decide how to distribute to their readers based on something a reader must do (e.g., follow the review site's Twitter account and then tweet a link to the review). Promo codes are precious commodities, though, so don't send these over until someone has agreed to do an app giveaway with you.

Gift This App

> A newer feature that Apple introduced into iTunes is called Gift This App. As you now know, you get only 50 promo codes; the Gift This App feature can help overcome that limitation. The added benefit to this approach is that you can use it in conjunction with further growing your email list, since gifting requires that you know the email of the recipient. You could create a page on your website dedicated to this promotion (e.g., the first *X* people to subscribe to our newsletter get a free copy of our app), or use one of the tools covered in Chapter 3, such as Google Docs, Wufoo, or Unbounce, to do something similar.

> Initially, Gift This App might seem expensive to you. For example, if your app costs just $0.99, it would cost you $1,000 to gift 1,000 copies of it. Remember, though, that you'll get 70% of each sale back. So, it actually would only cost you $300 to gift 1,000 copies. Because of the time constraints for giving away that many copies at once, you probably won't proceed with such a large promotion—but the point still stands.

The Gift This App option is a powerful and cost-effective tool for you to buy goodwill and grow one of your key communication channels. By the way, this feature does not impact ranking, so don't try to buy your way up the charts.

Contests

As you saw, Gift This App is a way to conduct a contest. In the preceding example, there were multiple winners and the "prize" was a free copy of your app. Contests, though, are an area where you can get really creative. Some contests occur over a period of days or weeks and involve multiple steps, such as following a Twitter account and tweeting about joining the contest. The prizes for some contests involve winning much more expensive items, such as iPads or even computers.

Develop your contest around a goal and budget. If you want more followers for your Twitter account, focus on providing an easy way to do that while verifying that it occurs. You also don't have to spend a large amount of money to make a contest successful. Your prize might be related to your app. If your app is focused on productivity, consider your prize to be a new bestselling business book. I generally recommend creating contests in which there are more prizes that cost less, yielding a greater opportunity for more people to win.

If you do proceed with a contest, clearly set the guidelines either on the page or with a link to them. The guidelines should include what constitutes entering, prize details, the length of the contest, and other limits and liabilities (e.g., no more than one entry per person).

Promotional pricing

Offering a temporary promotional price for your app can be a way to infuse activity back into your app. You can automatically start and end promotional pricing periods using the Price Tier Effective Date and Price Tier End Date, described in Chapter 7.

One of the immediate benefits of changing your price is that there are a number of sites and Twitter accounts that watch for price drops. They'll automatically post your price drop, with your app's App Store link, when your promotional pricing period goes into effect.

Dropping your price typically makes sense when you have a major update coming, are celebrating or trying to spur an event (e.g., getting to 500 Twitter followers or 1,000 sales), or are about to release a new app. You should also experiment with different prices throughout the week and during holidays, because general trends are that downloads increase 10% to 20% through the weekend and spike even higher during holidays.

Cross-app promotions

One concept I touched on in Chapter 1 is that you increase your chances of being successful with future apps once you've released your first app. That's even truer if that app has gotten some attention and buzz and helped make a name for you. Not only will customers be excited for other apps you are working on, but you'll also have the opportunity to use your most popular apps to cross-promote those new ones.

There are a couple of more common ways to do cross-app promotions, and you'll often find that they are combined. A more basic approach is to run an advertisement in your most popular app that promotes your newest app, linking to it in the App Store. Some developers use their own advertising framework to accomplish the cross-promotion of their own apps, but AdMob's AdWhirl and other third-party advertising options can also help with that integration (see Figure 8-16).

Figure 8-16. Harbor Master HD's cross-promotion of other Imangi iPhone games

A more aggressive cross-app promotion is to make one app free. When Imangi Studios launched the Harbor Master HD iPad version of its popular iPhone app Harbor Master it decided to make it free. It then cross-promoted its iPhone games, including Harbor Master and Hippo High Dive (see Figure 8-16). Its strategy can be considered doing a promotional "price" of free combined with cross-app promotion.

Mobile advertising

Leveraging mobile advertising to increase exposure for your app is definitely something to explore. You can run campaigns on mobile ad networks to drive awareness and, ultimately, more downloads for your app. Tapjoy also offers an innovative "pay per install" model, whereby you set the price you are willing to pay for someone to install your app (*http://tapjoy.com/Company/AboutPPI/*). Of course, you need to be smart about how you use these options; spending money makes sense only if it helps you achieve your goals or, at the very least, allows you to break even.

Networks

A popular approach, for games in particular, is to have your app be part of a "network." Imangi Studios—the creator of Harbor Master—is part of a network called App Treasures (*http://www.apptreasures.com/*), which consists of a number of small, independent game developers. Each app in this network contains an area dedicated to promoting the apps of all members of the network. Mentioned in Chapter 2, larger options in the game space include Plus+ (*http://plusplus.com/*) and OpenFeint (*http://www.openfeint.com/*), which also provide tools for game developers.

The lack of formalized networks for other categories is actually an opportunity for you. Seek out apps complementary to yours, or talk with your colleagues in the development community and explore forming your own network. This will give you another channel through which to promote your app and further strengthen your ties with peers.

Local media

Like smaller review sites and less popular bloggers, local media outlets are often ignored. With everyone clambering to get attention with app review sites and nationally known publications, you'll have significantly less, and possibly no, competition for your local community news sites. If your city or town also has a local print publication, pitching to it may also mean your name winds up in print. Remember that you are still in a relatively new industry, and that although iPhone or iPad stories are a dime a dozen in larger publications, it could represent a scoop for a local news outlet.

Obviously, much of what is covered in this chapter is useful beyond the pre-launch and immediate post-launch of your app. You can consider adopting many of these same principles and processes throughout the existence of your app, whether for a simple update or for a more significant release.

Tweeb Buzz

Although Tweeb launched into the App Store as a pre-release app (v0.9), it still received buzz from several reputable outlets, including Social Times, Twitterrati, and ReadWriteWeb, as outlined in the following list. Realize that most apps go into the App Store as v1.0, and my plan was unique to my strategy with the app (recall that my interests in Tweeb were acquired in June 2010).

Social Times

"Tweeb: Twitter Analytics for the iPhone" (*http://www.socialtimes.com/2010/02/ tweeb-twitter-analytics/*)

Twitterrati

"Tweeb: Analytics and Stats for Twitter" (*http://www.twitterrati.com/2010/04/02/ tweeb-analytics-and-stats-for-twitter/*)

ReadWriteWeb

"Weekend Fun: New Apps for Your iPhone" (*http://www.readwriteweb.com/ archives/weekend_fun_new_apps_for_your_iphone.php*)

Interviews

tap tap tap: Phill Ryu

COMPANY: tap tap tap

POSITION: Partner

BACKGROUND: Phill Ryu is part of the leadership team at tap tap tap and MacHeist. He co-created the bestselling app Classics, and when he's not cooking up cool app ideas, he's cooking up ways to craftily get those apps into customers' hands.

LINKS: *http://taptaptap.com/; http://www.macheist.com/*

Ken: *The folks at tap tap tap have been in the Apple world for quite some time. Is familiarity with the Apple mindset and way of doing things a key part of making it on the App Store?*

Phill: It may be the most important single part of making it in the App Store. Apple has worked extremely hard over the years to create a strong culture of high standards, in UI design, user experience, and marketing and launching products, and you can see how that culture affects every inch of their product line. It's similar with iPhone app development—there are apps you can just take a glance at and realize, yeah, these developers have grown up adoring Apple culture and ideals, and these apps will tend to do very well. They have the "special sauce" down.

Ken: *Having been on the App Store since the beginning, what are the major differences with it now compared to then, and how has that influenced how you approach building and releasing iPhone apps?*

Phill: The major difference is it's a much larger, more mature market, which means more customers to potentially reach, but also more intense competition, and more possibilities to just get lost in the crowd.

This is where some critical mass, whether it is through a powerful, growing brand or a fan base, can provide some level of insurance. We've accrued some of this over the years, so one thing we're doing now that we weren't doing then is working with some developers to help them hedge their app launches when we see an app that really deserves success.

Ken: *You've had an incredible number of hits to this point, including WhereTo, Classics, Convert, and Voices. How have you been able to ensure that you weren't a "one-hit wonder"? What do you consider the core elements for creating a successful app?*

Phill: There's just one very important question I like to ask myself before diving into a project: "How big is the vacuum?"

This will answer pretty much all your questions; the bigger the vacuum, the better. You can find vacuums of all sorts in the App Store if you look around. There might be a quality vacuum in a certain popular app genre, a vacuum of developers leveraging free for their paid app sales, or a vacuum of booby apps because Apple just removed a ton of them. There are always vacuums, and vacuums are the easiest things to fill in the world, because they inherently want to be filled. There's huge pressure and demand for it. And when you fill large vacuums, releasing that potential energy and pressure for your own benefit, you will do well.

If you look at our apps so far, you'll see a pattern of successful apps in fairly popular/crowded genres that then took those app categories a step or two forward, usually in the design and user experience department, filling those vacuums. For us, on a much smaller scale, we're trying to replicate the magic of the iPhone launch: the release of a product that's so much nicer to use than the status quo that it feels slightly magical. If you can nail that, you should do fine.

Ken: *Once you release an app, what metrics and signs are you watching to gauge success and what tools do you use to view them? If an app starts off more slowly or seems "in trouble," what sorts of steps would you take to get it back on track?*

Phill: App launch month will involve fairly compulsive viewing of the App Store "top paid" and category charts for your app's charting position—since Apple doesn't provide real-time sales information, it's the best we have in terms of gauging an app's trajectory, and that means madly refreshing pages in iTunes and on your phone while cursing Akamai when things randomly get cached for hours and don't update.

From our experience, if an app isn't cut out to chart high, it's not worth the trouble trying to prop it up. It's best to learn your lesson and move on, with a slightly better idea of the App Store demographics' tastes, than fall victim to the sunk cost fallacy.

Ken: *In your post "The Cookie Cutter Guide to Charting in the App Store"* (http://www.taptaptap.com/blog/the-cookie-cutter-guide-to-charting-in-the-app-store/) *you discuss how you pushed a completely unknown app to the top of the charts very quickly. You mention that this approach was experimental. Would you do it again? What are the right situations to take that approach versus teasing an app and building excitement for it before release?*

Phill: Teasing an app and building excitement for it before release can fit right into the "shaken-up soda bottle" model of building up pressure for release at launch, but just be careful to implement a way to notify interested people instantly that your app is out. Interested people coming back to the page a week after your app launched after bookmarking it two weeks earlier won't help you too much for your initial bid at the Top 100 chart.

You should always try to take at least some form of this kind of app launch if possible, even if it's on a much smaller scale. If you take one thing away from that post, it should be this: a concentrated blast is much more powerful than longer sustained promotion, because higher charting (from the concentrated sales) starts bringing in more and more customers the higher you get in a feedback cycle of increased visibility/freshness.

Ken: *In that same post, you write about MacHeist being a "rocket" to launch your apps. Although you mention that the rocket could be considerably smaller for other developers, many of those in that category don't have any mailing lists at all. If they have no lists and can't partner with someone, what should they do to get attention for their apps?*

Phill: I'm going to start with the assumption that this is an app that the developer really cares about, and believes is great. If so, this is where I recommend the Classics style approach—get it pretty much totally ready or submitted with an adjustable release date set, then at least throw up a teaser page with an email sign-up on release notification for visitors and start promoting that page as much as you can. This is by far the best approach for collecting potential energy in the form of interested, probable customers signing up to hear about when the app is out, then releasing it at your cue when the app is out and you're trying to chart.

Ken: *What is your guidance and philosophy on pricing apps? How is pricing a strategy, and do you think about it per app or just have a general approach that you apply across any app you launch?*

Phill: We believe in affordable software (you can see some of that belief shine through in our past history in the Mac community with MacHeist, our other business). With the App Store, we have an extremely efficient distribution and sales system set up on everyone's iPhone and iPod touch, and if anything, this means if your app becomes a hit you can price your app at $0.99 and make a bundle. We see some niche apps where it makes sense to price higher and do low-volume, high-margin business off of people who really need your app and go out to find it, but ultimately at tap tap tap we do focus on producing mainstream-friendly apps, so as a rule of thumb we price low and aim for high volume.

It's definitely situational, though; there are some apps where you'll look at them and a "freemium" model makes perfect sense. Or just free with ads, or dirt cheap aiming for a chart blockbuster, or high for a more niche business. It's just important for developers coming from other ecosystems to banish the idea that selling an app for $0.99 and making a living off of it is impossible. The App Store makes it possible now; it's tough to make it happen, but it's possible.

Ken: *Do you consider apps to have a certain life span to them? For example, at some point do you stop worrying about tinkering with the price and no longer invest in adding features to them?*

Phill: The App Store approval process is not very tuned for constant minor maintenance fixes and updates. We're interested in shipping a really, really solid 1.0, updating it with any critical fixes if necessary, then rolling out major (usually free) upgrades on a slower cycle. I actually find super-frequent app updates really annoying personally as an iPhone user (they can really stack up when you have dozens of apps), so I can see why Apple subtly pressures toward less frequent updates, with minor provisions for pushing out emergency bug fixes quickly.

Sales-wise, apps do tend to have a certain life span to them. It's pretty rare that an app will chart multiple times—you need something major like being featured in an Apple television ad, or a heavily promoted major upgrade, to boost you back into the top 100. This is another reason we're interested in concentrating on less frequent, but really meaty updates. They're something worth posting about from the perspective of media and bloggers, and for us, they're worth promoting heavily for another good shot at charting and a "second life" of sales, so to speak.

Grades: Jeremy Olson

COMPANY: Skookum

POSITION: User interface designer

BACKGROUND: Jeremy Olson is a UI designer and app developer. As part of the creation of his first application, Grades, Jeremy chronicled his marketing strategies on his personal blog, Tapity.com (*http://Tapity.com*). Grades went on to be featured by Apple on the App Store. It quickly climbed the charts, becoming the second ranked app in the Education category a week after launch.

LINKS: *http://skookum.com/; http://gradesapp.com/*

Ken: *You began talking very early about your app, Grades, probably even before it was built. Describe why you did that and how it plays a part in building a successful app.*

Jeremy: Taking the time to journal my design, development, and marketing of Grades on my Tapity blog was one of the best "marketing" decisions I ever made. I started the blog after reading *Tribes* [Portfolio], Seth Godin's inspiring book on leadership. The back cover of that book says, "If you think leadership is only for other people, you're wrong. We need YOU to lead us." At that time, I didn't really believe him, but it did inspire me to try to learn how to build successful iPhone applications and to see if anyone would want to follow along. Keep in mind, at this point I hadn't the slightest knowledge of how to design, develop, or market for the iPhone. I was a nobody in the iPhone development community, armed only with a passion for user interface design, a web development background, and an inspiration to lead.

I was astonished to see it actually work. After a few months of painstakingly blogging into the air (hey, I did get a few comments), tap tap tap—one of the most successful iPhone development shops out there—noticed the blog because I had been discussing some of the strategies they used. They blogged about it. Since then, Tapity has grown in influence and has given me the opportunity to learn from and engage with some of the most successful developers out there.

But so what? Why should you care about gaining respect in the iPhone developer community? I wondered the same thing. After all, my target market is college students, not iPhone developers. The answer to that question, I found, is twofold.

First, Apple does a decent job at documenting the basics of the App Store process, but much of the way the App Store works remains a mystery. Luckily, the iPhone development community is tremendous. By earning their respect by sharing my own experiences, I have gained access to a wealth of anecdotes, data points, and seasoned advice that fill a good number of the gaps Apple neglects to talk about.

Second, iPhone app marketing is largely about connections. Maybe I didn't get too many college students interested in Grades directly by writing a blog, but I certainly got the eyeballs of some influential people in the press, and, more importantly, the attention of the customer every iPhone developer should do anything to woo: Apple. Apple employees—the people who decide what gets featured on the App Store—are real people; they read these kinds of blogs. I bet that doing the blog played a big role in being prominently featured by Apple the week after Grades launched.

Ken: *While you are an actual student in college, you are also a student of the App Store. How did you first begin learning about the inner details of the App Store, and how have you discovered many of the tips and tricks that are now in your toolkit?*

Jeremy: Apple doesn't like to talk about the mechanics of the App Store, but there is definitely a wealth of information available; you just have to dig for it. I started by absorbing all the information developers have posted on their blogs: sales, diagrams, ups and downs, lessons learned.

I also did a lot of "primary research." It's simpler than it sounds. A lot of data and insight can be found by simply observing the App Store and the apps that do and don't make it. Look through the Top 100 chart and think about why those apps appealed to people. Starting with their website, try to see what kind of marketing they did. You can also use Google and Twitter search to see what kind of buzz they've been getting (and through what venues).

Read reviews—what do people appreciate in an app and what do they tend to complain about? You'll notice that people will often leave bad reviews simply because the app doesn't include a feature they imagined it should. Based on this, I realized that my app had to be extremely focused on the task at hand: calculating the grades you need. I could have included all kinds of neat class management features like assignment due dates and scheduling features (the more features the better, right?). Doing that, however, would cause users to desire infinitely more features in a category I really couldn't compete in (class management). The result would either be unsatisfied users or a cluttered mess. So, definitely read reviews, especially of apps in your niche.

In the end, though, the iPhone developer community is far and away the most valuable resource for figuring out how the App Store works. This goes back to the importance of developing a network of iPhone developers you respect and who respect you—and who are willing to share their experiences and insights.

Ken: *Expound on the importance of the iPhone developer community. Provide an example where you have seen that interacting with them helped you learn something you didn't know.*

Jeremy: I'll share how I came upon a trick that made Grades stay at the top of the Education category's front page for an entire day. A few days before I launched Grades I wanted to know what I should set as the release date, so I asked my developer friends on Twitter. I learned from another developer that you can set the release date to some time in the future and then on the day you plan to launch, set it back to that particular day.

With that information, I discovered an amazingly valuable trick. The front page of any given category (in my case, Education) on the iPhone App Store, by default, is sorted by Release Date. By looking at several category pages, however, I realized that it is sorted not only by date, but by time as well (with the most recent apps showing up first). Since most developers don't tinker with their release dates, most new apps show up around midnight. Knowing this, I set my release date to some arbitrary date in the future, then at 6:00 a.m. on launch day (Monday) I set the release date back to Monday. Since the other new apps came out at midnight and mine came out at 6:00 a.m., mine was technically more recent and, thus, remained at the top of the new apps list for almost an entire day!

Moral of the story: tapping into the experiences of other developers can help you come up with strategies and tricks of your own. Note that the App Store is constantly changing, so I cannot promise that this technique (or any, for that matter) will always work.

Ken: *Grades had a very specific marketing plan, and when it launched, you began getting buzz even before anyone really wrote about it. What did that marketing plan include and how did you ensure that you successfully executed it?*

Jeremy: I would make a distinction between my marketing plan and my launch plan. I started "marketing" Grades a year before it launched by simply writing about the ups and downs of development on my blog and getting noticed in the development community. My general marketing plan also included the following:

- Build a following on Twitter by tweeting about iPhone design and marketing strategies.

- Set up a beta program months before launching—by launch time I had an "army" of beta testers who loved the app. This was crucial in establishing a solid base of glowing reviews on launch day.

- Design a good-looking pre-launch website where people could sign up to be notified on launch day.

So, my marketing really started many months before launch, but a few weeks before my planned launch date, I started putting my launch plan into action, which included the following:

- Engaged a lot of the top bloggers, influential techies, and Apple employees on Twitter. I never mentioned Grades explicitly, but in some cases the mere act of "following" them on Twitter was enough to spark their interest in Grades since I mentioned it on my Twitter profile.

- Allowed MacStories, a large Mac blog, to post a preview and promo code giveaway.

- Submitted review requests to all the major review websites prior to launch. It is best for reviews to be concentrated around launch day, so send your requests a week or more before launch in order to give them time to write their reviews.

- Engaged with local press and scored a video interview as well as a Facebook post to the unofficial North Carolina Facebook page (48,000 fans) and a post to the official Facebook page for my university, UNC Charlotte (7,000 fans). As you noted, this generated quite a bit of launch buzz (especially on Twitter) and that buzz alone pushed the app into the Top 100 list in Education even before it received any press coverage.

Ken: *What is the most important element when launching an app? Once launched, what are some ways to keep an app charting high in the rankings?*

Jeremy: Two words: Apple (oh, wait, that's one word). This applies especially to hit-based apps (mentioned earlier), but any kind of promotion you get pales in comparison to being featured by Apple. This isn't all about luck, though. I was fairly certain my app would be featured by Apple (and was delighted when it was featured just a week after launch). It starts with the app itself: your app must meet or exceed Apple's standards of quality and polish, and the idea behind it must be solid. As I mentioned earlier, I think gaining the respect of the iPhone developer community also greatly increases your chances of being noticed by Apple. Finally, you've got to make your own splash if you want Apple to make you a bigger one. I built up a bunch of pre-launch buzz and then launched with quite a bit of fanfare, scoring some decent press along the way. If you don't bother to do great marketing yourself, don't expect Apple to do it for you.

It's tough to stay high on the rankings. Even most of the top apps fall out of the Top 100 eventually. If you are doing the hit-based approach, you want the initial spike to be as high as possible and the fall to be as gradual as possible. Major updates can help; including Facebook, Twitter, and email sharing features within the app can help; being featured by Apple in staff picks can really help. If you've priced your app high enough you can experiment with advertising within other apps or online. I haven't tried this since it would be difficult to have a great ROI for a $0.99 app. These things may help your app have a soft landing somewhere on the Top 100 chart of your category, which will also help with sustained sales.

TouchArcade: Arnold Kim

WEBSITES: MacRumors; TouchArcade
POSITION: Owner
BACKGROUND: Arnold Kim (often referred to as "Arn" online) is the owner of MacRumors, a popular Apple rumors website. Seeing the importance of the iPhone platform, Arnold opened TouchArcade in 2008, dedicating it to game reviews. It is extremely popular, with more than 40,000 active members.
LINKS: *http://www.macrumors.com; http://toucharcade.com*

Ken: *Touch Arcade is one of the most popular iPhone gaming review sites on the Web, and as such, you probably receive a very large number of review requests. What makes a request stand out? What are the biggest mistakes developers make when they submit review requests? What almost automatically prevents them from being considered?*

Arnold: Yes, we do get a large number of requests for reviews and we try to examine each one. Even so, the volume can be overwhelming at times. Given the number of apps coming out for the iPhone, TouchArcade is about game discovery as much as it is about reviews. While I can't say there's any one thing that a developer could do to automatically prevent them from being considered, there are many seemingly obvious things that developers should be doing.

When submitting a game for review to TouchArcade or any review site, I recommend that developers include their game information (name and description), screenshots, iTunes URL, and a link to a video. While each of these items may seem incredibly basic, a great many requests we receive don't include all these items. Anything a developer can do in their review submission to give us a sense of what the game is about is going to be incredibly helpful and will help them stand out from the pack.

Basic information like the iTunes URL is often omitted and can make it harder for us to even find the game in the App Store. Screenshots are eye-catching, and in our case, a video can easily convey the game play both to us as well as potential players. At that point, an app has a much better chance of standing on its own merits rather than potentially being lost in the crowd.

TouchArcade also hosts a very active player community that is always on the lookout for great new games. Preparing a game play video for launch serves the additional purpose of advertising to your customers. Due to the unpredictability of Apple's approval process, I've seen many developers' games launch without videos in place, and I think that's a huge opportunity lost. An app's launch in the App Store is a critical time and frequently results in a large spike in sales. Everything you can do to build buzz, sales, and interest at that time will build momentum for long-term success.

Ken: *If someone submits a request to you (or to other sites) and gets no re-sponse back and never receives a review, how persistent should this person be in trying again? When should the person give up trying? Is there anything that can be done that would change your mind and make you want to review the app? Similarly, if a developer who has had a review in the past submits a review request to you, what types of changes in the app would you look for to find it worth writing about again?*

Arnold: Unfortunately, we have trouble replying to each review request. I know this can be frustrating for developers not to get some acknowledg-ment back. Unfortunately, due to the pace of the App Store, if we've already evaluated an app and decided we aren't going to review it, it's unlikely we'll return to it in the future. Sending in a couple of requests is fine, as things can get lost in the mix. Major updates to games, however, will have us re-consider games for review, so it's always worth keeping us updated with those changes.

If we pass or miss your game, we might change our minds if we see a lot of interest and reaction to a game in our forums. As we said, our forum community is very active and developers have had a lot of luck generating interest in their games there. There have been occasions that we might have skipped a game, only to return to it due to the popularity in our community.

Ken: *From all the games you've played and reviewed since the App Store opened, what do you consider the elements for a long-term successful app? What do you think developers need to do to keep apps thriving once the buzz of a review is over?*

Arnold: That's a bit of a tricky question. Long-term success with a single game or app is such a rare thing in the App Store. There are probably a handful of apps that can really be considered long-term successes. I think what is a much more reasonable goal is trying to attain long-term success as a developer potentially across multiple titles. The TouchArcade commu-nity has brought developers and players together, and I've found that many of the successful developers have been able to build up a fan base for their games. So, building your own personal brand and community of customers will help you establish long-term success, and also helps you get noticed by review sites.

Recap

Here's what you learned in this chapter:

- Marketing is a process that occurs in parallel with development. Like the development process, it incorporates customers, who are the gatekeepers of an app's long-term success, once the initial buzz dies down.

- Twitter is a key channel to build influence with potential customers and peers. "Being useful" on Twitter is the best way to gain credibility with those you are attempting to engage.

- Having a web presence will provide a central communication hub for your app. Initially, the website will be a "splash" page, representing an extension of your app's early design while helping set the tone for its future aesthetics.

- Pitching your app is the most time-sensitive part of creating your marketing crescendo. Be smart about whom you pitch, how you pitch, and when you pitch, in order to maximize buzz around the launch of your app.

- Promoting an app does not stop after it launches. There are a number of ways to keep people interested in your app once it's in the App Store. You can try using some of the proven tactics, but you should also be creative when developing promotional opportunities.

9

Measuring Success and Future Development

REGARDLESS OF WHETHER YOU ARE fortunate enough to have had your app written up on a blog, received stellar ratings and reviews on the App Store, or achieved some of your initial goals, you'll need to be diligent and proactive with ongoing development of your app. Whether you have tasted success or are still seeking it, you'll need to keep interacting with customers and determine how your app should evolve over time…or if it should.

In this chapter, you'll explore:

- Monitoring feedback and analyzing your app's performance

- Keeping customers interested and involved in your app

- Preparing and submitting updates to the App Store

- Assessing the future of your app

Into the App Store

Some congratulations are due if you've made it this far. Launching an app into the App Store the way you did is no small feat. You know, of course, that your job is not done yet. Depending on how everything proceeds, you may in fact just be starting your job…literally. Going forward, it's possible that your app may allow you to dedicate much more time to it than before you shipped it. You could, for example, become focused exclusively on apps at work, have apps represent an extra or even a sole source of income (through sales or building apps for others), or just see them as a serious (yet fun) hobby.

That type of change will be influenced, in part, by how your app fares in the App Store. Everything you've done up to this point has put you in a position to be more successful than your competition. To continue to be at an advantage, you'll need to recognize that you aren't at the finish line yet and that there may indeed be no finish line. Before thinking too long-term, however, you'll want to begin monitoring feedback and looking at the performance of your app once it's available in the App Store.

Monitoring Feedback

More broadly, you can think about two types of feedback for your app: *qualitative* and *quantitative*. Qualitative feedback is what people will be saying about your app on websites, blogs, Twitter, App Store reviews, and other channels. This feedback may come directly to you, such as through email, or it may require you to be on the lookout for it, as with a blog review of your app.

Quantitative feedback is numerical in nature, consisting of analytics (you did install analytics as recommended in Chapter 7, right?) and data that Apple provides. By using qualitative and quantitative feedback in conjunction, you'll have a very complete picture of how your app is performing.

Qualitative and quantitative feedback will provide actionable insight and often requires you to do more significant activities in response to it (e.g., fix or update your app). In this section, you'll be focused exclusively on where to monitor and collect feedback. Taking more substantial action in response to this information will be covered in the next section. In the meantime, be sure you are answering support requests through Twitter, email, and other channels, as well as engaging customers and media where appropriate (e.g., commenting on a blog post that reviews your app).

Qualitative feedback

Qualitative feedback is generally text-based and will sometimes require you to infer conclusions. Here are some examples of where you can go to find qualitative feedback:

Twitter

> Twitter acts as a gateway for what's happening on the Web. This means you'll be able to monitor what customers say about your app directly through mentions (when they send an update with "@<yourusername>"), and indirectly when, for example, a blogger may review your app and subsequently share that link on Twitter. The second situation is possible through monitoring keywords related to your app, which I wrote about in Chapter 8.
>
> Once your app is launched, you may want to expand the keywords you are tracking based on how you see customers or the media discussing your app. Although your app probably has a core set of keywords that are most relevant, consider tracking keywords for specific features. Continue to experiment with what keywords to track based on the results that emerge. As you get more comfortable, include search operators to create more advanced and useful queries to track (*http://search. twitter.com/operators*).

Google Alerts

> Twitter will not catch every review or mention about your app on the Web. To help gain more comprehensive coverage, you will turn to Google Alerts (*http://www.google.com/alerts*).
>
> Google Alerts (see Figure 9-1) is a powerful tool that, like Twitter, allows you to monitor keywords. The two differences are that Google will look across the entire Web (five categories, including news and video sources) and will send you results via email (or if you're more technically inclined, an RSS feed). The alerts will include links to sites that

have written or somehow reference something about your app or your app's features, depending on what keywords you are monitoring. The monitoring options are very customizable, allowing you to receive an alert immediately, once a day, or once a week. You can also specify the number of results you want in an email. The challenge with Google Alerts, which you also face to some extent with Twitter, is to make the keywords you monitor provide relevant results. Since the Web is considerably more expansive than Twitter alone, the likelihood of spam and irrelevant alerts is higher with Google Alerts. Beyond tweaking your keywords, as with Twitter, try using some of Google's search operators to make your alerts more effective (*http://www.google.com/help/cheatsheet.html*).

Figure 9-1. A very basic Google Alert for AudioBookShelf

Customer reviews

Your customer reviews on the App Store can represent some of the richest feedback you'll receive about your app. It's typical for them to trend on the negative side—especially for $0.99 or free apps—because there is a low barrier to download them and price-sensitive customers will not read your application description. If you are mostly receiving one- or two-star ratings and poor reviews, though, it is a clear indication that there's a problem with your app.

If there are outliers, and the majority of your reviews are positive, don't lose your cool. In fact, you'll want to be aggressive about engaging the most negative critics of your application.

Email

Email is another of your most direct means to receive feedback. Unlike with customer reviews on the App Store, emails from customers require a response from you. Timely support responses are a key component of keeping your customers happy and engaged with your app. I will cover that aspect in more depth in the next section, but note that it should not prohibit you from answering any questions that may arise in the interim.

It's possible that you have some other channels to receive qualitative customer feedback. For example, if you are in a larger organization, you may offer phone support. You may have also implemented a support tool mentioned in Chapter 5. In general, however, these are some of the key channels to monitor feedback about your app.

Quantitative feedback

The quantitative side of feedback is numbers-based. You'll be able to use information from Apple and your analytics provider to give you a broader, more data-driven perspective on how your app is doing.

Sales and trends

iTunes Connect is where you'll find all of the Apple-provided data about your app. The first place you can visit is the Sales and Trends area, which is available from the iTunes Connect home page. By clicking that link, you can preview or download the daily or weekly reports for your app, which shows information related to what app was downloaded, the number of downloads (Units), the *royalty* price (i.e., your portion of revenue from sales), and the currency and country code associated with the download or purchase. A Monthly Free report will also consolidate all free downloads into a monthly report that corresponds with financial periods.

Note that the daily and weekly reports represent trends and should not be considered the financial accounting for the royalties Apple will pay you for your paid app(s). You can find that information in the Financial Reports (discussed momentarily). The reports in this area are purged regularly by Apple, with the daily reports being removed after seven days and the weekly reports after 13 weeks. So, you'll want to download and archive these reports somewhat regularly.

I'm going to bias you pretty heavily when it comes to the Apple-provided data. You will save yourself some serious headaches and frustration if you use a third-party tool to help interpret this data. The main reason is that these "reports" are really not reports at all, but instead are more like raw data. If you are very handy with spreadsheets, you can manipulate this data in something such as Microsoft Excel or Apple's Numbers to make better sense of it.

Very intuitive tools are available, however, that provide actual sales reporting and simplify the iTunes Connect data download process. And depending on what analytics platform you implemented in your app, you may be able to see both your sales and your analytics data in one location. The analytics providers can often also collect other diagnostic information such as crash reports, or even help check for piracy (again, depending on how you integrated them). I'll highlight the options I recommend in the following list, identifying the key differences among them.

Most cases of piracy occur in regions where an actual app sale would have never occurred in the first place. As a result, many developers don't bother with piracy checks. If you do pursue them, your options include tools such as mtiks (*http://www.mtiks.com/*), plug-ins from analytics providers, or your own custom solutions.

AppViz (http://www.ideaswarm.com/products/appviz/)

AppViz is a paid Mac OS X application (offering a 30-day free trial) that was developed by Ideaswarm and will download your iTunes Connect application data and subsequently visualize it for you. Unlike what you receive in iTunes Connect, in AppViz you'll be able to see data grouped by an app across all regions (which is particularly useful if you have several apps). AppViz can optionally pull in your iTunes reviews and ranking information, giving you a single dashboard to assess key feedback about your app.

appFigures (http://www.appfigures.com)

Compared to AppViz, the distinctions for appFigures (see Figure 9-2) are that it is web-based, offers automatic daily syncing with iTunes Connect, and thus can deliver daily email reports of how your app is doing. Since you are going to be busy with your app, the latter two features are particularly useful. With appFigures, you won't have to worry about your reports being purged by Apple before you obtain a copy of them, since they will be downloaded each day for you. Ariel Michael, the co-founder of appFigures, is interviewed at the end of this chapter.

Heartbeat (http://www.heartbeatapp.com/)

Like appFigures, Heartbeat is web-based. One of the key differences is that depending on whether you choose to integrate Heartbeat into your app as your analytics provider, you can view both sales and analytics information in the Heartbeat dashboard.

TapMetrics' TapMini (http://tapmetrics.com/tapmini)

TapMetrics is another analytics provider (and, like Heartbeat, is also mentioned in Chapter 7) that can give you a more comprehensive sales plus analytics display of your app's performance. The TapMini tool (Mac OS X download) will automate your iTunes Connect download data and sync those reports with TapMetrics daily.

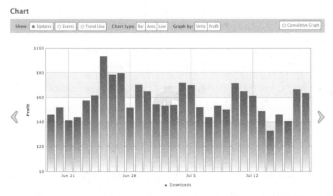

Figure 9-2. appFigures chart; charts such as this one are not present in iTunes Connect

Analytics

Data about downloads and sales only gives you a bird's-eye perspective about the fact that customers are downloading your app. What it doesn't help you understand is how many customers are actually using your app over time and what specifically they are doing in it. As you know from Chapter 7, that's the reason analytics exist.

In general, the analytics you'll want to pay attention to include the number of sessions for your app (where "session" represents one application open by a customer), sessions per month (also called "frequency of use" by platforms such as Flurry), average session length, number of active users, and number of new users (versus those who might have redownloaded your app). See Figure 9-3.

Figure 9-3. Analytics from Flurry showing the number of sessions

You may also be tracking a number of events in your app. Because the actions that are important for an app can vary widely, events are extremely important. So, if you didn't initially add any events to track in your app (e.g., identifying when a customer uses a particular feature or completes a certain task), you should consider adding one or more to give you additional insight. Peter Farago, VP of marketing at Flurry, discusses what you should be learning from analytics and events at the end of this chapter.

Crash logs

Crash logs were mentioned in Chapter 6, as part of beta testing. At this point in your app's existence, they serve as the most technical quantitative feedback you can receive. You can use the same methods described in that chapter to have your customers send you any crash logs generated by your app (see Figure 9-4); hopefully there are few, if any. Once your app is in the App Store, though, Apple provides a way to view the logs that were submitted by your customers through iTunes, which occurs in the background when they sync their devices (unless they previously opted out of this function). You can view these logs in iTunes Connect within the Version Information screen for a particular application by clicking Crash Reports.

Figure 9-4. The Crash Reports link in iTunes Connect

A much more aggressive (and fairly un-common) way to deal with crash logs is to intercept the events causing the application to crash when they occur, and then prompting a customer to send the reports directly to you when the app is reopened. To explore integrating this type of option, take a look at Plausible CrashReporter (*http://code.google.com/p/plcrashreporter/*) and MacDevCrashReporter (*http://macdevcrashreports.com/*). See Figure 9-5 for an example of the latter.

Figure 9-5.
MacDevCrashReporter in Icebird

Financial reports

The third-party sales tools mentioned earlier can help you understand the actual payments you should receive from your paid apps. Because Apple has some unique accounting principles that affect when you can receive payments, it's worth detailing them for you.

To start, select the Financial Reports link from the iTunes Connect home page. When you first visit this area, you will likely not see any reports. Apple only provides financial reports once a month, based on its fiscal calendar. When they're available, you'll find seven reports representing the United States (and Latin America), Canada, Europe, United Kingdom, Japan, Australia (and New Zealand), and "Rest of World." Apple will only provide you a payment when your app sales in any given region are greater than $150. In such cases, you will also see a Payment Advise file for that region, indicating the payment that was made. When the $150 threshold is not met, Apple will withhold payment, rolling it over until the sales are greater than $150 for that particular region in a given fiscal month.

You should also note that payments are typically made three to four weeks after the close of a fiscal month. So, depending on when your app is purchased, it's possible you might not receive your first check for at least two months. Apple's most current fiscal calendar is available from the Sales and Trends area of iTunes Connect via the Fiscal Calendar link (see Figure 9-6).

Figure 9-6. The Fiscal Calendar and User Guide, where you can learn more about Apple's reporting

Keeping Customers Engaged

By this point, you are going to be sorting through all types of information and data. As you did with the feedback you received through the pre-App Store development of your app, you should be funneling all of this feedback to make sense of it. This could be as simple as directing customers to a single support email address and internally managing a spreadsheet, or leveraging some number of tools that you implemented to interact with customers and track issues (as discussed in Chapter 5). The point is that after you monitor and collect this feedback, to make smart decisions about how to keep customers engaged you are going to need to prioritize and synthesize it all to make it actionable.

Listening and Learning

You've probably noticed that the qualitative insight supports the quantitative data and vice versa. It's unlikely, for instance, that you had tens of thousands of downloads when your app launched, only to receive all negative reviews. You will, however, sometimes find anomalies or aberrations between the two, and when you do, you should hone in on why that's the case.

To help make that happen, you need to have the same customer-focused mindset you had from the outset of this process and throughout your app's existence. You may have a strong vision and instinct about what should happen with your ongoing app development, but keep listening to and learning from your customers. That's particularly true of your most strident critics, who might tweet some frustration about your app or write a scathing review about it. Now, you should recognize that your app will never please all customers, and sometimes, no matter what you do, you won't win over critics. But for each critic who is turned from a foe to a fan, your app will become that much better and less susceptible to these sorts of critiques.

I recommend that you facilitate discussions with some of your customers at least on a monthly basis once your app is in the App Store. These discussions should be prompted by you and could focus on how your customers are using your app, what they like and dislike about it, and what's missing in it, and inquiring about what new apps they are using (whether competitive, complementary, or just interesting). These conversations don't necessarily need to be as formal as what you did during the customer interviews. Your purpose with them is to ensure that you continue to have opportunities to listen to and learn from customers so that you can keep delivering on the promise of your application.

Obsessive customer support

A very "cheap" way, at least in terms of actual development costs, to show your commitment to customers and keep them engaged is to obsessively answer their support questions and feature requests. I can't tell you the number of times I've seen App Store reviews that talked about a developer's responsiveness (e.g., "The developer responded to my email within 15 minutes") or that were subsequently edited because a developer implemented a feature a customer requested. In many ways, even if your app is not perfect, you will earn goodwill with customers when providing them with outstanding support and being attentive to their needs.

When it comes to support specifically, set a goal for how long it should take you to respond to an inbound query. If you determine this to be five hours, for example, it doesn't mean you will necessarily solve the problem within that time (unless that's possible). Instead, you'll at least acknowledge that you received the request and are working on it. If you have a dedicated support email inbox, you might want to create an auto-reply, indicating your support hours and typical response time. Third-party customer support solutions such as ZenDesk and Tender will automatically assign a ticket to a customer issue and send the customer an email from a template you create.

It is worth reiterating that one benefit of support solutions is that customers will always have visibility into the status of their issue(s). Giving customers this type of real-time transparency helps set their expectation regarding response times while also providing them the confidence that their inquiries are indeed being tracked. Whether through email, Twitter, or other channels, do your best not to keep your customers hanging. Although that's always been true, it's particularly important in an "on-demand" world.

App Store listing changes

Altering the App Store listing for your app can have a positive impact on the interest in your app by highlighting press reviews (see Figure 9-7), awards, or new and upcoming features. You can change a number of items in the App Store without submitting an actual app update (i.e., a new binary) to Apple. The allowable changes include editing the App Store description, URLs (application and support), contact email address, application icon and screenshots, and price. Changing these elements may seem trivial, but they can have a big effect individually and even more so when combined. You can edit these items by selecting Manage Your Applications from the home page of iTunes Connect, choosing the desired app, and then clicking the Edit Information button.

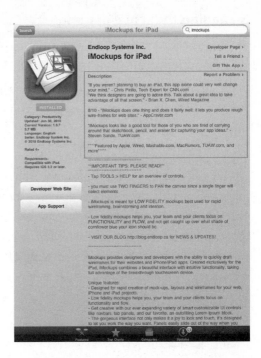

Figure 9-7. The Endloop team's method of highlighting press about iMockups in its App Store listing

As touched on in Chapter 8, some of the more useful changes you can make include incorporating quotes from customers and reviewers in your App Store description, including "What's Coming" in the App Store description to highlight the features you are working on, or testing different pricing points, whether as a promotion or to find what spurs the most demand. Click Save Changes at the bottom of the screen, and the changes will usually appear within several hours on the App Store.

App Updates

For the most part, submitting updates for your app is the best way to keep your customers engaged. These updates may respond to customer feature requests and criticisms, fix bugs, or simply execute on your vision and road-map for your app. In all cases, these updates will show that you are actively maintaining the app and are committed to improving it. Of course, you'll need to identify what goes into an update, test and get feedback on an update, and subsequently submit the update to Apple. Much of that will flow from what you've done to this point in the development of your app, but I'll outline some update-specific information now.

Managing the scope of updates

There are many different ways to approach how you release updates for your app. Some developers release updates weekly while others may take months. There's no right or wrong way to do it necessarily. What's more important is to be clear about what you are working on and be consistent on when you indicate you are going to release your updates.

A good way to approach setting the scope of your updates is to add to and reprioritize your app's backlog features from your roadmap with the qualitative and quantitative feedback you have for your app (see the section "Creating your initial roadmap" in Chapter 5). If "feature X" is the most requested item from customers but it's currently ranked low on the backlog, its importance should be reassessed. Similarly, if your analytics indicate that customers are not using a particular feature that you were planning to expand, you might consider spending your energies elsewhere.

You're going to need to constantly balance working on more significant features with resolving critical issues or getting easy wins in your app. If your app is currently crashing under certain common conditions, you'll need to focus all your attention on getting that update submitted immediately. Similarly, if a large amount of customer feedback concerns complaints about the size of a button, you can easily resolve that and thereby reduce noise for you while making customers happy. As discussed previously, you can categorize these types of updates with either bug fix or minor version number changes (e.g., 1.0.1 or 1.1) when you submit the update to Apple.

As I wrote before, readjusting your roadmap based on feedback is something you'll do frequently. It matches the same paradigm you used to initially build your app; you'll continue to start with your own assumptions and then validate them against customer input and the data you have at your disposal.

More "beta" testing

It's a good practice to test your updates the same way you did leading up to the initial release of your app. In fact, you may have learned a thing or two after launching your app, so be sure to incorporate those lessons as you begin testing your update internally and with customers.

As with the pre-App Store version of your app, you'll need to test your update with customers who have provided their UDIDs. If you still have some of the 100 device spaces left in the iOS Provisioning Portal, you may want to add some new customers. In either case, you'll still need to follow the ad hoc distribution process to put your update into your customers' hands (see the section "UDID" in Chapter 6) for them to test it outside the App Store.

You should only send your app update to customers who previously agreed to continue testing your app. When you send it to them, as you did during the beta testing, let them know what is new, updated, fixed, or outstanding. These release notes will also be used when you submit your update to Apple.

Submitting your update to Apple

Getting an update for your app submitted to Apple is relatively straightforward. To submit your update, you'll need the following information:

Version Number
> Try to adhere to the *major version.minor version.bug fix* paradigm (see the "Release Numbering" sidebar in Chapter 5). This number should match what your developer specified inside your updated app's binary.

Name
> You are allowed to change the application name when submitting a new binary. There's a good chance there's no reason to, but you may want to experiment with a more descriptive name. For example, I tested "Tweeb - Twitter analytics" versus "Tweeb" and saw varying impacts on downloads.

Keywords
> Keywords are another element that is editable when you submit a new binary. As with your application name, you should experiment as needed.

What's New in this Version
> These are your release notes. They will appear to those who have already installed your app in the Updates area of the App Store. If you have a Universal app, group this information by application version (i.e., iPhone and iPad). Also, use categories to help identify new

features versus bug fixes. I recommend using "New," "Updated," and "Fixed." Some developers include the release notes from the past several updates, which is especially useful if updates are being produced regularly. You may also consider including this information in the app itself (see Figures 9-8 and 9-9).

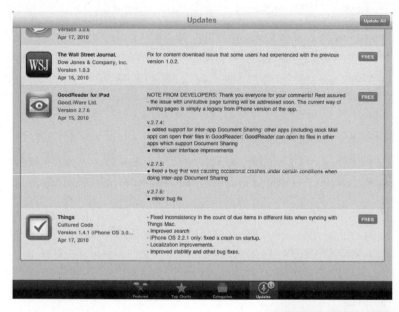

Figure 9-8 (Above). How Apple uses the What's New in this Version information on the App Store

Figure 9-9 (Right). Outside's innovative display of release notes to customers upon first opening the app after the update

Updated Application Binary

This represents the binary for your app update. Ensure that your developer uses the same credentials that created the initial app (technically, the same distribution provisioning profile) when building the binary update. Again, the version number in the binary should also match what you are submitting in the Version Number section in iTunes Connect.

Once you have this information available, you will again select Manage Your Applications from the home page of iTunes Connect and choose the desired app. From there, click the Add Version button under the Versions section of that particular app's App Summary screen. The next screen will only request the Version Number and What's New in this Version information. If you also want to edit the Name or Keywords, you'll need to revisit the newly created entry (click the View Details button for this version— New Version—of your application on the App Summary screen) and edit either the Version Information section for the application name or the Metadata section for the keywords. Submit the updated binary through the Application Uploader, as you did when first submitting the app (see the "App Summary and binary upload" section in Chapter 7).

Upon your update being approved, you will receive a fresh set of 50 promo codes (awesome!) and a reset of your ratings for the current version of the app (not so awesome!). The ratings reset can temporarily impact your download and sales numbers, but if your update is seen as valuable to customers, they should rebound within a week or so. This cycle means you should largely focus your updates on critical bug fixes or major feature releases. For another perspective, check out Apple's guidance on how frequently to submit app updates (*https://developer.apple.com/ios/appstore/managing.html#submit*).

What's coming

It is important to share what you are working on with your app in all of the usual channels. This includes not only editing your App Store description, as mentioned earlier, but also sharing this progress on Twitter, your blog, your website, your email newsletter, and similar outlets.

If you haven't figured it out yet, the same strategies you've used throughout the marketing and development process will continue to be useful. This can include teaser previews of new screens or features, reaching out to review sites when you are about to launch a major update, or distributing promo codes.

Considering the two extremes of either engaging with customers too much or being completely absent, you are better off with the first over the second. Apps that go months without any updates and no communication from developers are usually considered abandoned. Existing customers will let prospective customers know of that perception and scare off downloads by discussing your lack of interaction and updates in their reviews. Don't let that happen.

Cultured Code's "Arrivals"

If you really want to be aggressive in informing your customers about what you are working on, take a look at Cultured Code's "Arrivals" (*http://cultured-code.com/status/*; see Figure 9-10). Maker of the popular task management software Things (available on the iPhone, iPad, and Mac), Cultured Code created a highly visible (and visual) status page of the features that are soon "arriving" across its different apps.

Figure 9-10. Cultured Code's "Arrivals"

Assessing Your App's Future

When you first began this journey, I asked you to do your best to quantify your app by thinking about your app's goals and potential (its addressable market). By the time you've done a couple of updates and your app has been in the store for three to four weeks, you should start to have enough data to consider how your app is doing relative to those initial goals and estimates.

It's possible that you might be shocked—in a good or a bad way—when you take a step back and compare your initial analysis with the reality of the data you now have. Depending on this comparison over time, you may soon be at a crossroads where you need to determine whether your app is a worthwhile investment or a lost cause. Regardless of what becomes apparent, do not be discouraged; even the top apps in the App Store don't stay on top forever.

Closed for Business?

Determining the health of an app can vary drastically from app to app, but there are some broader warning signals that indicate your app is on a path to its demise. Although this list is not exhaustive, it should help you to recognize patterns that indicate your app is headed for trouble within its first two weeks of launching.

No downloads or sales

> Yes, it's a "duh" signal, but worth mentioning. If your app has been out for several weeks and has no or very few downloads or sales, that's a problem. Although I am tempted to ask that you keep trying for press and media attention, it's likely that there's a more systematic problem with your app. Reach out to customers and advocates and find out if there are any issues with your app. Ask why they did or did not download your app.

No App Store reviews

> If you have no App Store reviews, it's a sign that your customers aren't very engaged with your application. That's especially true if you specifically requested reviews. It's possible that your customers are busy, but

it's also possible that they just don't find your application interesting or useful enough to take the time to review it. Find out if that's the case and ask how you can change that.

Mostly negative App Store reviews

Although not common, some apps receive hundreds or thousands of downloads when they are first released, but then receive an excessive number of negative reviews. Typically, this occurs because customers feel deceived about what the app is about or the app has major bugs and performance issues. A developer who doesn't recognize the problems and fails to quickly address them directly (e.g., through the App Store listing) is destined for failure.

Low frequency of use

Your analytics will tell you how often your customers are using your application. The general trend on the App Store is that many apps will be used less and less over the first 30 days. But if your app's frequency of use seems to be dropping at an alarming rate, it may be perceived as a gimmick (of course, that's OK if you have a "gimmick" or "seasonal" app) or as something that lacks long-term value.

Low number of active users

Remember, there's a difference between new users and active users. If your app is being downloaded consistently but its analytics show that most customers using your app are new users, your app is clearly not delivering on the feature set or experience you've described in the App Store.

Low number of In App Purchases

If your business model is to entice customers to buy features, credits, or virtual goods, you'll want to see a good conversion rate of free to In App Purchase. A low number could mean you have not implemented In App Purchases in an intuitive manner or that you did not compellingly break down the free and paid features of your app.

Low amount of customer interaction

If you are receiving a very low number of customer inquiries through Twitter, email, and other channels, it's unlikely that this is happening because your app is perfect. Instead, customers probably aren't using your app frequently or simply don't care enough to send you any ideas to improve or fix it.

Low number of updates

You will be able to track how many customers update your application. If you've shipped two or three updates to Apple and you've noticed that there's a low number of updates compared to the total number of users for your application, customers may be not using your app or are not finding your updates worth installing.

No media reviews

I'm a little hesitant to suggest that no media reviews is problematic, because it is hard to get a review today. Still, if you followed my previous advice, you should be getting some kind of attention, even if from smaller outlets such as a customer's blog. Receiving no reviews can indicate that people consider your app boring or uninteresting.

Beyond Warning Signals

As you look through my recommendations about early warning signals, keep in mind that one of these indicators alone doesn't mean it's time to shut down your app. In fact, catching these problems early enough may allow you to quickly recover or even discover an improved or new vision for your app.

If your app has been out for a couple of months or more, however, and you've tried some of the post-launch promotional techniques in Chapter 8 (see the "Additional Promotion" section in that chapter), yet you feel like the early warning signals are now permanent attributes of your app, you are going to need to take a closer look at what you are doing. You know the opportunity cost for continuing to maintain this app. So, if you find that your app has no hints of life, is not achieving any of your goals, and is costing you considerably more time, money, and effort than it's worth, you should consider severing ties with it or at least putting it on the back burner while you explore other opportunities.

This advice shouldn't come as a surprise. In Chapter 1, I made it clear that pursuing an app is risky, especially under the wrong motivations, and that even following all of the principles I outlined for you wouldn't guarantee a favorable outcome on the App Store, but would only improve your chances for that to occur.

You also should recall that being successful on the App Store is often about a portfolio of apps and not a single app. One particular app may be what you become known for, but that's often not the first or even second app. Ultimately even a "failed" app is part of a larger mobile strategy because it will provide you with intangible experience, as well as tangible creative and code assets. By making a hard but prudent decision to stop subsequent development of an app that shows no life earlier in its existence, you'll be positioning yourself to more quickly find the right opportunity. Only this time, you'll be much more experienced and prepared for the challenges of the App Store.

Toward the Future

Even if your app is doing well or is a critical part of a longer-term strategy (e.g., it's a companion to an existing product or service), it will likely experience some of these warning signals throughout its existence. All apps have ebbs and flows, often resulting from updates you release, reviews you receive, changes in the App Store, new operating systems and devices released by Apple, and many other factors that will likely be out of your control. That's why it is so important to stay disciplined and follow through on what is under your control—discovering ways to innovate in the App Store, working with customers to validate ideas, rigorously testing your app and its updates before they go into the App Store, and continuing to marry your marketing and development cycles together.

Essentially, you should make sure that each app update follows the principles described in this book on a smaller scale. By being methodical and staying customer-focused, you will constantly be increasing your chances of being competitive in Apple's always-growing and ever-changing App Store.

Interviews

Flurry: Peter Farago

COMPANY: Flurry

POSITION: VP, marketing

BACKGROUND: At Flurry, a leading mobile application analytics provider for Apple's iOS and Google's Android platforms, Peter is in charge of corporate and product marketing. In the past, Peter led product marketing at Electronic Arts, where he managed The Sims franchise, the #1 PC game of all time.

LINK: *http://www.flurry.com/*

Ken: *What are the biggest misperceptions developers have about analytics? In general, do they understand the value of them or just see installing them into their apps as a chore?*

Peter: Analytics is something our developers choose to add to their applications, so we believe they see value in them. We think they understand the value of learning how consumers interact with their applications. Beyond this, we believe developers can also learn things like where to best place ads, how effective cross-selling is working, or understand click-through conversion rates on offers placed within the application.

Ken: *The apps in the App Store range quite a bit, from games to utilities. At a more fundamental level, though, what types of metrics (analytics or otherwise) are important for all developers to pay attention to and track when an app goes into the App Store?*

Peter: Engagement and loyalty metrics are important to understand beyond simply the number of times an application is downloaded. These include metrics like frequency of use, length of use session, and retention of users over time. Working to increase these metrics, depending on the application, typically means that developers are focused on increasing customers' satisfaction. Also of interest is the geographic distribution of users, what operating system and device version they are using, and whether they are connecting through WiFi or carrier networks.

Ken: *Are there any baselines for assessing the health of an app? For example, if an app is opened three times per week, is that good or bad? How can developers best compare their apps' analytics to similar or popular apps?*

Peter: This primarily depends on the category of application (e.g., games versus utilities). Flurry has considered but not yet released the ability for a developer to benchmark his application performance within relevant categories. Flurry released some data on this at *http://blog.flurry.com/bid/26376/ Mobile-Apps-Models-Money-and-Loyalty.*

Ken: *Those who are not familiar with analytics probably have never heard the word "event" before. What are events and why do developers create them? How does tracking events influence the evolution of an app?*

Peter: Events (called "goals" in Google Analytics) are created to count the number of times a consumer completes a specific action or task within an application. For example, a developer who makes a game may want to see which game mode users play most often, which power-ups are selected most frequently, or what percent of users completes the entire game. For books, perhaps the developer would like to know how many sessions it takes to read a book, or which chapter the user is currently reading.

Ken: *How can developers use analytics to decide if an app is no longer worth investing in? What sort of changes in metrics might indicate that the app has stabilized or previously reached its peak? Are there early warning signals that can help prevent that from happening?*

Peter: It depends on the app, but for apps that seek to hold the attention of a large audience (e.g., news) the developer can look at "active users," which shows the total number of users that have downloaded an application versus how many have used it recently. If this number continues to decline, indicating *churn* even after making a few updates, that can indicate a problem. Or perhaps the application operates on a free-to-paid micro-transaction model (e.g., In App Purchases). In this case, the developer would want to track both the active users as well as the percent of those who purchase goods. If this number is declining, then it might be time to either refresh the current app or build another one.

Lumos Labs: Romain David

COMPANY: Lumos Labs

POSITION: Director of Mobile Products

BACKGROUND: Romain David is a mobile professional with more than 10 years of experience. He currently serves as Director of Mobile Products at Lumos Labs, Inc., the creator of Lumosity.com, a leader in online cognitive training.

LINK: *http://www.lumosity.com/*

Ken: *The Lumosity product has been around for several years now. What were the initial plans to port that experience to a mobile platform, and specifically to the iPhone?*

Romain: Less than three months after the iPhone platform was launched, the number of devices, monetization capabilities, and incredible user experience made it obvious that the iPhone would become our initial targeted mobile platform. We first collected input from our users visiting our site on their iPhone and iPod touch. This gave us a sense of what our users expected to see on the device, and what cognitive area they were most excited to train on the go.

We decided to start by porting one existing game available on Lumosity.com based on different criteria including user experience, session length, and popularity. We introduced Speed Brain in November 2008 as a paid application. iPhone users were able to play this game and improve their speed processing. Due to encouraging early results, we decided to invest more resources on the platform and developed more standalone brain games, before launching Brain Trainer, a complete portable brain training program.

Ken: *Because you had an existing product, what were the biggest challenges you faced in this process? Where did you make compromises? What aspects of the iPhone, if any, helped improve your product?*

Romain: It is very challenging for companies to be successful on more than one platform. You usually see winners on the Web not doing so well on mobile, and vice versa. Being successful on one platform requires a different skill set and a different culture. We understood that mobile was going to be a key component of our business moving forward, and the challenge was to overcome these limitations while offering a consistent experience to our users, whether they want to train their brain on their computer or on their mobile device.

It is very tempting to port all your assets from one platform to another. Our approach, however, is to develop products that take the most advantage of the platform's unique capabilities, interface, and monetization opportunities. One of the compromises we had to make was to not port very successful games on Lumosity.com, since they were not going to provide a good enough experience on the iPhone.

Ken: *Once you launched into the App Store, describe your approach for improving existing apps and launching new ones. What part does analytics play in influencing your decisions? What other factors inform the development process and updates that get pushed to Apple? How do you determine what does or does not go into an update?*

Romain: Many of our decisions come from what we learn from our users. The iPhone is no exception, and analytics has played a key role in our decision-making process. In our iPhone apps, we survey our users, so we can prioritize our features accordingly. For example, many of our iPhone users have told us they wanted more scientific information and an explanation about the Brain Performance Index (BPI) we use to measure their cognitive performance and progress. We took this feedback into account and provided a lot more information in our latest app update.

Ken: *Without sharing anything proprietary, what are some of the ways that you measure the success of your iPhone apps? Are there other ways to monitor them besides looking at the number of downloads or revenue generated?*

Romain: When Brain Trainer became a Top 25 app, we demonstrated that our brain training program could be appealing to a wide range of iPhone and iPod touch users. Beyond the number of downloads and premium users, the number of daily active users combined with the session length gives us a good idea of how engaging our application is. Engagement is a very important measure, since brain training is most valuable if practiced on a daily basis.

Ken: *As a customer of your products, I know that you launched many individual paid apps over a period of time and that recently you launched a new free app that supports In App Purchases. Was this approach part of your original plan or something that evolved based on customer feedback and changes in App Store policies?*

Romain: Even before we launched Speed Brain—our first application—we knew that at some point we were going to launch an app that will provide a complete brain training experience, similar to what we offer on Lumosity.com. When Apple introduced In App Purchase and made it available for free applications, it became obvious that we should adopt this model. We were finally able to provide a similar approach to our website. In addition, our iPhone and iPod touch users have always mentioned they wanted more games, so adopting this approach was the best way to meet their demand.

appFigures: Ariel Michael

COMPANY: Fileitup Media

POSITION: Co-founder

BACKGROUND: Ariel Michael is the co-founder of appFigures, a product of Fileitup Media. appFigures is a reporting platform for iPhone and iPad developers that brings together App Store sales data, worldwide reviews, and hourly rank updates into a single, intuitive, and informative reporting solution.

LINKS: *http://www.appfigures.com; http://www.fileitup.com/*

Ken: *Most developers launch their apps to a global audience because that's the default setting. Is that a good approach? How does that complicate the reporting process in iTunes Connect?*

Ariel: While iTunes Connect reports are not pretty to the naked eye, they do in fact contain data that's easy to interpret programmatically. Although the U.S. is by far the largest market for apps, it's extremely beneficial for developers to release worldwide.

Ken: *What are the biggest misperceptions and frustrations developers have about reporting? How does appFigures address some of those issues?*

Ariel: Most developers expect Apple to provide reports directly. The reality of the situation is that they don't provide reports at all; just tab-separated text files that get purged after seven days.

That's exactly why appFigures was developed! appFigures was born out of the need to have meaningful reports that can easily be viewed and used to enable us as developers to maker better decisions instead of spending time doing spreadsheet analysis.

Today, appFigures helps developers by automating the entire process of downloading and interpreting sales reports, turning them into meaningful charts and tables. We also extend these reports by tracking ranks and reviews from all App Stores.

Ken: *The apps in the App Store range quite a bit, from games to utilities. At a more fundamental level, though, what are the types of metrics (downloads, sales, or otherwise) that are important for all developers to pay attention to and track when an app goes into the App Store?*

Ariel: There are several key places developers can look at to better understand their place in the App Store:

Reviews

> This is an extremely helpful area developers most often neglect. Reading reviews gives developers direct insight into the minds of their users. This information can then be used to expand the app and even fix flaws, and at the end show your users you care about them by listening.

Sales/downloads

> This is the most obvious one, as it is the bottom line. Developers should, however, keep a close watch, not only on the actual number but also on how external events such as marketing campaigns, PR work, getting reviewed, etc. affect downloads.

Returns

> Most developers are unaware of the fact that apps can be returned. It's especially important to track the number of returns and try to keep those as low as possible. All developers see some returns here and there; it is important, however, to ensure they are not consistent.

Ranks

> Although developers have no direct control over the rank of their app, watching rank trends can give developers a real-time indication of their app's performance, which is not available when just using sales reports. By keeping a close watch on rank trends, developers can react fast. A good example would be reacting to an increase in rank by lowering price.

Ken: *Can you provide a simple description of the way Apple pays out revenue? Assume, for example, that an app launched globally today and made $5,000 across all App Stores in its first month. When would the developer see the first check? How long could it take to see some of those checks?*

Ariel: Getting paid by Apple is not as simple as that. There are actually a few things about getting paid that many new developers are unaware of:

- Apple operates on a fiscal calendar that's different from the normal calendar.

- Payments are distributed separately by region. The seven payment regions include United States, United Kingdom, Australia, Japan, Canada, Europe, and "Rest of World."

- You'll only get paid if your profit in a region exceeds $150. If it doesn't, it will roll over to the next month, or until you reach $150 in that region.

- Payments are usually sent out three to four weeks after the end of the fiscal month. This was not the case before, but Apple has gotten much better at making payments on time over the past few months.

Ken: *Are there any baselines for assessing the health of an app? For example, if an app is making $10 per day, is that good or bad? How can developers best compare their apps' download and sales numbers to similar or popular apps?*

Ariel: Because apps vary ever so much on the App Store, it's hard to compare one app to the other. At a very basic level, developers should set goals for their apps and use trend analysis to see if those goals can be achieved with current capabilities. If not, the developer should make a decision whether to stop development or invest more resources.

Making $10 a day is certainly not enough to keep a developer, indie or studio, alive. At such a point, the developer should examine why the app is selling so few copies and whether to end development and move on to bigger and better apps, or to invest more in advertising and PR. This depends on the quality and scope of the app.

Because financial data is kept privately by most developers, there is no way to compare an app's financial performance. Many developers, however, use ranks as an indication of performance when comparing their app to a competitor's.

Ken: *What guidance would you provide to developers about pricing and the "race to the bottom" of the App Store? How can they find the "sweet spot" for their app to maximize returns, that is, the price that yields the most revenue and not necessarily the most downloads?*

Ariel: The "race to the bottom" is very tempting, but should not be the first choice for a new app. If there is one thing to learn about the App Store it is that one price does not fit all. That's even more so on the iPad App Store.

Finding the sweet spot will depend on the app and the competition. The best approach is educated trial and error. Try different price points and see how the App Store reacts. The best time for a price change is with the release of an update.

The freemium model has become a great sweet spot for many developers, ever since it was made possible by Apple in mid-2009. The freemium model has great potential in my opinion because it sucks in users who would otherwise not be interested in paying and increases the potential to get those users to pay via In App Purchases. The model does have its cons, and so developers should not consider it for all apps.

With the recent release of the iPad, many developers have enjoyed the ability to charge a much higher price for the same app when on the iPad. This is a trend I believe will continue because of the iPad's increased capabilities and larger screen. These capabilities will allow developers to target larger industries such as retail, hospitality, and entertainment, which would open up the market to a wider audience that's used to spending large amounts for applications.

Ken: *How can developers use reporting to decide if an app is no longer worth investing in? What sort of changes in metrics might indicate that the app has stabilized or previously reached its peak? Are there early warning signals that can help prevent that from happening?*

Ariel: When looking at reports, developers should always look for trends and try to analyze them. Trend analysis will give developers an indication of whether the app is still in motion or if new efforts are needed to bring an app to life, and also allow developers to react fast.

There are many trends to watch for, but most would depend on the type of app, market conditions, and the competition. Here are some more common trends that are easy to spot:

A slow decline

> This is the most common trend to spot, and is a clear indicator that more needs to be done. Limited-time price drops are one way to change the trend; another is by releasing an update or promoting the app.

A zigzag

> This is common for niche apps or apps with very little/no promotion. One way to capitalize on the zigzag is to increase the price of the app. To turn the zigzag into an upward trend a developer should consider releasing an update or promoting the app.

A sudden sharp increase in sales

> This is the most desired trend and usually means the app got featured. When an app gets featured its sales will skyrocket for about a week. Reacting fast (by changing the price, releasing a press release, mass mailing, asking for reviews, etc.) can make the difference between re-maining on top and disappearing completely after the featured week is over.

Developers should also read reviews. I've mentioned it before, but stress its importance once again. Reviews can tell you if your app is healthy. Not having reviews means it probably isn't.

Recap

Here's what you learned in this chapter:

- Once your app is in the App Store, you'll immediately begin monitoring feedback about it. In general, you can think about feedback as being qualitative (e.g., App Store reviews) and quantitative (e.g., analytics).

- Apple's reporting features are somewhat limited and confusing. Third-party tools such as appFigures can help you quickly make sense of your app's download and financial data.

- Listening to customer feedback does not stop once an app is in the App Store. Continuing to gather customer insights and offering obsessive customer support will keep customers engaged and happy with your app, even when it has shortcomings.

- Application updates should follow from your app's initial roadmap and the feedback collected about your app. Updates should be balanced between short- and long-term needs and should always be tested before being submitted to the App Store.

- Deciding to stop development on an app should not be considered a failure. Apps have various life spans and will experience ups and downs throughout their existence.

Afterword

When Mobile Is No Longer the Exception

INITIALLY, LAPTOPS, SMARTPHONES, TABLETS, and netbooks all represented new yet complementary options to the traditional desktop computer. Today's reality, however, is that mobile devices are increasingly becoming the primary means of accessing and interacting with information. In fact, Morgan Stanley's prescient Internet analyst, Mary Meeker, predicts that in the next five years, "more users will connect to the Internet over mobile devices than desktop PCs."[1] The stationary desktop and its counterparts, the physical keyboard and mouse, are being replaced by portable, touch-enabled interfaces that have always-on connectivity. With this trend, you absolutely must understand that advancements such as Multi-Touch on the iPod touch, iPhone, and iPad will not be isolated to those devices alone. Apple knows this, and it's why the company already renamed its operating system from "iPhone OS" to "iOS" as part of the announcement of the iPhone 4.

Beyond Apple, every major technology innovator is trying to make sense of and be a leader in the mobile touch era. Microsoft Surface became popularized in the 2008 elections by facilitating advanced manipulation of large electoral maps through gesture recognition. Cisco has a business tablet focused on mobile video conferencing called Cius, powered by Google's mobile operating system, Android. Android has also flooded the smartphone market, with estimates of more than 150,000 Android handsets being activated per day.

---

1 *http://www.morganstanley.com/institutional/techresearch/mobile_internet_report122009.html*

The coming paradigm shift is also supported by considerable anecdotal evidence. One major observation is that iPhones and iPads have become the babysitter du jour for many parents, providing distraction, er...entertainment for their children through games and videos. Somehow, these young minds require no training or formal education on touch devices; they just touch and go. Touch is such a natural means of interaction that friends have shared stories of their children trying to interact with other screens, such as televisions, in the same way, swiping left or right to change the channel.

Although not quite yet the way the Class of 2024 would prefer, television itself is again being reinvented due to more robust data networks. Time-shifted programming was powered with the introduction of TiVo in the late 1990s, which allowed people to watch recordings of their favorite shows. Now, always-on connectivity for mobile devices is providing location-independent viewing of live events over high-speed networks. Even though soccer fans couldn't be home on their couch or at the bar with their friends, they were still able to watch games of the 2010 FIFA World Cup while on subways and in similar obscure locations using their smartphones. Unfortunately, that offered the opportunity to once again watch the United States lose to Ghana like they did in 2006; the smaller iPhone screen did not make it less painful.

All signs point to these new, more portable, more interactive, and more connected devices becoming the next major computing paradigm. It's not quite here yet, but soon enough, mobile, touch-enabled, always-on devices won't be the exception; they'll be the standard.

Tips and Tools

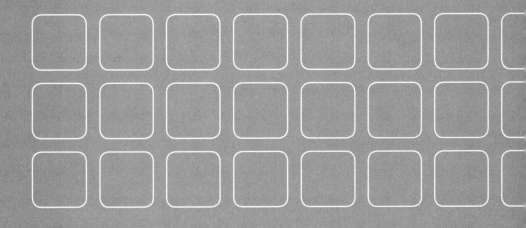

Appendix

Tips and Tools

THE iOS DEVELOPER PROGRAM, iOS SDK, and many third-party tools are often mainly used by designers and developers who are responsible for the creative and technical aspects of developing an app. However, a number of extremely useful resources and tools are available for people who don't fall into those categories, yet are daring enough to understand them. The good news is that you can be slightly less daring because I'm going to highlight just the parts that are relevant to you.

iOS Developer Program

By being a registered Apple Developer and enrolling in the iOS Developer Program, you'll get access to tools and information not available publicly. The iOS Developer Program itself is what will allow you to actually submit your app to Apple for review and will grant you access to a number of important areas, including the iOS Provisioning Portal and iTunes Connect, which are mentioned in the last four chapters of this book. The program will also enable you to get support through the private Apple Developer Forums and the Developer Support Center.

Registration and Enrollment

As I mentioned in the Preface, tackling iOS Developer Program enrollment when your app is almost completed or after your app is completed can delay your entrance into the App Store. So, you should begin registration and enrollment at the outset of this process. The first step is to register as an Apple Developer (*http://developer.apple.com/programs/register/*). This registration will create an Apple ID for you (if you don't already have one), and collects only basic information. Completing this free registration will give you access to download the iOS SDK (discussed next) and documentation related to iOS.

Once you've completed the registration, activated your Apple ID, and logged in, you should navigate to the iOS Dev Center (*http://developer.apple.com/iphone/*). You will see some information in the righthand sidebar about joining the iOS Developer Program. Follow those links until you reach a page asking if you want to enroll as an Individual or Company. Choose the appropriate option. The second choice (Company) will have a more significant impact on how long your application process takes, as it will require additional supporting documentation as part of Apple's identity verification process. Note that generally you should select Individual only if you will be releasing your app under your own name.

After you've completed the enrollment and submitted any required documentation, you'll need to wait for Apple to process, verify, and approve you into the program. Upon receiving your approval into the program, return to the iOS Dev Center and you'll be able to access four new options in the righthand sidebar: iOS Provisioning Portal, iTunes Connect, Apple Developer Forums, and the Developer Support Center. Right now, you'll want to focus on iTunes Connect.

Paid Application Contract

iTunes Connect is more fully explored in Chapter 7, as it's the place where you'll submit your application. Currently, however, you'll want to select the Contracts, Tax & Banking Information link on the home screen. If you plan to distribute only free applications, you are already done and will see that Free Applications has a green checkmark for Contract in Effect (see Figure A-1). If you want to offer paid applications, you'll need to request a contract for that and agree to its terms before you can distribute paid applications.

You'll then need to complete the Contact Info, Bank Info, and Tax Info sections for this contract. These aren't the worst forms in the world to complete, although no forms are really ever fun. You may need to look up some information related to your bank for the Bank Info section, or consult with an accountant or tax professional regarding the Tax Info section. Try to complete all of this information promptly because it can take up to several weeks for Apple to process your contract once you've submitted all your information. The implication is that you won't be able to distribute paid applications until the paid contract is in effect.

Figure A-1. iTunes Connect – Manage Your Contracts

Pay attention to the three bullets at the bottom of the Manage Your Contracts screen. The first two are relevant for developers in Canada or Australia. The last one is for all developers distributing paid apps in Japan. Unless you complete the additional paperwork, your earnings will be subject to an additional 20% withholding, as deemed by the Japanese government. Although it's more tedious compared to other forms, not completing this paperwork can have a significant impact on revenue you receive from Japanese sales. If you don't know yet, Apple takes 30% of the revenue from the sale of all apps, meaning that you may only receive 50% of the revenue for apps you sell in Japan.

Tools

Both Apple and third parties offer a number of iPhone-specific and general software development tools, which can help you better guide and oversee the development of your app. Apple's iOS SDK, which includes its iOS development tools, requires an Intel Mac, as do the other tools detailed in the following subsections.

iOS SDK

The iOS SDK (software development kit) is generally used only by developers. It includes their development environment, Xcode, and a number of other tools to aid in the programming side of applications. There is one application, which is part of Xcode itself, that can also be extremely useful for you and make installing the SDK worthwhile: Organizer.

By registering as an Apple Developer, you will be able to access and download the iOS SDK from the iOS Dev Center. There's really no risk for you to try out these tools, with the costs being the time it takes to download and install the 2 GB to 3 GB iOS SDK disk image file, which includes the SDK as well as Xcode. Of course, you can kick off the download and subsequently run the installation while you busy yourself with other tasks.

If you are officially enrolled in the iOS Developer Program, you'll possibly have the option to download two different SDKs, the second of which is usually a private "beta" of what Apple has coming next. Stick with the publicly available SDK unless your app requires functionality available only in the beta version.

Organizer

If you allow the SDK installation to use its default settings (recommended), a new top-level folder called *Developer* will be created on your Mac's hard drive after installation is complete. The easiest way to access that folder is to select your hard drive under Devices in the Finder application. Inside the *Developer* folder, you'll want to access *Applications*, which is the folder that contains the Xcode application. Open that application and you should be greeted with the first useful tool, called Organizer. If you don't see it, it's also available via the Windows menu item of Xcode. Organizer will let you take screenshots of anything open on a connected device and access diagnostics information such as crash logs (Figure A-2). Using these functions of Organizer is described in the "Organizer" section in Chapter 6.

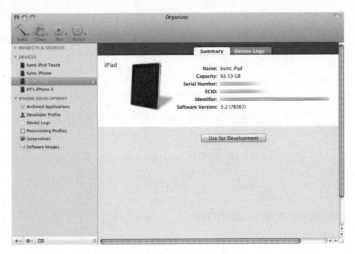

Figure A-2. Xcode's Organizer

Building onto a device

In the "Screens and Prototypes" section in Chapter 5, I first mention that when testing your in-progress app, developers should be building apps onto devices instead of relying on the iPhone Simulator. As part of the "Development App" section in Chapter 6, I discuss the process of installing your app through iTunes or the iPhone Configuration Utility after your developer sends you the latest version. But with Xcode installed, a few other tools, and some configuration help from your developer, you too can build your app directly onto your iPod touch, iPhone, or iPad.

The benefit of you being able to do this is that it allows you to always have access to the very latest version of the app. Once developers distribute an app, they usually continue to work on it. This means that even minutes after you install your app, a bug fix or other change may be available that you won't be able to see until your developer provides you with another version. Not only is that inefficient for you, but it's tedious for your developer. So, by spending some time to get this environment set up properly, you'll also make your developer more productive.

For this situation to be possible, you'll need access to your app's source code. Because of what we covered in Chapter 5, you should already have access to your code's repository (see "Repositories and source code" on page 168). Using the latest version you pull down from the repository, you'll open it in Xcode and build the app straight onto your device. Thus, this method makes installing your app with iTunes or the iPhone Configuration Utility obsolete.

If you are already starting to feel overwhelmed, don't feel bad if you need to depend heavily on your developer through this process. In fact, I'm purposely not going to provide all the required details because this setup can get fairly complicated and frustrating for someone with no experience.

It's simple enough to pull down the source code and open it in Xcode. You'll be looking for an Xcode Project File (see Figure A-3) in the folder of the source code, which ends with the extension *.xcodeproj*. Double-clicking that file will open Xcode.

Figure A-3. Xcode Project File

On the other side, what's not so simple is the configuration required to actually build the application onto your device. You are going to need to rely exclusively on your developer to help you with these steps. An overview of this process includes using Keychain Access and the iOS Provisioning Portal to request and install certificates, as well as ensuring that you have the proper provisioning profile installed. After these steps are completed and you've verified with your developer that the settings are correct, connect your device. Choose your device from the Overview drop down and set your configuration to Adhoc. If everything is done right, by clicking Build and Run (see Figure A-4) you should be moments away from Xcode installing your app onto your device. Work with your developer until that occurs.

If you feel beaten down by this process, remember that once you have everything set up the right way, your main task is just pulling down the most recent code from your repository. You then only need to click Build and Run in Xcode with your device attached. The ongoing benefits outweigh the complications of the initial setup.

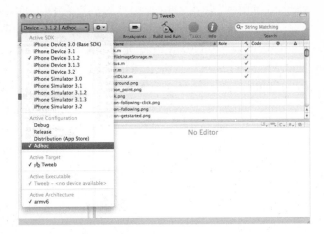

Figure A-4. Xcode – Ready to "Build and Run"

Third-Party Tools

One of my greatest frustrations in the development process, and particularly in testing apps, has been dealing with screenshots. Screenshots are incredibly helpful to show both creative and functional issues, and I almost always include them when logging bugs.

Screenshots aren't that bad when done through Organizer. You can use the Capture tool under the Screenshots tab to grab a screenshot and then drag it to your computer. But your device may not be connected to Organizer when you need to grab a screenshot of your app. In fact, if you are testing your app in live, real-world conditions, you often should not be sitting in front of your computer. In this case, the screenshots you take on the device itself—by pressing the Home and Power buttons at the same time—are stored on the device's Camera Roll.

In this case, my preference in transfering these screenshots has been to use two third-party tools. The first is Infinite Labs' Mover+, which operates on the iPod touch, iPhone, iPad, and Mac (*http://infinite-labs.net/mover/*). When the devices are on the same WiFi network, opening the app on any of them allows you to "slide" photos from one device to another. Mover+ really is the quickest way to move stuff from one device to another, and more specifically, one-off screenshots from an iOS device to a Mac (see Figure A-5).

The second tool I frequently use is called PhoneView (*http://www.ecamm.com/mac/phoneview/*). After connecting your device and opening PhoneView, you can easily drag one or more photos to your computer (see Figure A-6). I find PhoneView to be the fastest way to get multiple photos (screenshots), which are already stored on my device, onto my machine. For one-off screenshots, I would be remiss if I didn't mention Tapbots' apps, Pastebot and Pastebot Sync (*http://tapbots.com/software/pastebot/*). You may also want to read the interview with Tapbots' Paul Haddad and Mark Jardine at the end of Chapter 5.

Figure A-5 (Right). Mover+ transferring a screenshot to my Mac

Figure A-6 (Below). PhoneView – Selecting multiple photos and dragging to the computer

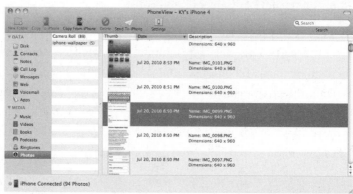

To edit screenshots, especially when preparing them for submission in iTunes Connect, check out iPhone Screentaker (*http://fabian-kreiser.com/ public/iPhone-Screentaker.app.zip*), Acorn (*http://flyingmeat.com/acorn/*), or Pixelmator (*http://www.pixelmator.com/*). iPhone Screentaker, in particular, provides a streamlined interface, where those without image editing experience can accomplish the key tasks required for manipulating iOS screenshots (see Figures A-7 and A-8).

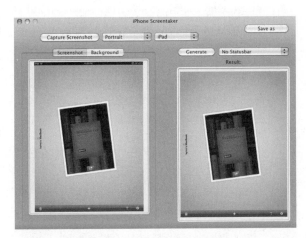

Figure A-7 (Top). iPhone Screentaker – Editing out the status bar in a screenshot

Figure A-8 (Bottom). iPhone Screentaker – Creating a screenshot in an iPad

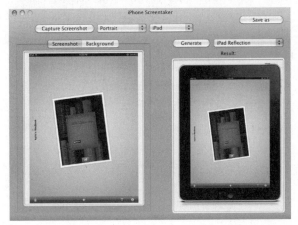

Additional Resources

The best way to stay sharp and attuned to what's happening in the App Store ecosystem is to continue to foster relationships with fellow developers, read blogs, and stay active on Twitter. Here is a list of some other places where you can continue to learn and look for help:

Apple Developer Forums (https://devforums.apple.com/)
> The Apple Developer Forums are accessible through the iOS Dev Center, once you've enrolled in the iOS Developer Program.

iOS Reference Library (https://developer.apple.com/ios/library/navigation/index.html)
> This is Apple's documentation on the iOS, including the Human Interface Guidelines mentioned in Chapter 5.

Answer sites (http://stackoverflow.com/; http://answers.oreilly.com/)
> Stack Overflow and O'Reilly Answers are great places to find answers to commonly asked questions. Although Stack Overflow is programming-oriented, it can save you from having to email your developer.

OnStartups (http://answers.onstartups.com/)
> Consider Answers OnStartups to be the product-focused version of Stack Overflow. It's not tuned into apps specifically, but you can get answers related to building startups (i.e., your app) and small businesses.

Of course, don't forget to check out *http://kenyarmosh.com/appsavvy*, where I'll continue to list new or updated resources and, more generally, help keep you app savvy!

Numbers